To David
glad yo

Alan Bissn

June 2023

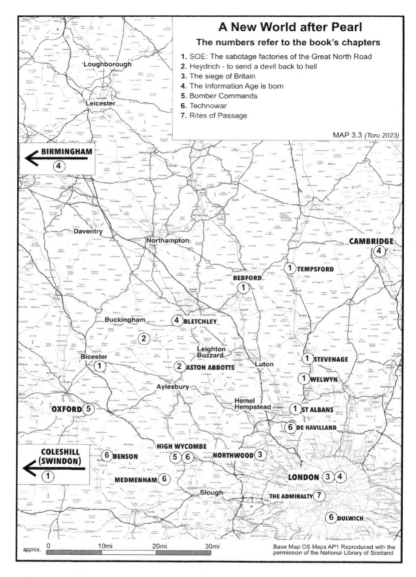

A New World after Pearl

The numbers refer to the book's chapters

1. SOE: The sabotage factories of the Great North Road
2. Heydrich - to send a devil back to hell
3. The siege of Britain
4. The Information Age is born
5. Bomber Commands
6. Technowar
7. Rites of Passage

MAP 3.3 *(Toru 2023)*

Loughborough

Leicester

← **BIRMINGHAM** (4)

Daventry

Northampton

CAMBRIDGE (4)

(1) **TEMPSFORD**

BEDFORD (1)

Buckingham (4) **BLETCHLEY**

(2)

Leighton Buzzard

Bicester (1)

(2) **ASTON ABBOTTS** Luton

(1) **STEVENAGE**

Aylesbury

(1) **WELWYN**

Hemel Hempstead

OXFORD (5)

(1) **ST ALBANS**

(6) **DE HAVILLAND**

HIGH WYCOMBE

COLESHILL (SWINDON) ← (1)

(6) **BENSON**

(5)(6)

NORTHWOOD (3)

LONDON (3)(4)

MEDMENHAM (6)

Slough

THE ADMIRALTY (7)

(6) **DULWICH**

approx. 0   10mi   20mi   30mi

Base Map OS Maps AP1 Reproduced with the permission of the National Library of Scotland

(This book is a sequel to *The Intelligence Zone*. For an overview of the chapters in both books, please see the map at the end of this book.)

A New World after Pearl

(the sequel to *The Intelligence Zone*)

Alan Biggins

with Maps and Illustrations by Kai Toru

Previous books by Alan Biggins
A Normandy Tapestry: a portrait of rural France
Selling French Dreams - tales of property, France and family
30 Great days out in Brittany
The Intelligence Zone

First edition March 2023
Published by Kirkdale Books
Website - theintelligencezone.com
Contact - theintzoneuk@gmail.com

ISBN; 978-1-7393299-2-1 – Paperback
ISBN; 978-1-7393299-3-8 – eBook

Cast up thine eyes to the hills; from thence cometh thy salvation
Alan Biggins (with a nod to the King James Bible)

I dedicate this volume to all the friends with whom I have walked over the years. My chums in the RAF, the Gunslingers, a Dave or two and especially Uncle Colin and the long-suffering Roger Spittles.

Contents

'If I have seen further, it was by standing on the shoulders of giants.'
Isaac Newton (1675)

Who is the most important person in the history of physics? Some physicists give the palm to Newton, some say Einstein, a few cite Rutherford. When I asked three leading physicists their opinions, they differed. One was for Newton, another Einstein. The reply I liked best, however, was from the American, Adam Riess (who I am in correspondence with as he is the holder of the copyright for his grandfather's definitive book on Goebbels). In his opinion:

"In modern physics, Einstein. In pre-Einstein physics, Newton."

As Professor Riess holds the Nobel Prize for Physics, I humbly bow to his opinion.

Newton's birthplace is now a museum, near Grantham, fifty or so miles up the Great North Road (A1) from the Intelligence Zone.

Introduction

In the prequel to this book, *The Intelligence Zone*, I wrote of the period between Hitler's accession to power (1933) until late 1941. I spoke there about the development of key tools which were used by Britain in the war, such as radar, communications, penicillin and the interception and decryption of enemy broadcasts, and how they were used.

In this book, *A New World after Pearl*, I take the story forward to when Russia, Japan and America joined the conflict, making it a truly global war. Here I tell how the tools, weapons and techniques developed in the Intelligence Zone would be used by all of the Allies. As well as the military aspects, it also tells of the seismic shift in world power, from Europe to America.

Apart from the massive change in the scope of the war itself, there were also a couple of practical reasons why I split *The Intelligence Zone* into two separate books. Firstly I am not a fan of thick books; they are bulky and not easy to handle. Then, there is expense. I reasoned that a reader would rather try a reasonably priced book and, if persuaded by it, buy its concluding part, than risk spending the same amount and possibly end up with something they might not enjoy (or finish). The fact that you are reading this means, I suspect, that you have already read *The Intelligence Zone*. If not, may I strongly advise you to do so before you read this one.

The story of what went on in the Intelligence Zone after Pearl Harbour is at least as exciting as its earlier days. Some stories here are:

- In the Chiltern Hills, MI9 organises escape lines for shot-down RAF and USAAF flyers – instructing the airmen in almost biblical terms on when and from whom to seek succour:

    'Not in the morning but at the end of the day. Women in preference to men. Old rather than young. Poor rather than rich. Country people rather than city. Priests and doctors rather than merchants or shopkeepers.'

Thousands of Allied airmen will be saved by the 'ordinary' people of Europe. Many of their saviours will die by rope and bullet.

- In Norway, a saboteur crouches under a pier atop a pile of mines originally designed in the public baths in Bedford. He bides his time, waiting a couple of days until his target-ship docks, reading a P.G. Wodehouse novel as a German guard marches overhead.

- In Prague, two Czech saboteurs, trained in Hertfordshire, wait on a corner with British guns and bombs, to kill the foulest of the Nazis. The murder will slow down arms production and help the Russian front.

- Under the waves of the Atlantic, a German submariner is driven close to insanity as his 'iron coffin' is bombarded hour after hour by weapons developed in 'Winston Churchill's Toyshop' near Aylesbury.

- High drama among the gods of war in Whitehall – as General Eisenhower threatens to quit as supreme Allied commander because RAF and USAAF generals 'quarrel like children' over where to drop their bombs to bring victory in Europe.

- In the sky above Berlin an American airman, flying out of East Anglia, releases a bomb which will kill Hitler's hangman, Roland Friesler. Around him, Flying Fortresses fall from the sky into the burning city. Enraged Berliners thrust parachuting airmen into the flames.

- In Russia, the Russian dictator Joseph Stalin is told of Nazi attack plans by Bletchley Park, saving countless Russian lives and hastening the defeat of Germany.

- Over a city in Japan, an RAF Group Captain witnesses the apocalyptic legacy of experiments made in Cambridge, England, 12 years earlier, when Cockcroft and Walton produced the first man-made nuclear reaction.

- In a dock in Bremerhaven, Germany, Patrick Denzel-Job, an officer working for Ian Fleming (and perhaps the original for James Bond) lowers the British flag on a captured German ship and hands it over to the United States Navy. This is symbolic of a passage of power worldwide.

1. SOE and the sabotage factories of the Great North Road

SOE – the army in the shadows

The British are sometimes accused of being insular. Britain has, however, always been open to foreign ideas: and in World War Two it adopted two of them - sabotage and guerrilla warfare - with great enthusiasm, refining them as never before.

Sabot is the French word for a clog: and if the word sabotage did not quite originate from throwing clogs into industrial machinery, that was certainly what SOE was about. It made stuff to wreck things, trained people how to do it and delivered explosives and agents to where the job needed to be done. Sabotage was the perfect word for SOE, as much of its work was in France.

The Special Operation Executive - SOE - was formed in July 1940 under the Minister of Economic Warfare, Hugh Dalton. Dalton was a politician who had been anti-appeasement and a close ally (although in a different political party) to Churchill. He wrote to the Secretary of State for Foreign Affairs:

> 'We've got to organise movements in enemy occupied territories, comparable to the Sinn Fein movement in Ireland (which)... must use many different methods, including industrial and military sabotage, propaganda, terrorist acts against traitors and German leaders.'

This was passed to Winston Churchill who (in July 1940), instructed Dalton to 'Set Europe ablaze.'

The building blocks of SOE were three organisations, each of which had been set up in 1938, in direct response to Hitler marching his armies into Austria.

The first was Section 'D' (for destruction) of SIS/MI6, the British foreign secret service, under Colonel Laurence Grand (whose boss was 'Quex' - Admiral Hugh Sinclair).

I spoke about the second in *The Intelligence Zone*. It was MI(R) of the War office. That was Colin Gubbins' baby – he

1

who shared an office with Millis Jefferis, the creator of Winston Churchill's toyshop at Whitchurch.

The third was based at Electra House in London and had been set up by the Foreign Office, mainly for propaganda.

These organisations were already of some size: Section D, for example, had 300 staff by then. Dalton advocated that the three be merged and Churchill agreed.

The SIS/MI6 were not very happy to see Section D taken from them as they considered themselves the 'real' home both for spying and sabotage. SIS still kept their spies (for example Marie-Madeleine Fourcade's *Alliance* Network) but SOE took over sabotage. This, at times, led to competition and even, on occasion, enmity between SIS and SOE. This lasted throughout the war and was sometimes a brake on efficiency.

That a department dedicated to sabotage existed at all in a democratic state is, perhaps, surprising. As the historian of SOE – M.R.D. Foot said:

'It is at first sight quite amazing that Churchill, the grandson of a duke, should advocate guerrilla warfare for the destruction of another state.'

It can, convincingly, be argued that this was a case of fighting terror with terror. If your enemy fights dirty, then you will not defeat him by 'playing fair'. More pressingly, perhaps, it was a matter of necessity. Churchill, in 1940, was acutely aware that if the British and German armies met in the field, the German army would win; as had happened very recently in France. Nor had that defeat been a surprise to him – he had been screaming its likelihood from the rooftops for years. Guerrilla tactics were one way to redress the balance. Churchill, an inveterate student of history, was well aware that the word *guerrilla* comes from the Spanish for 'little war'. It was coined to describe the harassing tactics that the Spanish and Portuguese peoples had used to help Wellington's British army defeat the French armies of one of Europe's previous would-be great dictators – Napoleon Bonaparte.

Churchill knew from his own experience that Britain herself had at times been in a position of overwhelming strength and still come off worst. In the Boer war (in South Africa) 25,000

Boers nearly defeated ten times as many British soldiers. Churchill himself, at the age of 25, when reporting on that war for *The Times* newspaper, was captured by the Boers. He escaped... and wrote a book about it. If ever there was a warrior-bard it was Winston Spencer Churchill.

More recently, in the Irish War of Independence ('the Troubles'), two or three thousand Irish Republican Army fighters had fought against 80,000 British troops and won independence. M.R.D. Foot says that the origins of SOE could be traced back to the streets of Dublin during the Troubles, when two young British majors called John Holland and Colin Gubbins had been struck by the comparative efficiency of gunmen working singly in plain clothes over soldiers working in massed battalions in uniform. Both Holland and Gubbins were to end up in charge of SOE.

The Peninsula War, the Boer War and Ireland. All three conflicts were fought in areas where the 'partisans' had the populace overwhelmingly on their side. The parallel with Nazi occupied Europe was exact.

SOE was known affectionately as The Baker Street Irregulars. This was a reference both to their headquarters in London's Baker Street and also to Conan Doyle's fictional detective, Sherlock Holmes, who also lived in Baker Street and who used street urchins - his 'irregulars' - to gather intelligence for him as they were streetwise and observant and ignored by all. SOE (in order to confuse) operated under several names during the war, including ISTD – the Inter Service Topological Department.

Poland, Czechoslovakia and France

Over 20,000 Polish troops came to Britain after the collapse of France, making them, at the end of 1940, by far the most numerous foreign army in Britain. They largely organised their own sabotage. In hopeless circumstances, they fought with courage and tenacity. The Polish resistance struggle was the longest and bloodiest of any country's in the war. This included the Warsaw uprising, crushed by the Nazis as the Russians stood back and refused to allow Britain and America to use their airfields to help. That tragic history is too large for this volume, except to say that the Poles, as befits the nation who had replicated and gifted to Britain the Enigma machine, had a first class intelligence service and were talented engineers. The radio sets they produced at Stanmore were of a very high quality.

The Czechs, too, had significant forces (about 6,500) in Britain. They achieved what could be called the most significant sabotage – or terrorist if you were a Nazi - attack of the war. This had such a profound effect that I will devote the next chapter to it.

The most important occupied country in Europe in SOE terms was France. It is worth re-iterating that France did not have a government in exile in Britain. It's government was at Vichy; largely following Nazi orders. The United States recognised the Vichy Government as the legitimate government of France and so, at first, did most of the population of occupied France. Britain, however, did not recognise Vichy; and nor did the French resistance.

One side-effect of this schism in French politics was that there were two 'brands' of SOE French resistance SOE(F) and SOE(RF). While both were wholly supported by British resources, SOE(RF) was controlled by de Gaulle's *France Libre* (based in London). French agents who worked for SOE were given an option (at first), which of these organisations they reported to. Many of them did not recognise de Gaulle's authority and preferred to work under British control. That there were two different SOE sections in France was not merely confusing but sometimes created friction. Noreen Riols, who was fluent in French and worked for SOE during the war says that 'SOE was destined to fight a war on three fronts... Germany, General de Gaulle and SIS.'

Why was de Gaulle considered an 'enemy', though? It is perhaps best not to try to distil reason from the chalice of rancour stirred up by France's humiliating defeat. One is unlikely to reach enlightenment by sipping old poison. It is important, however, to be aware of the bitterness that de Gaulle felt towards his British saviours. That was to sour relations between Britain, France and Europe long after the war.

Apart from the two 'allied' French SOE sections, France had various other resistance groups too, most noticeably – after Hitler invaded Russia – the Communists.

A fruitful source of agents for SOE was the Royal Patriotic School in Wandsworth, where escapers were interrogated. (I talk about this place in *The Intelligence Zone*. It was where Marie-Madeleine's brother had had a run-in with his father in law.)

Other SOE recruits were British nationals who had lived, or been brought up, abroad. After training in Britain, SOE recruits would return to Europe where they trained further agents on the ground.

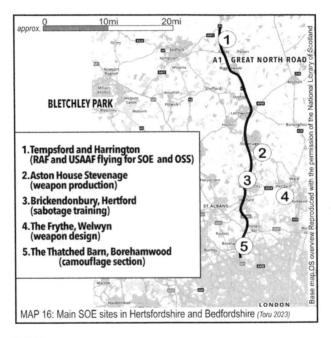

MAP 16: Main SOE sites in Hertfordshire and Bedfordshire *(Toru 2023)*

BLETCHLEY PARK

1. Tempsford and Harrington
(RAF and USAAF flying for SOE and OSS)

2. Aston House Stevenage
(weapon production)

3. Brickendonbury, Hertford
(sabotage training)

4. The Frythe, Welwyn
(weapon design)

5. The Thatched Barn, Borehamwood
(camouflage section)

How SOE grew

Because of the dozens of houses and estates that SOE requisitioned during the war, some asserted that the initials stood for 'Stately 'omes of England'. That doesn't do the organisation justice though; for it spread beyond England's borders. Its basic physical training, toughening up and weeding-out were done in Scotland, with over 10 different requisitioned estates in the highlands; and there was a marine testing base in Wales. There were also a couple of stations outside the British Isles.

Beaulieu in Hampshire was a major base, RAF Ringway (now Manchester airport) in Cheshire was used for parachute training and there were several other SOE houses and bases dotted around England. Most of the SOE sites (about 25), however, were in the Intelligence Zone: the headquarters was at Baker Street in London and it had many large properties in the counties of Bedfordshire, Hertfordshire and Buckinghamshire. A glance at a map of the bases show that they more or less straggled along a stretch of the Great North Road (the A1) – that ancient backbone of Britain that links England and Scotland.

Collin Gubbins, a Scot with a distinguished military record, was a driving force in SOE throughout the war and would become its chief. Gubbins had been in Poland when it was invaded by the Germans and he also had strong links with Czechoslovakia. He produced three main handbooks for the SOE. One of them was the *Partisan leader's handbook*, a 30 page pamphlet which covered how to organise an ambush (road and rail), how to immobilise a railway engine, who to tap for information (innkeepers and hawkers were best), wiring diagrams and more. As the title of the booklet makes clear, SOE were training leaders who would, on their return to their countries, train others. Those who passed SOE training were an elite – the strongest and most able among the bravest of their nations – the officers of the underground European struggle for freedom.

All three booklets were essential reading for those intent on

The Partisan Leader's Handbook

mayhem and were updated and reprinted throughout the war.

The nature of SOE, its industrial scale and thorough planning, can be seen from looking at how it handled weapon production, sabotage training, communications and movement of agents in SOE's heartlands, in the Intelligence Zone.

Station 12 - Aston House, Stevenage, weapon making

Aston House was SOE's centre of weapons production. A commandeered stately home, Aston (since demolished) was a great 16th century pile with 80 acres of grounds churning out endless 'toys' for SOE, the Commandos, the SAS and the SBS. Surrounded by wire with armed guards, this factory of industrial mayhem was a hive of industry, with over 500 staff by the end of the war. It supplied the tinder with which Europe was 'set ablaze'. Among the weapons made at Aston were plastic explosives, pressure switches, incendiary bombs and time fuses. The unit, set up by 'Quex' Sinclair, originated at Bletchley Park; but the coding staff there, intent on deep thoughts about the relationship of letter frequency in German secret signals, complained about the bangs, causing section D to be moved to Aston House (in November 1939).

The first commander - when it was still an SIS establishment - was Lieutenant Commander A.J.G. (John) Langley. Langley was a science graduate (a Fellow of the Institute of Physics). It was he who developed Time Pencils to facilitate sabotage. These were timed fuses linked to explosives and were used on, for example, aircraft and railway points, so that the saboteur could set an explosion for, say, three hours' time and then run in the other direction, hoping to get clear of the explosion and the hue and cry that inevitably followed.

Langley realised that he was going against the military grain; so he kept quiet about what he was up to, knowing that were he to mention it to a fellow member of the armed forces they were likely to '...edge away, muttering "Gad sir, that man has no idea of the Marquis of Queensberry rules."'

He expected that his opponents in Germany must also have had a parallel organisation, but:

'We found out later that they hadn't. That was probably because they had not bothered about what to them would have appeared... utterly insignificant... you don't waste your time on feather dusters when you are making sledgehammers capable of crushing entire nations at one blow. Poland (crushed) in 18 days, France in a month.'

A reflection that more or less sums up why the British had an SOE and the Germans did not (Otto Skorzeny was probably the closest they got, much later in the war).

After Dunkirk, an order was placed with John Langley for 10,000 'Time Pencil' (delay) fuses, a thousand incendiaries and half a ton of plastic explosive as soon as possible. 'Plastic', developed at Woolwich Arsenal in London, was easily mouldable and yet safe to handle. It was the explosive of choice for saboteurs; indeed captured SOE plastic explosive was to be used by Claus von Stauffenberg in his attempt to assassinate Hitler in 1944 (ironically the reason that the Fuhrer didn't die seems to have been because his wounds were treated with captured penicillin; which means that a bit of British technology which should have killed him was countered by another which saved him).

When SIS's weapon facilities were taken over by SOE, John Langley decided he wanted to stay with SIS (a decision made easier as Richard Gambier Parry was eager to use his services at Whaddon Hall). Lieutenant-Colonel Leslie Wood then took over at Aston House.

Aston House designed explosives for specific raids. Amongst these were those it produced for a naval attack on the Lofoten Islands (off Northern Norway). Lofoten is a good example of how organisations in the Intelligence Zone worked together. The raid, ostensibly to blow up German fish-oil tanks, was a cover for the successful seizure of an Enigma machine and code books for Bletchley Park from an armed trawler. Through naval gunfire and demolition parties, 18,000 tons of shipping was sunk. The British experienced only one accident; an officer injuring himself with his own revolver; and returned with 228 German prisoners, 314 Norwegian volunteers, a number of Norwegian collaborators and, of course, the Enigma machine and code book.

Colonel (as he became) Wood took part in agent training, but was not always enamoured with his students: 'I ought to have had a VC because anyone who teaches – or tries to teach – a Frenchman to use high explosives deserves a VC.'

His criticism appears to have been justified. Showing a French Major how to blow a railway track with a very small charge:

'I almost had to frog march him back a quarter of a mile and force him down: I tackled him low and a second later there was a clang! As a piece of rail went through the metal signpost just where his head had been.'

Wood was known to the Free French as 'Captain Blood'

Aston House's explosives were much in demand. On one occasion the production department at Aston worked for three days and nights non-stop. Many of the staff were female; Wood said of them:

'Most of them were Geordies, and when they were doing their work they sang a repertoire of songs that made even me blush.'

One visitor to Aston early in the war was an American, Colonel Bill Donovan. President Roosevelt had asked Donovan to visit Britain to assess whether the country was worth military support or was already finished. Aston House was one of his ports of call. Colonel Wood loved 'Wild Bill' and gave him a fighting knife. He also invited him to a demonstration he gave at the end of a VIP visit when he put a lot of old explosive in a pond and detonated it. It did not go quite to plan:

'I positioned the viewers where I thought they were absolutely safe, lit the fuse and the pond went up in the air and the wind changed and the whole bloody lot shifted across and fell on top of them! All this ruddy water. Luckily it was a summer's day but they were not prepared for it. I will never forget Donovan, with a straight face, saying out of the corner of his mouth as he passed me, "Wood, you know, old boy, I personally wouldn't treat senior officers like this." …oh dear, dear, dear.'

Donovan reported back to his President that Britain still had plenty of fight in her and was worth supporting. Indeed, he took the SOE so much to heart that he used it as the template for a new organisation of his own: the OSS – which later became the CIA.

Aston didn't just make explosives for SOE. In the desert, the Special Air Service, amongst others, was a major customer. Paddy Mayne, the SAS's commander after David Stirling's capture, blew up many German aircraft behind the lines using Time Pencils and explosives. During the course of the Second World War he became one of the British Army's most highly decorated soldiers. On one raid he and his troop destroyed 47 aircraft in a single action. (Eric Lock, the RAFs highest scoring ace during the battle of Britain shot down 21.) Mayne was awarded the DSO four times. If he had been a bit more liked by those in authority he would have got the Victoria Cross.

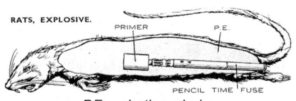

P.E. = plastic explosive

Aston could make most things explode – or at least make explosives look like most things. One order was for 16 pieces of explosive coal, 65 explosive rats, 40 explosive logs and 50 explosive Fish Plates (railway sleeper mounts). The name of the explosives – 'dogs' breakfasts' (a kind of incendiary sausage to make sure that things stayed alight), 'pencils', 'rats' and the like annoyed the War Office …'they must be catalogued and given a proper number in future.' It was pointed out that Commandos would still ask for dogs' breakfasts and pencils and as such they remained.

There was even a (characteristically) impractical design from Churchill's scientific advisor Frederick Lindemann ('the Prof') - for a bicycle pump that would fire a poisoned dart.

Colonel Wood's section also supplied the weapons for Coleshill House, near Swindon, where Peter Fleming (Ian's brother) trained the stay-behind units who were to go to ground and be overrun by the Germans if they landed. This was the section, it may be remembered, for which Gambier Parry's Whaddon team had provided the communications. In February 1941, Aston House provided 1,000 cases of mixed stores for them.

Lieutenant-Colonel Fairburn and Captain Bill Sykes, the double-act ex-Shangai Police combat trainers, although normally in Scotland, were at Aston House on several occasions, training agents. Fairburn taught unarmed combat – silent killing; Sykes the use of revolvers. Both were experts in killing. Together they developed the commando knife now used world-wide by special combat forces. They allegedly concluded all sessions with the instruction, "and then kick him in the balls".

There seems no end to the range of equipment made at Aston: including scaling equipment (used at Dieppe) and the charges used to blow up the lock gates at St Nazaire, which denied French anchorage to the German battleships. They made a training film 'how to blow up a power pylon' for the Free French (the local police arrested the trainers during filming). They had fun at Aston House. According to Arthur Christie (a laboratory Assistant there) this included playing japes on prominent visitors:

> 'Nobody was too sacred. One of our favourite tricks was to rub gelignite around the inside band of the hat of anyone visiting our explosive store at an inopportune moment or who did not not approve of our type of warfare. When perspiration mixes with gelignite it has the effect of the worst hangover ever experienced.'

On another occasion, the car of a visitor (Lord Inverchapel) was booby trapped by the addition of 'a couple of limpet mines and time fuses to its petrol tank':

> 'Unfortunately the car left quickly before the mines could be revealed and removed. This led to a high speed chase, eventually catching him up at Station IX, The Frythe (near

Welwyn, yet another SOE establishment). Boy! The expression on their faces when they saw us remove the live limpet mines from the fuel tank!'

Aston House also mass-produced some of the devices developed by 'Winston Churchill's Toyshop'; Millis Jefferis's establishment at Whitchurch. One of these was the Limpet Mine. Aston also manufactured a gun to fire a nail into the side of a ship (Limpet mines couldn't stick onto barnacles). There was a large crossover between Aston and Whitchurch. Nobby Clarke, he who developed the Limpet with Macrae at Bedford public baths, worked at Aston before going on to SOE's saboteur's training facility at Brickendonbury. He later worked at Whitchurch.

Aston house had a NAAFI and later even a theatre. It seems to have been a very good posting – and a happy place to work. Many were the marriages there (about a quarter of the personnel were female). On one occasion Aston came close to playing a decisive part in the war - when they nearly killed Churchill while demonstrating a new type of mine to him, placed under a car. In Arthur Christie's words: 'Bang, the vehicle whizzed through the air and landed quite near him. He didn't even miss a puff on his cigar!'

Section 17 – Brickendonbury Manor, Hertford, industrial sabotage

Brickendonbury Manor, near Hertford (Station XVII) was another property that SOE took over from SIS. It had been requisitioned at the start of the war and specialised in the training of industrial sabotage techniques. Captain 'Nobby' Clarke (whom we have met before at Bedford public baths and Aston House) took over at Brickendonbury in December 1940. Stuart Macrae, of 'Churchill's Toyshop' at Whitchurch, describes the reception he afforded to his visitors:

'He (Clarke) had no guards on the gates of his magnificent estate. One just drove in and found the vehicle being battered by rounds from the spigot mortars set off by trip wires. Nobby would emerge smiling and point out that, if they had been live rounds the occupants of the vehicle would no longer be in this world. But this was little consolation to the driver who had to explain how the bodywork of his vehicle had been badly bashed.'

The training at Brickendonbury was hands-on. Clarke himself had designed quite a few of the weapons, such as the explosive device for planting on board Axis bombers, triggered by a change in air pressure and set to go off at a certain height. This was manufactured in thousands. Nobby himself did much of the

Nobby Clarke wearing an early limpet mine in the position a swimmer would carry it.

training for that one. Clarke was keen to give the agents he was training a realistic experience. One night he took a team out, who scaled the walls of Luton's main power station and fixed dummy charges. Clarke then forged a document giving him permission to inspect the station. Once inside, he showed the (very shaken) officer who escorted him the dummy charges, saying to him:

'Alright old man, you say nothing about this and I'll say nothing about it. But you've learnt your lesson.'

The decoys were retrieved and the unconventional training operation was over. The (Free French) team that he had trained parachuted into France and blew up a power station serving the French Port of Bordeaux, putting the German U-boat complex out of service for months. The saboteurs all escaped. The Germans shot twelve of their own guards for negligence.

Clarke was considered rather a loose cannon and was transferred to Whitchurch. He was replaced by George Rheam, who is considered a pioneer of industrial sabotage. Resistance fighters from the occupied countries would be trained here and then parachuted back into their homelands.

One officer who was trained at Brickendonbury was George Millar. We last saw him on the *Madura* back in 1940, fleeing from France with Sefton Delmer. Quite a bit had happened to him in the meantime. He was commissioned into the Rifle Brigade and fought in North Africa, where his platoon was overrun by the Germans and he was captured – meeting Rommel himself (for whom he had a high regard). A prisoner of war in Italy, his repeated attempts to escape landed him in a high security POW camp. Escaping from a train taking him to Germany, he made his way through France to Lyon and escaped into Spain across the Pyrenees and so back to England where he was awarded the Military Cross and joined SOE. He learned unarmed combat and how to shoot with a pistol at Warnborough Manor in Surrey. Then, perhaps because he was an army officer already, he was given a foreshortened, one week course (it was normally three weeks):

'In the grey Hertfordshire country house, Rheam, in a series of engrossing lectures, taught us the vital point of power stations, telephone exchanges, factories, reservoirs, canals, railway systems. A few pounds, or ounces, of plastic explosive on a single turbine or transformer might do more significant damage to the enemy than the attentions of one of the fleets of Allied bombers that passed over us so frequently at night.'

Benjamin Cowburn, another SOE agent who also went through training in industrial sabotage and who operated in Paris and elsewhere in France, makes the same points in *No cloak no dagger:* the ideal targets for destruction were key components such as vital and difficult to replace parts of machines. Locomotives were very often attacked; there was a very strong resistance movement within the French railways (SNCF) itself.

He also says that:

'The necessity of not causing the execution of hostages was an important consideration when planning sabotage. One of the frequent manifestations of resistance was the killing of a German soldier... bi-lingual notices would appear ...in the metro giving names of hostages who had been shot in reprisal with a warning that worse would follow if such an act was repeated. The unwritten rule of the game seemed to be that as long as no Germans were injured there would generally be no reprisals.'

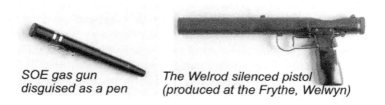

SOE gas gun
disguised as a pen

The Welrod silenced pistol
(produced at the Frythe, Welwyn)

Many of the lessons were 'one-off', such as training in the use of the specially designed explosives which Aston House had produced to destroy the high pressure pipes at the Norsk Hydro plant in Norway. Station 17 built a mock-up of the hydro plant in the grounds for the men to practice on. The trainers were very highly qualified engineers. Rheam looked for a degree in engineering in his instructors; this at a time when tertiary education was very rare. Many of the weapons were very 'James Bond' – and this is where Ian Fleming got his inspiration for 007's gadgets.

Station 15 – The Thatched Barn

Yet another site in the vast SOE empire was the Thatched Barn in Borehamwood, on the northern edge of London. The Thatched Barn was built in the 1930s and had been a Butlin's holiday camp. It was home to SOE's camouflage section. Much of the work of this station involved the final equipping of agents before they were sent into Europe. Typical of the work was reproducing the right clothing for the relevant country. The styles were copied from newspaper photographs, catalogues and so on; and had to be perfect down to the last stitch and button.

Maps were hand-sewn into silk underwear. Labels in clothes were in the language of the target country. Forged travel passes, ration cards and work permits were also produced in industrial quantities by the Thatched Barn and its sub-contractors. Other work included packing hand grenades into tins labelled as fruit.

The labels were reproduced by skilled artists to look like the real thing. Logs were made from plaster of Paris, with guns hidden inside them – while explosives from Aston House were disguised as coal, and the droppings of horses, mules and dogs.

No detail was too small for SOE. George Millar, for example, had his teeth fillings taken out and replaced using French amalgam. Gilbert Renault, chief of the Notre Dame resistance circuit, in Northern France, was given a paunch – which interfered with his digestion. In fact Renault's appearance had been altered so much – by professional make-up artists from Denham film studios – that he was unrecognisable even to his nearest and dearest. Agents were issued with cyanide pills if they wanted them – some in false teeth, some in signet rings, some in coat buttons.

Once trained, armed and disguised, the next step for the agent was to go into Europe.

Tempsford, Tangmere and Harrington – secret flights

In the summer of 1942, Squadron Leader Hugh Verity was deep underground at the headquarters of Fighter Command at Bentley Priory, acting as a link-man between the radar plotters and the RAF's fighter stations; his job being to target fighters onto incoming raiders. One of his assistants was a 'Y' service officer who logged Luftwaffe and RAF radio traffic. Verity was intrigued by the single RAF aircraft – 'Specials' - that flew in and out of British aerospace on moonlit nights - which the 'Y' man identified and told him to ignore. The 'Y' man told him that the Specials were ferrying spies, saboteurs and their weapons and supplies into occupied Europe. There were quite a few such planes. Verity, who already had much night-flying experience with Coastal and Bomber Commands and who was growing bored with 'flying a desk', investigated further. He found that the aeroplanes were from 161 squadron, based at RAF Tempsford, near Bedford. The squadron had two flights, one of which dropped agents and supplies by parachute, the other (which flew Lysanders) landed in enemy territory to deliver and pick up agents and supplies. The Lysander could transport two (or if they were very friendly and lightly built and conditions were ideal, three) adult passengers.

The Westland Lysander

Verity was 24 years old and married with a baby son. Like many fine young men and women in the war years he was prepared to risk his life for his country: 'Once I had calmly accepted what seemed to be the high probability of death …I went to Tempsford to offer them my services as a Lysander pilot.'

Hugh Verity was heartily welcomed by the officer in charge of the flights, Wing Commander Percy Pickard. Verity - being an above average pilot with a lot of night-flying experience and who, as an added bonus, was fluent in French - was just the man Pickard was looking for. He there and then offered Hugh Verity the job of running the Lysander flight. Verity turned down promotion and a safe non-flying job to take the post.

In the early years of the war, the aircraft that flew SIS and SOE agents back and forwards to Europe were based at several places. In 1942 their headquarters was finally fixed at Tempsford, just up the Great North Road from the training and camouflage bases. Even so, the Lysander flight was somewhat nomadic, spending two weeks of each lunar month at Tangmere, in Sussex, which was much nearer the coast than Bedfordshire. Both sites were highly secret. Very few people, even in government and the RAF, knew of their existence. The Westland Lysander was ideal for the job of agent ferrying because of its comparative lightness, strength, and ability to take off and land on a short runway.

For all his-night flying experience, Hugh Verity had to train up for the taxing demands of his new role. The Lysander was a single crew plane, so the pilot had to navigate as well as fly, and that in darkness – or rather in moonlight. With, initially, no radio plotting aids, he would have to find and land on a small landing strip many miles behind enemy lines, drop off an agent or two and their luggage (normally transmitters weapons and money), perhaps pick up another agent, and leave. The skill of the pilots in finding the fields at night was extraordinary. The pilots would prepare a strip map from Tangmere to the landing field with the main features, towns, rivers, coast, flak gun batteries, etc, plotted on it and follow it with the aid of weak cockpit lights which, when used, would cause the loss of night-vision. Hence the need to fly a week before and after full moon – clouds, storms and fog permitting. Verity studied the map for each flight for around two hours before leaving. The work called for mental fitness and concentration of a high order – which was why the pilots had to be above average. Here is Hugh Verity aloft on a January night:

'I kept my head down studying the map for a few seconds too long. I looked up and found that I was flying straight at a huge wireless mast, one of several in a group. The heavy 'g' loading as I pulled the stick back must have increased my apparent weight two or three times. I was badly frightened by this near miss and the sudden charge of adrenalin in my blood left me trembling.'

As for the frequently filthy weather:

'... in the strong up and down draughts, the four tons of my little Lysander were tossed around like a cork in a whirlpool. Flashes of lightning temporarily ruined my night vision and St Elmo's fire flickered with blue light round... my aeroplane. My gyro compass toppled and I came to the conclusion that hell could hardly be worse. Then it got worse, because I felt air sick. I opened a sliding window, took off my oxygen mask and vomited, meanwhile doing my best to fly the Lysander through the storm. I wondered how much I should tip the airmen who would clean out the cockpit.'

There were plenty of ways to lose planes. When Verity first took charge of the Lysander flight, he didn't like the fact that his aircraft were painted matt black all over:

'...in the mistaken belief that this would make them invisible at night. While this may have been true for searchlights, the night fighter's view from above on a moonlight night was a very different matter. The silhouette against low cloud was far too positive. So I had the upper surfaces recamouflaged in dark green and pale grey.'

Another fear was of ambush. What if the lights below were operated by Germans and not friends? To counter this, the correct recognition letters had to be used by both sides. In fact, as time went on, this became less of a threat. The Germans tended to keep to the towns and larger villages. To stage an ambush would have taken many troops and the landing grounds were remote, frequently changed and guarded by resistance workers armed with Sten guns. However, when they did find a landing site, or a possible one, the Germans would put up wooden stakes to stop landings.

A further and unexpected enemy was treachery. Verity trusted one agent, Henri Déricourt, to a specially high degree, as did his fellow aviators. Verity's boss, Wing Commander Pickard, however, had an old English sheepdog called Ming who 'was very truculent' towards Déricourt when he visited his home. Ming would not remain in his presence and had to be confined to the kitchen when Déricourt was in the house. *Ming was never belligerent to any other person or dog* (my italics). Ming was right. Déricourt was in it for the money. He betrayed many of his French fellow agents to the Nazis. They were tortured and died in concentration camps.

The landing grounds had to be marked by 3 lights. The first one was lit at the agreed landing time (or when they heard the plane approach) by the agent on the ground for the aircraft to see. To see this light – Verity describes the torch lights as 'pin-pricks' – called for superb eyesight and, of course, outstanding map-reading. The pilot replied by flashing an agreed recognition Morse letter. Then the ground force lit the other two lights to make an 'L' shape, pointing roughly into the wind. The landing area had to be flat, not boggy and treeless, with no tracks or roads across it and of a certain length (the long side of the 'L' where the Lysander would land, turn round and take off, being 150 yards). The turnaround time to unload passengers and cargo and load new passengers and cargo was three minutes.

Marking out a landing zone took experience and practice. If it was not done properly, the pilots could not find the rendezvous. Even worse, the RAF lost pilots and planes by landing in ploughed or rutted fields. As time went on, they insisted that the reception committee be trained at Tempsford on a week-long course. George Millar in *Road to Resistance* describes how he did a course there, covering; 'Reception committees, containers, Lysander and Hudson landing grounds, new radio and radar aids.'

Increasingly, the aircraft themselves were fitted with radios by engineers from Whaddon: and SOE developed the 'S' phone so that the ground party could talk directly to the pilot.

As well as flying in agents for SIS and SOE, the Lysanders were used by MI9 to pick up escaped allied airmen. One of them went on to join 61 Squadron.

The half dozen Lysander pilots met most of the resistance leaders; Verity flew Marie-Madeleine Fourcade and Benjamin Cowburn; and they transported the great and the good of the French resistance, including two future French Prime Ministers and also General de Lattre, the only French general who tried to fight the Germans when they marched their troops into Vichy France, in 1942. He had been imprisoned and escaped and would become the leader of the Free French armies.

A French agent said of landing in England:

'At last one can breathe freely. No more prison, no more continuous terror, no more need to watch everything, note everything; no more black fear as in a bottomless well.'

As for the agents arriving in France, they were greeted like the saviours that they were. Benjamin Cowburn (who arrived by parachute) says that the French showed an awed respect for the deviousness and ability of the British secret services:

'It was touching to see how their conviction blinded them to the obvious lack of intelligence of any kind whatever that had led to the Munich agreement, Dunkirk and other weird "strategic conceptions" which had distinguished our war-making up to date... but now Winston Churchill would alter all that... and victory would soon follow... the prestige of Churchill was immense and I felt proud. We had the good fortune to have an incomparable leader who was also the greatest living orator in the world.'

Verity made around thirty successful landings in France, perhaps the most of any RAF pilot, and was given several decorations. On one occasion he flew 12 nights in a row:

'The end of my tour of operations released the tension on the spring which I had more tightly wound than I had realised. I suddenly collapsed and was good for nothing but staying in bed for the best part of a week.'

Shortly after this (in December 1943), 3 of the 4 Lysander pilots in his flight were killed on operations. His boss, Percy Pickard, died in a tree-top raid on Amiens prison which was carried out to free imprisoned resistance fighters.

The scale of the operations from Tempsford and its satellites was astonishing. In late 1943, an SOE agent, Wing Commander Yeo-Thomas ('Tommy' to the SOE) made a direct appeal to Winston Churchill for more aircraft. Churchill went to the Americans, who obligingly gave him one hundred aircraft, which flew from nearby Harrington (where today there is a wonderful small museum on them and SOE). The USAAF flew mainly Liberator ex-bombers. These were used for parachuting agents and supplies. In all, the RAF and USAAF made some 25,000 'Special' flights (3,000 of them American), delivered 46,000 tons of supplies to them (4,000 of them by the USAAF) and flew in over 7,000 agents (of which over 500 were American).

Once the agents were in France, they communicated with headquarters by radio.

They talk to their agents – Leo Marks

Until June 1942, SIS supplied SOE's radio traffic from the Whaddon Web (as described in *The Intelligence Zone*) – but SOE complained of delays and so, in June 1942, they were given control of their own communications. Those communications were centred on Poundon and Grendon Underwood, near Bicester, in a very rural area on the borders of Buckinghamshire and Oxfordshire.

The man who was in charge of SOE's coding was Leo Marks; the only (and rather spoiled) child of antiquarian book sellers of 84 Charing Cross Road, London (If that address seems familiar, it is because of the book of the same name written by Helene Hanff, an American, who wrote movingly about her dealings with Leo Marks' father as she built up her book collection by post). Leo was obsessed with codes. He cut his teeth deciphering the coded prices of his father's stock and was, after much effort on his part, recruited onto a cryptography course (run by John Tiltman, of Bletchley Park) in Bedford in January 1942.

Marks was precociously clever; solving cryptographic examinations at a speed which confused the course tutors. Later during the war he was (as a part-time task) to compile crosswords for *The Times* – a hobby he had taken up as a boy at St Paul's school. Of the twenty five graduates of the Bedford course, Marks alone went to SOE – all the others to Bletchley Park. Tiltman described him later as 'the one that got away.' Apart from training agents in the use of codes, Marks also trained SOE's radio operators.

Initially the messages were based on coded references to poems, some of the poems chosen by the agents and many of them ditties written by Marks himself, often witty, sometimes obscene, sometimes very moving, as was the one he wrote for the twenty-two year old Violette Szabo:

The life that I have
Is all that I have
And the life that I have
Is yours

The love that I have
Of the life that I have
Is yours and yours and yours

A sleep I shall have
A rest I shall have

Yet death will be but a pause

For the peace of my years
In the long green grass
Will be yours and yours and yours

Violette Szabo was not fated to sleep in long green grass. She was shot in the back of her head in the concentration camp of Ravensbruck along with two other SOE agents, Lilian Rolfe and Denise Bloch. They held hands as they knelt down together. Then they were flung into a furnace.

The greatest coding problem SOE faced during the war was the number of indecipherable messages that agents sent. If the poems were misremembered, or mis-keyed, the message would need to be retransmitted; in which case the agent in the field was increasingly in danger of detection by the Germans, who monitored traffic from a central office in Paris and gave immediate instructions to detector vans who would close in on the agents. The searchers, when they got close, would then turn off the electricity in individual buildings (the fuse boxes in France being on the outside of the buildings). If the transmission stopped when the power was cut off from a building, the agent must be inside. That was one of the dangers of having a set which was powered from the mains. Only when SOE produced a new set with its own (pedal-powered) generator would this part of the problem be solved. Marks tells us:

'The slightest mistake in the coding, a second's lapse of concentration, would render the entire message undecipherable. Frequently as much as 20 per cent of SOE's traffic could not be decoded due to agents' errors.'

The agent traffic was handled at Grendon Hall, near Bicester, where teams of women worked on transmitting and receiving – and cracking undecipherable messages – round the clock:

'They were all FANY (First Aid Nursing Yeomanry), a volunteer organisation whose members could resign at will. The average age of these girls was twenty. After the briefest of training they were dispatched to one of the most secret establishments in England.'

As I mentioned earlier, there was much tension in SOE between the British F Section and de Gaulle's RF Section. The transmission and receipt of both was handled by Marks's stations, although the French insisted on using their own codes. When a French agent working for de Gaulle was caught by the Gestapo while retransmitting an undecipherable, Marks decided that enough was enough. He personally cracked the codes of de Gaulle's RF section and worked out any undecipherables before passing the message on. He never let on that he had done so, but now that any De Gaulle undecipherables were dealt with by Marks, there were far fewer retransmits – and far fewer dead radio operators.

Marks was a mathematical genius. He also had compassion, poetry and common sense. It was he who later introduced the use of one-time codes, randomly generated and printed on silk. One 'silk' was given to the agent, a second kept at Grendon Hall. Once used, the code would be destroyed by the agent.

Marks was as sharp as a needle; the ideal person to be in charge of SOE radio codes. His suspicions were aroused by what was happening in the Dutch section of SOE: or rather, what was not happening. While all other sections had their large number of undecipherables, the Dutch section did not have any. Not one:

'Why were the Dutch agents the only ones who never made mistakes with their coding... were their working conditions so secure that they had as much time as they needed to encode their messages and didn't have to worry about Germans on the prowl?'

As he looked more closely at the Dutch section, Leo Marks saw some other anomalies. All agents were issued with security checks. For example, one of the Dutch agents was required to make a spelling mistake every eighteenth letter and insert three dummy letters at the end of each message. The Dutch agent omitted these checks. Was it feasible that these super-agents, who made no mistakes in coding, were incompetent enough to omit security checks? Nor did the Dutch ever ask for repeats of messages sent to them by Grendon Underwood...

Radio tends to be a two-edged weapon; it is difficult to be sure that the cipher messages plucked with difficulty out of the ether are genuine or enemy disinformation. Both sides successfully used captured radio operators to deceive the other – sometimes briefly, sometimes over an extended period with devastating results. The Germans called the process *funkspiel* (radio game). Marks suspected that the SOE Dutch operation was a *funkspiel*. He was right; the entire operation had been discovered by the Germans. The reason why agents omitted their security checks was either because they were under German control, in prison or dead. Every scheduled landing was known by the controller of the Abwehr in Holland, Herr Hermann Giskes; his troops were picking up every supply drop and agent. The British were being played. Marks had difficulty getting his masters in SOE to believe him. He had little respect for some in his own organisation – hardly surprising in the circumstances:

'Nothing could persuade them their traffic was blown, and if I'd told them that none of their agents had ever made a mistake in their coding, they'd have sent a message to the field asking why not.'

The sparring game of bluff that Marks played with Hermann Giske is described in Marks' book *Between Silk and Cyanide* (silk being the one-time message pads he devised, cyanide the alternative for many who did not use them). It was a game that Marks won – but the real losers of the 'England Game' as the Germans called it were the Dutch agents. In 1942 and 1943, 51 British trained agents fell into German hands during their parachute landings in Holland, as well as tons of weapons, radios, explosives and other sabotage material. Several were murdered in the concentration camp of Rawicz, in Poland. In September 1944 the rest were moved to Mauthausen, where thirty five more were butchered.

The tale of what happened at Mauthausen is very dark indeed. The camp had been set up specifically for the murder of intellectuals. One of the refinements was the 'stairs of death' at the stone quarry. The SS guards would force prisoners to race up the 196 stairs carrying 50 kilogram blocks of stone. As can be imagined, many collapsed, rolling backwards, in falling killing and maiming those behind them. Those who survived the ordeal would often be placed in a line-up at the edge of a cliff known as The Parachutists Wall. At gun-point each prisoner would have the option of being shot or pushing the prisoner in front of him off the cliff.

Of the fifty-one Dutch agents captured in the 'game', four survived.

What agents did in the field

Trained, armed and into the field, the agent now had to carry out his or her tasks – the disruption of the German war effort by the destruction of transport and material. For their part, the Germans did all that they could to destroy their hidden enemy – by identity checks, searches, the employment of double agents (such as Cole and Alesch); any means to find and, if possible, break into agents' traffic – as they did so successfully in Holland.

Sometimes it was mere luck, courage or the degree of German vigilance which dictated whether or not an agent was caught. Some bluffed their way through terrifying encounters with aplomb.

SOE saboteurs were especially effective in damaging the French railways. In the year before D-day (June 1943 to May 1944) they damaged or destroyed nearly 2,000 locomotives and 8,000 goods trucks. U-boats were often penned in port as they could not get spare parts. The Peugeot tank manufacturing plant and around 90 other factories were put out of action. In France, SOE persuaded several factory owners to collaborate with them in the sabotage of their own factories; under the threat that if they didn't the RAF or USAAF would do it anyway. The factories were paid after the war to fix the damage. This 'blackmail sabotage' was SOE at it very best: cutting the involvement of the middle man (themselves or the air forces) to the minimum and saving the lives of many civilians and airmen. In this they were helped by the BBC.

The BBC played a vital role in the secret war. Often they would furnish the proof that was needed to show a waverer that the person who asked them to fight the Nazis was not an agent provocateur. The Peugeot factory is one example of this. The owner, Rodophe Peugeot, was asked by an SOE agent, Harry Ree, to supply plans and aid the sabotage of his factory. Peugeot was, naturally enough, somewhat suspicious: so Ree asked him to supply a message which would be read out over the BBC to prove that the appeal was genuine. The Frenchman asked that the phrase *la guerre de Troie n'aura pas lieu* (the Trojan War will not take place – the title of a French play) be read out. It was, and on the strength of that confirmation, Peugeot helped SOE sabotage his own factory; which was put out of action for several months at the expense of a little plastic explosive. Furthermore, Peugeot's workforce did not die under Allied carpet bombing.

The BBC was the great Allied broadcasting success; it was listened to religiously across the continent even under pain of imprisonment or death. It aided the resistance on a massive scale, for example broadcasting coded messages giving the timing, place and number of packages of the night flights from Tempsford and Harrington.

On the eve of D-day, when the BBC announced to the SOE the message *les carrots sont cuites* – the carrots are cooked – 960 sabotage attacks against railway lines were carried out and every train from southern France to the front was derailed at least once. The movement of the Das Reich armoured division toward Normandy was delayed by weeks.

There is a huge literature of the works of SOE across Europe and rightly so. Theirs is the story of how the British helped the subject peoples rise against their oppressors and help to overthrow the strongest and most evil regime in the history of mankind. The books are not only exciting and moving but have a value far above mere fiction, for they are the unvarnished truth and tell us of the best and worst that man has been and can be. These are lessons worth learning. The numbers of resistants who died in the concentration camps ran into their thousands. They fought knowing that they would probably be captured: and that if they were, death would be almost guaranteed and probably welcomed. I will finish this chapter with a couple of tales of the Norwegian resistance.

Norway

The Norsk Hydro and the atomic bomb

'Heavy Water' (deuterium oxide) is a moderator which can be used during nuclear fission to both promote and control certain chain reactions. It was believed that the German plan to make an atom bomb involved the use of Heavy Water in a so-called 'breeder reactor'. Heavy Water was only produced in quantity at the Norsk Hydro in Norway. The importance of Heavy Water was recognised by all atomic scientists – high amongst whom were the French Nobel prize winners, Madame Marie Curie and her husband, Pierre Joliot. This esteemed couple deemed the liquid so important that they purchased the Norsk Hydro's entire supply and shipped it from Bordeaux to Britain in the custodianship of their daughter, Eve. That was in 1940: the same year that the Nazis gained control of the Norsk Hydro as a fruit of their invasion of Norway.

The first successful attack on the Norsk Hydro works was in February 1943. It was carried out by Norwegian saboteurs trained by SOE. The agents entered the heavily-guarded and seemingly impregnable factory and blew up key components. A year later, SOE agents struck again: blowing up and sinking the ferry which was carrying the Heavy Water which had been produced in the intervening period. These tales are extraordinary but far too large for this book. As I mentioned earlier, the agents were trained at Brickendonbury, where models were set up of the Norsk Hydro plant, its surroundings (a deep chasm had to be crossed to get to it) and the machines and pipework inside. The attacks took a lot of resources; three saboteur raids and a USAAF bombing attack.

In fact, the attacks were not as urgent as were thought at the time as the Nazis were not close to producing an atom bomb. Britain and America had to assume that the Nazi bomb was imminent, however, for they knew better than anyone what such a weapon would mean. As I've explained elsewhere, Britain had already started to build a bomb at the start of the war (the

Norsk Hydro - Vemork hydroelectric plant at Rjukan Norway circa 1947

MAUD project) and handed over her research to America. This information was left to gather dust on a shelf in Washington for nearly a year until a determined British scientist, Mark Oliphant, finally managed to bring it to the attention of two influential Americans - Ernest Lawrence and Robert Oppenheimer. Then America moved atomic research forward with astonishing rapidity, pumping vast resources into it; taking over the lead from Britain. Both countries, then, were well aware of the importance of Norsk Hydro and would do just about anything to destroy its output.

The effectiveness of SOE's pinpoint targeting is revealing. A USAAF air attack on Norsk Hydro used 174 bombers and 435 tons of bombs to destroy 120 lbs of Heavy Water. The SOE attack used 11 lbs of explosive and destroyed 3,000 lbs of Heavy Water.

Max Manus

A less well-known Norwegian resistance story concerns the work which was carried out by Max Manus and his Oslo Group. Manus was a Norwegian hard man who had knocked about

South America before the war; working as the foreman of a gang of joiners in Chile:

'We earned good money, and we spent it on wine, women and song. There was always fighting at Laguna Verde, usually with knife-play. Life was cheap.'

When war came, he returned to Norway. When the Germans invaded his country he joined the underground fight against them, ever watchful, ever fearful:

'No one who has not experienced an occupation can imagine what terror the name of the Gestapo inspires. There were countless tales of their sadistic orgies, the best way out of which was death.'

Max Manus

Manus was working on an illicit newspaper *Vi vil oss et land* (we want a country) and was also involved in more violent resistance. He was returning to his flat one evening when he was jumped by six armed men. In his rucksack were weapons, illicit newspapers and a plan to kill one of Quisling's deputies (Quisling was the puppet governor of Norway – a collaborator with the Nazis). Manus dived through the window (he was on the first floor):

'I was resolved to take my life rather than submit to interrogation... I was convinced, and still am today, that I could not hold out under interrogation... I have never reckoned on any normal person being able to hold out under torture.'

When he regained consciousness he was in an ambulance, handcuffed, being taken to hospital. The Norwegian hospital doctor lied to the Germans that Manus had broken his back and was at death's door – and so his captors waited for him to recover sufficiently to be interrogated. He lay in bed for days until he regained enough strength to escape. He then bluffed his way through the resultant German manhunt, proving his bona fides at one tight moment by singing... 'the song which was almost the German national anthem during their occupation of Norway "Wir fahren gegen Engeland' (we drive against England).'

Manus then escaped to England (via Russia, Turkey, Africa, Trinidad and Canada), arriving there in December 1941, seven months after breaking out of the hospital:

'It is hard to describe the feelings which filled me on realising that I had arrived in England – that I stood on English soil and would be able to fight side by side with the people which I set above any other in the world, this strange race whose unshakeable calm could be so exasperating, but who always won the last battle because they never gave up. We felt like pilgrims arriving at Mecca.'

Manus was put through the usual agent training:

'For the first time, perhaps, in history ordinary young lads were scientifically turned into criminals pure and simple. We went through special courses (at Brickendonbury) in which we learnt how to to blow up anything from a railway track to a safe... we learnt how to kill with a knife... we also learnt to kill without weapons ..we learnt to draw swiftly and shoot quickly; we realised that sooner or later, which of two men could draw quickest would be a decisive factor.'

Manus was also taught how to forge identity cards, how to lie, how to distribute propaganda as well as going through commando training in Scotland and parachute training at Ringwood. He learned with Norwegian thoroughness and speed. George Rheam, the father of sabotage at Brickendonbury, said that the Norwegians impressed him above any other nationality: 'for their readiness to run risks and for their steadfastness in facing the dangers of sabotage.'

Manus was exceptional, even for a Norwegian. He was parachuted into Norway along with weapons and explosives. His plan was to get hold of canoes and paddle into Oslo harbour, there to place Limpet mines on German shipping.

31

Manus tells many tales of what he and his Oslo Group got up to in his superb book *Underwater Saboteur*. Here is one of them:

Manus and a companion, Gregers, dressed as workmen, are carrying a bag and toolbox along a quay in Oslo harbour. It's not easy; their loads are bulky and heavy. As well as Limpet mines they are carrying food, water, one of those guns which get round the barnacle problem by shooting a nail into the ship (to hang the limpets on) and a couple of books to read – for they expect to be under the quay for four days before their target ship arrives. Their chosen books are *Piccadilly Jim* and *Thank you Jeeves* – both by P.G. Wodehouse. They have to get onto the woodwork under the quay in order to sink the ships without being seen:

'I felt many pairs of watchful eyes on me. It would not be very pleasant if that disagreeable looking officer with the scars on his chin were to rouse himself and come up and ask what I had in the bag. I must take matters into my own hands. I went to the edge of the jetty where I was to go down, and asked politely if the sentry would mind moving a little. He asked what I was going to do, and I replied that I was going down to repair the electric cable which belonged to the cranes. It was a feeble story, but it was good enough for the sentry. Gregers came along lugging a heavy tool-box full of Limpets and had a considerable shock when he saw me talking to the sentry. He put down the box beside the bag; I clambered down the ladder and was going to take the things from him. Gregers' sense of humour, as usual, got the better of him, and he asked the sentry if he could not help us with the heavy box. The sentry was more than happy and carried it with pleasure. Our spirits rose again...'

The SOE could, and did, teach their recruits many things: but they could not teach them courage, or raw cheek.

Manus survived the war: but it must not be thought that he was a man without nerves, or feelings. As so many of SOE's agents, he suffered for years afterwards from nightmares, alcoholism and bouts of depression. Len Manderstam, another SOE man, said:

'I believe the post-war rate of divorces amongst those who served in SOE was the highest of all the armed forces. Our people had lived on lies and found it hard to readjust to a peacetime family existence. To live a lie, day in day out, is a very difficult thing. Gradually... you develop reflexes which in normal circumstances would be regarded as criminal. For months after the war I had to restrain an urge to open desk drawers and check the contents whenever I was left alone in someone else's office.'

I quoted Benjamin Cowburn earlier: 'The unwritten rule of the game seemed to be that as long as no Germans were injured there would generally be no reprisals.'

However, if the resistance did kill Germans, the reprisals were sudden, ruthless and terrifying, often involving hostages. Mostly these incidents are forgotten now, such as the attack in April 1942 on a German troop train on the Paris to Cherbourg line. Ten German soldiers died. For this, fifty-two hostages were immediately shot. These were men and women who had been pulled from the street at random and forced to travel on the troop train. If anything happened to the train, they died. It had. They did. The Germans suspected that it was a communist attack; they were almost certainly right. Most of the open attacks were by the Communists, who cared little for repercussions. The Germans rounded up a hundred Jews and communists and transported them to concentration camps in Germany where ninety of them were murdered.

There was a third possible target for what the Nazis leaders styled 'terror attacks'; and one of far greater importance to them than their machines or even their troops: themselves. The seemingly invulnerable Nazi state was run by individuals; the messiahs of the master race who had built concentration camps for the torture and death of all who stood against them. These, the high priests of racial evil, had ordered the invasion and subjugation of a continent – and had made and were overseeing detailed plans to murder entire nations and peoples: Jews, Poles, Russians, Ukrainians, Gypsies, the mentally defective, homosexuals.

If the 'terrorists' who were fighting for the liberation of their own countries could snuff out one of them, then the lords of Nazi evil, too, would know terror. One government, exiled in Buckinghamshire, was planning to do exactly that. With SOE help, they would kill perhaps the cleverest, most effective and evil devil of them all. But the strike would spark off rapid, and rabid, Nazi retribution...

2: To send a devil back to hell

Alarms of war

The starting point of all that I have written so far – the rise of SIS and SOE, the forests of their communications networks, their arms factories and agents, radar, the RAF's modernisation and the first steps towards computing – were Britain's response to Nazi belligerence after the election of Hitler to the leadership of Germany. Hitler's chief of intelligence, Reinhard Heydrich, was an integral part of the Fuhrer's plans and their execution. To understand just how important a part Heydrich played in the Nazi state, and how that led to his being targeted for assassination, it is worth looking back at the events which led to war and the part he played in them.

The first, bloodless, Nazi takeover was in 1936 with their reoccupation of the Rhineland, a large 'buffer zone' of western German territory which had been administered by the Allies after the First World War.

The Nazi annexation of Austria followed a little later. It was Hitler's second attempt to take over his homeland, the first having being in 1934, when he arranged the murder of the Austrian Chancellor, Engelbert Dollfuss. On that occasion the Italian dictator, Mussolini, had opposed Hitler, forcing him to back down. In 1938 the German army marched into Austria unopposed. The tanks were bedecked with greenery, flowers and the flags of both nations. The frontier barriers were raised. There was no resistance In the words of the Panzer commander, Heinz Guderian:

'Old soldiers from the First World War had pinned their decorations to their chests and saluted us as we drove by. At every halt the tanks were decked with flowers and food was pressed on the soldiers. Their hands were shaken, they were kissed, and there were tears of joy… children of one nation, split by unfortunate politics into two during so many decades, were now happily united at last.'

The remark that Austria and Germany were 'children of one nation' is interesting. Modern Germany was formed in 1870 by the Chancellor of Prussia, Otto Von Bismarck. Prussia and Austria were the strongest of the multitude of independent German-speaking states which had resulted when Napoleon kicked the Holy Roman Empire to pieces. When Bismarck united them, he did not want any challenge to his power within 'his' new nation, so he excluded Austria. Hitler's move to unite the two great German speaking states into his 'thousand year Reich' set off alarm bells throughout Europe. In 1914, the united powers of Germany and Austria (and its Austrian-Hungarian empire) were at the heart of the armies which defeated Russia and came within an ace of total domination of Western Europe.

When Hitler sent his troops into Austria, he also sent his secret police - the Gestapo. Potential opponents of the Nazis – 70,000 of them – were arrested within days. A referendum was then held to see whether the people of Austria approved of Hitler's occupation of their country. Those that the Nazis did not like - such as gypsies, Jews and communists – were not allowed to vote. Over 99% of those who did vote were recorded as approving the annexation. Hitler's brand of promises, violence, intimidation, propaganda and vote-rigging was all but unstoppable.

Some voices in the west - most famously Winston Churchill - warned that Hitler's demands would not stop with Austria. They claimed that unless he was challenged, the other European nations would fall one by one. Nazi demands would go on until they dominated continental Europe. Then it would be Russia's turn, then Britain's, then America's. There was no limit to Hitler's ambition. Churchill and his like were largely dismissed as fantasists – or worse, war-mongers. And so, Europe slid towards the abyss.

After Austria, the major powers that might fight Hitler - Britain and France - were to allow him one more 'easy' conquest. That conquest was Czechoslovakia.

In the spring of 1938, Hitler began to demand the return of the Sudeten region of Czechoslovakia to Germany. The Sudetenland was an area of Germany which had been

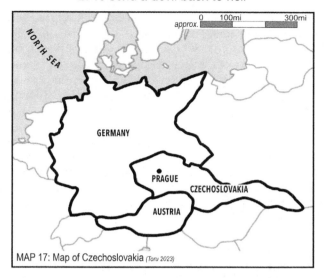

MAP 17: Map of Czechoslovakia *(Toru 2023)*

given to Czechoslovakia by the victors of the First World War as a buffer zone. It had a large proportion (around 90%) of German citizens. Czechoslovakia itself had been set up after the first world war partly from elements of the old Austrian-Hungarian empire with the object of curbing German power. Militarily, the hilly Sudetenland was of key importance to the young country as most of its border defences were situated there. If Czechoslovakia lost the Sudetenland, she would lose her defence belt, leaving the rest of the country an easy prey to German expansion.

Moravec – master of spies

The Czech Prime Minister was Edouard Benes. The head of Czech intelligence at the outbreak of war was General František Moravec. Moravec had been given the job ten years earlier; his workload expanding hugely as Nazi spies and agitators began to infiltrate Czechoslovakia in force. He worked long and hard to turn around his country's moribund intelligence services. The focus of his efforts was the enemy at the door - Hitler's Germany:

'We needed the secrets of a country where people already spoke in whispers, in constant dread of the Goering-Himmler Gestapo, whose spies and informers were everywhere. Concentration camps were already being built: the Reich's frontiers were closely guarded and every foreigner, like every citizen, was watched. Espionage was punished by long periods of imprisonment or – as was frequently the case in Berlin – death by beheading. How could this police state be penetrated? How could spies be found, willing to supply some of the most closely guarded secrets in Europe? ..although our recruitment of agents inside the Reich began from scratch we soon discovered that even a brutal police state like Hitler's could be penetrated. We were to find, in fact that... the Third Reich... could be completely riddled.'

František Moravec

The head of Czech Intelligence

Moravec was a very good spy master. He set up his networks very carefully, so that one agent could not implicate another. He was playing against a dangerous foe, one Reinhard Heydrich, who had been employed by the SS leader, Heinrich Himmler, to run his secret services, the SD and Gestapo. The two arms often overlapped; but essentially the SD controlled spying and the Gestapo provided the muscle. Heydrich was the man behind the flood of Nazi agents into Czechoslovakia – and many other countries beside. Moravec did not under-estimate Heydrich's men:

'We accepted it as a fact that no agent, or contact, could withstand the Gestapo's drugs and tortures, if arrested.'

One of the pieces of information Moravec got from Germany was the complete plan of their air force for 1936-7 including blueprints and performance figures on the new fighters and bombers they were developing. These he passed on to French and British intelligence (to be added to everything else they had). The German agent from whom he got these plans was arrested and beheaded by the Gestapo.

Another informant, who was highly placed in German military intelligence (the Abwehr), supplied Moravec with details of tank production and troop numbers. This agent, whom Moravec refers to as 'A54', was to become a key source of information on Nazi resources and intentions.

Munich

On September the 22nd, 1938, Hitler demanded the immediate surrender of the Sudetenland to Germany and the evacuation of the Czechoslovak population by the end of the month. The next day, Czechoslovakia ordered troop mobilisation. War seemed imminent, and France, which had a mutual defence treaty with Czechoslovakia, began a partial mobilisation. Neville Chamberlain, the Prime Minister of Great Britain, was in a less warlike state of mind. He said:

'How horrible, fantastic, incredible it is that we should be digging trenches and trying on gas-masks here because of a quarrel in a faraway country between people of whom we know nothing.'

Chamberlain and the French Prime Minister, Edouard Daladier, travelled to Munich and met with Hitler, agreeing to his demands on September the 30th. The Czechs (who were not represented at the meeting) seeing that no country would come to their aid, surrendered the Sudetenland. Hitler assured those at the meeting that this was the extent of his ambitions for expansion.

Chamberlain returned to England carrying a treaty signed by Hitler, which, he proclaimed meant 'peace in our time.' The British Prime Minister's wish for peace was, on the face of it, admirable. However, in implying that Hitler's action was of small consequence, he denied the growing threat to his own country, Europe and, indeed, humanity itself. The scope of the danger was worldwide because of the rise of the fascist powers. This group of expansionist and belligerent nations possibly had the military might to take over Europe and Asia and pick up the remains – Australia, Africa and the Americas – at their leisure. And the first among those nations – Nazi Germany – was an evil one.

In truth, Chamberlain knew a great deal about the victim of the quarrel, Czechoslovakia and even more about the aggressor, Germany. And he knew it through the press and through Sinclair's spies. He also knew it through a number of members of parliament. Perhaps the most important of these politicians (but not the only ones) were Clement Attlee (the leader of the Labour party), Anthony Eden (Chamberlain's own Foreign Minister, who resigned because of Munich), and a troublesome back bencher called Winston Churchill.

The opinion of the Czech head of intelligence, František Moravec, on the actions of Chamberlain and Daladier at Munich is interesting. He said that Czechoslovakia was betrayed by France – who he called 'corrupt and defeatist' – but he had no strictures for Britain. That seems odd – but then France had a formal treaty, Britain did not; and Moravec may well have been influenced by the fact that he would end up in Britain.

Reaction to Munich

Chamberlain's action at Munich was widely welcomed at the time, but British opinion was sharply polarised. Those who were against it thought it the greatest political error in their lifetime: possibly in the history of their country. Churchill said in the House of Commons (5th of October 1938):

'We have sustained a total and unmitigated defeat... and do not suppose this is the end. This is only the beginning.'

Clement Attlee's speech was profound and ominous; truly terrifying in its implications:

'We have seen today a gallant, civilised and democratic people betrayed and handed over to a ruthless despotism. We have seen something more. We have seen the cause of democracy, which is, in our view, the cause of civilisation and humanity, receive a terrible defeat... The events of these last few days constitute one of the greatest diplomatic defeats that this country and France have ever sustained. There can be no doubt that it is a tremendous victory for Herr Hitler. Without firing a shot, by the mere display of military force, he has achieved a dominating position in Europe which Germany failed to win after four years of war. He has overturned the balance of power in Europe. He has destroyed the last fortress of democracy in Eastern Europe which stood in the way of his ambition.'

After the outbreak of war, many who had been in favour of the Munich agreement said that it had given a breathing space to rearm. The argument is weak. Czechoslovakia was strong and, given any backing from the western powers, would have fought. In František Moravec's words:

'In the opinion of the (Czech) general staff the situation was that, had France and Britain stood firm and France kept her word, Hitler would have been compelled to back down, with probably fatal results for his regime, or, had he gone to war, he would have suffered a military defeat... the intelligence on which this was based was, in virtually every detail, in the possession of the French and British.'

These opinions were shared by most of the German army high command. They urged Hitler not to press his case, but their Fuhrer was in the habit of overriding his generals. He was a gambler and, until now, a successful one. The Munich gamble was high-stakes but shrewd. The Western democracies had lost millions of their men in the mud of Flanders and the Somme a mere twenty-five years earlier. The Fuhrer thought they lacked the 'courage' to spark a second Armageddon. He had no such 'weakness' and he was prepared to bet with the blood of his people. This time he was right.

With the Nazi takeover of the Sudetenland, Moravec believed it was only a matter of time before German armies swallowed up the rest of his country. When this happened, he intended to take his intelligence team to London:

'My collaboration with British intelligence was already long standing and close. Politically Czechoslovakia suffered as a result of Chamberlain's actions, but at least there was no element of betrayal, as we had no formal alliance with Britain ...I had made up my mind our new base would be in Britain ...whose intelligence service I rated then and rate now among the best in the world for efficiency and integrity.'

Britain would certainly welcome the Czechs. Major Harold Gibson, the SIS's man in Czechoslovakia, had promised them a safe haven should they need to flee their country.

After taking the Sudetenland without having to fire a shot, the Nazis were, indeed, poised to take over the rest of Czechoslovakia. Goebbels' propaganda machine was pumping out its usual pre-invasion justifications with stories about Czech 'provocation' – tales of brutalities and atrocities allegedly carried out by Czech police on the German minority. Moravec's intelligence agents were already reporting that German troops were mustering to take over his country and A54, their super-spy in the German Abwehr, confirmed this. He also passed on a copy of the black list that the Gestapo were to use to round up people that they wished to interrogate once they had crossed the border. Major Gibson offered Moravec a plane with 12 seats to get the Czech intelligence service out.

Moravec flees

After passing their most important files to the British embassy, and destroying all the rest, Moravec and ten of his companions fled to England. All of them were on the Gestapo black list that A54 had passed on. It was the 14th of March 1939. Moravec recalled later:

'As our plane passed over the frontier mountains, I put my head in my hands and cried.'

The next day, in the teeth of a violent snowstorm, the Germans entered Prague. Moravec and his intelligence section joined the exiled Czech President, Edouard Benes (who was already living in Dulwich, south of the Thames) in London. Shortly after his arrival, Moravec met Quex Sinclair, the head of SIS/MI6, who welcomed his Czech counterpart with open arms. As I mentioned earlier, the Czechs and the Poles, having more sophisticated and complete organisations than any of the other allies in exile, would run more or less independent intelligence organisations in Britain.

Moravec still had radio links with 'stay behind' intelligence staff in Prague and through them with his vitally important spy in German military security force (the Abwehr), codenamed A54. Moravec met A54 in Holland in June 1939 and was briefed by him on the upcoming German invasion of Poland, which was planned for the first of September. A54 also told of increases in German Panzer divisions (to 9). Moravec passed this information to French intelligence – who didn't believe it – and the British. The Poles themselves refused to listen. Moravec is scathing about the Poles, who had taken the opportunity of Germany's invasion of Czechoslovakia to annex a bit of his country for themselves:

'Their singular blindness and stupidity sealed the fate of both our countries.'

A54's reports influenced Chamberlain's decision to proclaim to the British parliament Britain's guarantee of Polish independence. As predicted, on September the 1st, 1939, the Germans invaded Poland. As a pretext, they dressed some concentration camp inmates in Polish uniform, murdered them, and then photographed their bodies at the German border, alleging that they had been part of a Polish invasion.

The organiser of this Nazi deception was one Reinhard Heydrich. Heydrich was a busy man after the German invasion of Poland, finding and killing all those whom he had identified as being a threat to the Nazis. To do this, he used mobile killing groups, the *Einsatzgruppen*. Heydrich's Central Security Office(SD) furnished lists of those who they considered to be a threat to the Nazis. In addition to intelligentsia and political opponents, the mobile squads murdered Jews wherever they found them. Heydrich is said to have boasted that within three weeks he had arranged the murder of over 90% of the Polish intelligentsia.

The abandonment of Czechoslovakia at Munich played a key part in the German attack on France. The Skoda Works, in Pilsen, was one of the largest armament complexes in Europe. The Czech tanks that could have fought Hitler were now part of the German army. In the words of Len Deighton, in his brilliant book *Blitzkreig*:

'It is doubtful whether any attack against France in 1940 would have been contemplated without the resources the Germans gained in Czechoslovakia. Discounting lightweight German training tanks, no less than one third of the German armour used against France originated in Czech factories.'

After the collapse of France, Moravec's star agent, A54 (by then working in Prague), reported on Operation *Seelöwe* (Sealion) the German plan for the invasion of England. This information was passed on to Winston Churchill, as Moravec tells us in his memoirs:

'We did not have to wonder what would happen to us if Hitler's invasion succeeded. Since August we had had in our hands a document compiled by the Reich's Central Security Office which listed over 2,000 people in Britain for 'special treatment'. My name was on there, as was Winston Churchill's... special German units had been trained for the task of dealing with the listed persons and were scheduled to come with the first wave of the invading forces. On their black list, after each name. was the number of the Bureau assigned to conduct the investigation. Mine was Bureau IV, the Gestapo.'

The 'black list for Britain' was just one of Heydrich's many such lists. Heydrich gave it to Franz Six, whose job it would be to direct police operations in Britain. The 'special units' Moravec alluded to were the *Einsatzgruppen* mobile murder units. They would have been particularly busy in the Intelligence Zone.

It was not surprising that Moravec's name appeared on Heydrich's death list. Even though far from the Reich, the Czech intelligence service constituted a menace to the Nazis. The Czechs aimed high; arranging the 1939 Munich beer-hall bomb attempt to kill Hitler, which the Fuhrer only escaped by changing his schedule (which he did frequently; a lot of people were out to get him). And they planted a bomb to blow up Himmler's train. The bomb went off on time but the train was late. Under Frantisek Moravec, the Czech secret service was the most active of the European secret services.

Moravec's intelligence unit was housed in three houses in Dulwich; directly under the Luftwaffe's flight path from France. They had a worm's eye view as the Battle of Britain was fought in the skies above them. As a break from his problems, Moravec and his wife and two daughters would garden at the end of the day. It was a beautiful spring and summer. His family would ever afterwards associate the smell of sweet peas with the 'undulating banshee call of an air-raid siren.' One evening in that August of 1940, they went out into the garden and stood on top of their bomb shelter and looked up at the waves of incoming aircraft:

'The whole scene looked unreal – tiny silver planes darting about like toys. But as the days went by, with sirens sounding 'Alert' and 'All Clear' almost continuously, there could soon be no doubt that we, along with all the millions of London's inhabitants, had suddenly been transported to the front lines.'

When the Germans switched to night bombing, Dulwich was hit hard in the indiscriminate attacks – and the three houses quickly became too bomb-damaged to live in. In September 1940 the Czechs were moved to the Cumberland Hotel, near Hyde Park, while night after night the Luftwaffe bombed London:

'The purpose of the terror clearly was to break the spirit of the Londoner and to render the great city uninhabitable. Fifty-seven apocalyptic nights in a row failed to accomplish either of these ends... I remember vividly one night in the Cumberland Hotel cafeteria (which was underground and was used as the hotel's bomb shelter)... Suddenly there was a shudder and I could feel the wall behind us undulate. The room filled with dust. A helmeted air-raid warden and a policeman rushed in, went to the wall along which a number of people, my family among them, were sleeping. He shook my daughter Hanyi by the shoulder, motioning her to get up. Everyone was ordered to the centre of the room, to lie on the ground with their heads under stacked tables, like the spokes of a wheel. In the morning we learned what had happened. A bomb had fallen next to the hotel and buried itself in the pavement. It did not explode but lay wedged against the wall, inches away from the sleepers. It was a delayed-action bomb and no one could tell when it would go off. One of the heroic squad who dealt with unexploded bombs dug it out during the night and removed it to Hyde Park where at 8 a.m. we heard it explode.'

Then the Czechs were evacuated from London, heading up Watling Street to that popular destination for the London exodus, North Buckinghamshire. Their new accommodation was found - as Bletchley Park and Whaddon Hall had been - through the good grace of SIS's contacts within the Whaddon Chase hunt. President Benes and his entourage moved to houses in Aston Abbots and Wingrave several miles from Aylesbury, while several Czech families, including Moravec's went to a country house in Addington, a couple of miles from Buckingham. They also took over a very nice mansion at Chicheley, for training their agents.

'Pop' Gambier-Parry's section set them up with a transmitting station at Hockcliffe, on Watling Street - the old Roman road, running south from Bletchley to London (the Czechs and Poles, retaining their own intelligence services, had their own transmitters).

After Hitler's lost battle with the Royal Air Force, he turned his eyes away from Britain. A54 reported on various German military plans, including the invasion of Greece; and the Nazi attack on Russia. Moravec passed the information to Churchill – who informed Stalin of the forthcoming attack on his country. Stalin regarded all of the warnings from Britain as a provocation and ignored them.

The Nazi invasion of Russia (the Soviet Union)
In 1941 the Soviet Union consisted of Russia and several of her client and conquered satellites (such as the Ukraine and the

Baltic states). I will refer to the Soviet Union here simply as Russia. On the 22nd of June 1941, German armies launched their 'surprise' attack on their Russian ally. The Nazi armies went through the Russian defences like a hot knife through butter.

The Nazis had been undermining the Russians for years – as they had been working against all of their neighbours. In charge of Nazi intelligence work was Heinrich Himmler's second in command, Reinhard Heydrich. He had played a long game. Several years before the Nazi assault on Russia, he had instigated a plan to dupe Stalin into believing that the Russian army was riddled with traitors. He had documents forged to 'prove' it. These he fed back to Stalin. In his Red Army purges which began in 1937, Stalin had 10 of his 13 army commanders, 57 of 85 of his Corps commanders and 110 of his 195 division commanders shot – as well as somewhere between fifteen and thirty thousand other officers. It is a matter of conjecture whether it was Heydrich's lies which triggered this massacre of the innocent; or whether Stalin was merely looking for an excuse to break the power of his army. 'Uncle Joe' was partial to mass murder. At any rate, the move suited the Nazi high command well; the Red Army offered no meaningful resistance during the first months of Hitler's invasion.

Incidentally, Heydrich fell out with Admiral Wilhelm Canaris, the head of the Abwehr (German military intelligence) over his deception of Stalin. Canaris did not think forgery honourable. Heydrich had no such scruples. According to one of his senior staff (Walter Schellenberg), he:

'...had to be the first, the best, in everything, regardless of the means, whether by deceit, treachery, or violence. Untouched by any pangs of conscience and assisted by an ice-cold intellect, he could carry injustice to the point of extreme cruelty.'

As Adolf Hitler launched his three million soldiers against Russia, he was not totally confident. How could he be, after his recent defeat at the hands of Dowding and the subsequent flight of his deputy, Rudolf Hess, to England? The Fuhrer had replaced Hess with a new High Priest, Martin Bormann.

Bormann would more and more decide who should enter the holy presence. Now, he whispered in his master's ear that all was well: 'Providence has appointed you as her instrument for deciding the future of the world.'

Victory in Russia was key to German victory in this global war. To exploit that expected victory and lay down the foundations of his 'Thousand Year Reich', Hitler looked to his SS deputy Heinrich Himmler – and Himmler looked to his own subordinate, Reinhard Heydrich.

Reinhard Heydrich's singular talents lay not only in deception and extreme cruelty but in mass murder. He was kept busy after the German invasion of Russia and the Baltic States in mopping-up operations behind the front; setting up further mobile *Einsatzgruppen* units to kill captured communist officials and Jews. He improved their working methods. Driving from place to place killing people was too slow. Quicker to get the locals or the victims themselves to dig mass graves. The victims were forced to strip first so that their money, jewellery and clothes could be taken, then shot, then buried. Meticulous records were kept. For example, the Nazis murdered more than thirty-three thousand that way at Baba Yar.

But being the best at streamlining the wholesale slaughter of the helpless was not fulfilling enough for Heydrich. His tireless and acute brain identified Czechoslovakia as a place where he could increase his power and move into the limelight. The Protectorate of Bohemia and Moravia (as the Germans called the Czech lands) was becoming a problem to the Nazis; the man who Hitler had appointed to run the country – Konstantin von Neurath – was too soft. True, he had shot a few students and closed the universities; but what about the factories?

Just as they had in France, the Nazis used Skoda tanks and guns in their assault on Russia; but Czech armament production was plagued by a wave of strikes. Deliveries to the Russian front fell by a third. As the summer of 1941 faded into autumn, the surprise attack on the east had slowed down; all means must be taken to restore momentum and take Moscow. The problems in Bohemia and Moravia had to be addressed quickly; but they called for special treatment. In Moravec's words, his country:

'was not to be crushed by indiscriminate naked brutality as elsewhere... yet the resistance movement had to be rooted out. This called for a special mixture of brutality and cunning.'

No Nazi combined brutality and cunning better than SS Obergruppenfuhrer Reinhard Heydrich.

Heydrich: puppet master of the Third Reich

What made Heydrich tick – and why was he so successful? According to Schellenberg:

'He was a tall, impressive figure with a broad, unusually high forehead, small restless eyes as predatory as an animal's and of uncanny power, a long predatory nose, and a wide full-lipped mouth. His hands were slender and rather too long – they made one think of the legs of a spider. His splendid figure was marred by the breadth of his hips, a disturbingly feminine effect which made him even more sinister. His voice was much too high for so large a man and his speech was nervous and staccato and although he scarcely ever finished a sentence, he always managed to express his meaning quite clearly.'

Heydrich was a sociopath. He had no moral compass, compassion or empathy. Hitler called him 'the man with an iron heart'; but it would be wrong to dismiss the man purely in terms of the good that was missing from him – 'the heart'. There was plenty within him; but it was all rotten stuff; manipulation, intimidation and violence. Heinrich Heydrich was a living cancer on mankind; malign; evil; a devil. Schellenberg relates that he had:

Reinhard Heydrich

'An ungovernable sexual

appetite. To this he would surrender himself without inhibition or caution, and the calculated control which characterised him in everything he did left him completely then. But in the end he always regained sufficient mastery over himself to prevent serious repercussions.'

Being in high office allowed him to get away with whatever he wanted in that direction. It hadn't always been so. In his earlier life he had been an officer in the German Navy but was court–martialled and thrown out for sexual misconduct. Being jobless was what had taken him into the Nazi party in the first place. As a complement to his sexual interests he ran a brothel in Berlin – the Salon Kitty – where the prostitutes were all committed Nazis. There he had all the visitors' pillow talk recorded on to vinyl disks; the recording devices being turned off when he turned up for his own orgies. When he considered that the recording engineers knew too much, he would have them drafted to the Russian Front. Schellenberg tells us that meetings with Heydrich often concluded with an orgy. He also records that:

'He was inordinately ambitious. It seemed as if, in a pack of wolves, he must always prove himself the strongest and assume the leadership ...he always knew more than others.'

He collated detailed dossiers on everyone he deemed important or a threat, including fellow Nazis, so that he could strike them down if necessary. He, was, he liked to think, Nazi Germany's 'C' – even going so far as to use the letter 'C' (for chef) to describe himself. He differed, however, in one vital way to Quex Sinclair, the head of Britain's SIS. His people were as wont to use the thumb screw as the brain to attain their ends. Although Heydrich's name was not as commonly known as that of his boss, Himmler, a continent lived in terror of his minions: the SS, SD and Gestapo. He was, arguably, the brains of the Nazi party. In Schellenberg's words:

'This man was the puppet master of the Third Reich ...the hidden pivot around which the Nazi regime revolved. The development of a whole nation was guided indirectly by his forceful power. He was far superior to all his political colleagues and controlled them as he controlled the vast intelligence machine of the SD.'

Heydrich takes charge of Czechoslovakia

In September 1941, the Fuhrer put Heydrich in charge of 'The Protectorate of Bohemia and Moravia' – as the Nazis had renamed Czechoslovakia. Heydrich did not waste time. On the very day that he was inaugurated in the magnificent Hradcany Castle in Prague he had the Czech Prime Minister, Alois Elias, arrested. He would be shot. Heydrich knew that Elias was talking to, and supported, the Czech government in exile, in England. On the same day he also moved against the Czech resistance. Over 4,000 would die in the purge. The action would earn Heydrich the nickname 'The Butcher of Prague'.

At the same time, the Reich Protector increased workers' wages and rations. Canteens were introduced to factories, workers' food, clothing and tobacco rations were increased and properties stolen from the Jews were set up as holiday homes for them. Heydrich, having a complete control of press and radio, gave great emphasis to the execution of black marketers. His mixture of stick and carrot worked well and arms production increased. The change was almost instantaneous. The leader of Czech intelligence, Frantisek Moravec said of this period:

'In London, the resistance activities of the occupied countries were regularly reviewed. Their rating depended on the degree of damage they had succeeded in causing the Nazis. The activity of each underground movement was regarded as its contribution to the war effort. In the second half of 1941, as a result of Heydrich's destruction of the resistance organisation, Czechoslovakia was always about the bottom of the list.'

The hunter becomes the prey

František Moravec knew Heydrich of old; and he knew what he was capable of. Within a week of the inauguration of the new 'Reich Protector of Bohemia and Moravia', Moravec recommended, and President Benes agreed, that they would try to kill him. The job was to be carried out by a Czech hit team –

trained by SOE. The plan was given the code name of Operation Anthropoid. President Benes knew the cost in Czech lives would be high; but believed that the killing was necessary for the good of the country. The Czech intelligence service got down to planning.

The agents and their training

After the German invasion of their country, a large part of the Czech army had fled to, and fought on in, France. Over 3000 of them took ship in the great evacuation to England from Bordeaux on the eve of the French surrender. They were based near Chester. Moravec visited their barracks to select volunteers for Operation Anthropoid. He interviewed only bachelors whose parents were dead. The two soldiers who would carry out the killing of Heydrich were Jan Kubiš and Jozef Gabčík. Both were sergeants in their late twenties; and both had fought with the Czech army in France. The two men were good friends.

They were put through basic SOE training in Scotland – where their trainer described them as 'near perfect' in jujitsu. Then they were sent down the Great North Road to Brickendonbury and Aston House, the SOE's sabotage schools in Hertfordshire. These, as I've mentioned previously, were run by 'Nobby' Clarke (of Bedford Baths fame) – and 'Captain Blood' – Colonel Leslie Wood. Here they went through the usual sabotage course; pressure switches, explosives and the like; then progressed to specialised training.

Clarke and Wood had modified one of their standard anti–tank grenades. The resultant bomb was about a third of the length of the original and fitted with one of their own Bakelite 'all–ways fuse' – designed to ignite irrespective of how the grenade landed. The grenade weighed just over a pound. Kubiš (the thrower) would have to unscrew the Bakelite cap, set the fuse and toss the bomb – then run. The two experimented on old cars at various speeds. It was tricky to get the grenade into or near enough the car to demolish it and the two Czechs preferred to rely on the Sten gun. They were only issued with one Sten (for Gabčík); they had enough other stuff to cart about, what with pistols, a dozen bombs, detonators, wire, ammunition, 40

pounds of plastic explosive and gelignite, fog signals, time
pencils, a tree spigot gun and a lethal hypodermic syringe.

Moravec briefed the two on the topography of Prague with
the aid of a large–scale map. The pair learned quickly.

Josef Gabčik

Jan Kubiš

Josef Gabčík and Jan Kubiš were flown to Czechoslovakia
from RAF Tangmere in Sussex. František Moravec drove them
there himself. He told them that they were probably going to
their death:

'Gabčík said he viewed the mission as an act of war and
the risk of death as natural. Kubiš thanked me for choosing
him for a task of such importance. Both said they would
prefer death to capture by the Gestapo.'

The men were told to act alone and contact no–one as the
Czech underground was riddled with Heydrich's spies. Josef
Gabčík's last words to František Moravec were:

"You can rely on us Colonel. We shall fulfil our mission
as ordered."

The four engine Halifax bomber took off from Tangmere at
10pm on December the 28th, 1941. It returned at 0819 the
following morning, having dropped Kubiš and Gabčík and two

other resistance groups into Czechoslovakia. During its mission, the Halifax was fired at twice from the ground and shook off two night fighter attacks.

Heydrich's work in 1942

The Wannsee Conference

As well as running The Protectorate of Bohemia and Moravia, Heydrich was busy perfecting a complex administrative problem for which he was uniquely suited; how to turn millions of peoples out of their homes and kill them. To further this plan he presided at the Wannsee Conference in Berlin (in January 1942).

The object of the Wannsee Conference was to define and initiate the methods needed to exterminate European Jewry as quickly, cheaply and efficiently as possible. Heydrich had several improvements to the inefficient existing processes to offer, based partly on his work with the *Einsatzgruppen*. Gas was quicker than bullets, and less distressing for the killers; more of the work could be done by the victims themselves. Then there was the pioneering work he had done at Terezin, where the whole of the Jewish population of Czechoslovakia (88,000) were taken. Many died there, the rest were sent on to extermination camps. Only 3,000 would survive the war.

A major 'deliverable' of the Wannsee Conference was Operation Reinhard (named in Heydrich's 'honour'); the building of three new purpose-built killing camps – Belzec, Sobibor and Treblinka.

Heydrich's master plan for the Czech lands

And then there was Heydrich's plan for the Czechs. The founding father of modern Germany, Otto von Bismarck had said that he who controlled Bohemia controlled Europe and Hitler agreed. Consequently Bohemia and Moravia would become part of the Thousand Year Reich. Once the war was won, the Czechs would be shipped out and replaced by Germans. After a while, no one would even remember that they had ever been there. But Heydrich was, as so often, playing a long game. There was lots to do first. In his own words:

'In order to have an idea which of the people in the area are capable of Germanization, I have to have a racial and national census. This involves the use of various methods and all kinds of back–door approaches so that I can classify the entire population by nationality and race.'

Heydrich thought that somewhere between 40 and 60 percent of the population – say half – were worth saving. These would 'wherever feasible' be resettled in Germany 'in a manner precluding their return'. They were to be used as labourers and slaves. The other half would be sent out east – to Stalin's Arctic concentration camps, which were expected to be captured soon by the German army.

Heydrich had set the appropriate wheels in motion in order to decide which half of the Czechs were to live and which to die. Buses were touring the country examining school pupils and workers under the pretext of an anti–tuberculosis campaign. The 'racial experts' in the buses used tables with graduations of shade – like paint charts – to determine race by the colour of hair, skin and eyes; providing the raw data for the box ticker who would assign who was to be a slave and who was to die.

The turning in Prague

Heydrich lived with his family in a small village near Prague called Brezany. His comfortable estate there had been confiscated from a Jewish family and extensively remodelled by his wife, Lina. She had a pool of slave labour provided by a concentration camp to carry out her wishes. Not for the Heydrichs the scream of air–raid sirens and the disturbing smell of sweet peas in Dulwich. The 'Reich Protector' was to be ambushed as he was driven to work in his office in Hradcany Castle, in Prague.

Kubiš and Gabčík had initially thought to attack Heydrich as he came out of the gates of his estate. After detailed study of his schedule, however, they had realised that a better place to get him was in Prague itself. Down a hill, as he approached the river, there was a sharp corner where his car would have to slow down.

The two assassins had a lookout man, Jozef Valchik.

On the morning of May the 27th, 1942, Heydrich bade Lina and his four small children goodbye and set off to work as usual. He probably felt pretty good that lovely spring morning. Things were going well for him. He had broken the Czech resistance and production levels were high. As he had reported to his boss, Adolf Hitler, the people were more interested in meat and cigarettes than fighting; and why should they not be? Germany controlled continental Europe and, while Hitler's armies had not reached Moscow, they would doubtless do so this year. He, Heinrich Heydrich, was lord of all he saw. He slew entire races at his whim – and could have any woman he desired. None could withstand him. Deportations, death marches, mass killing of Jews and of various conquered nationalities were his daily occupation. He was the purifier of the races, man become god; and he knew no fear.

He had recently had a fellow German, Paul Thummel, arrested. He was convinced Thummel was spying for Moravec. He was right. Thummel was 'A54' and would be shot by the SS.

He was also very close to realising a long–term ambition of his; to take over all of Germany's intelligence services, including the Abwehr (military intelligence). He was leaning heavily on Admiral Canaris, the head of the Abwehr and the signs were that he would prevail. Heydrich inspired fear in just about everyone: Canaris included. Heydrich had summoned the admiral and he was arriving in a few days. Then all policing of the Nazi state would be in his, Reinhard Heydrich's hand.

And what of the future? Heydrich was just 38 years old – what about the boss's job? Hitler was 53 years old and cracks were beginning to appear. Heydrich had a file on the man. The Fuhrer would not last for ever. Who better to replace him when the time came than the most ruthless, committed and intelligent Nazi of them all: himself.

Heydrich's soft-top car was not escorted and it was unarmoured. The top was down. Whatever fine self–conceit he may have been harbouring on that warm spring morning, the master of the most feared secret police in the world had made basic and stupid mistakes which would cost him his life.

Gabčík and Kubiš put paid to the tyrant in a most dramatic shoot out. As the car slowed to turn the steep corner, Gabčík

Scene of shooting of Heydrich - Prague, Czechoslovakia

stepped into the road, raised his Sten gun, aimed at the Reich Protector and pressed the trigger. Nothing happened. Perhaps in the heat of the moment, Gabčík had forgotten to release the safety catch, or maybe it had jammed. Stens had a habit of doing that. Heydrich saw Gabčík and ordered his driver, Klein, to stop, pulling out his pistol as his car slewed to a halt. In the meantime a tram had drawn up on the opposite side of the road. Kubiš stepped forward and flung his grenade, which, instead of going into the Mercedes, exploded behind it, sending shrapnel into the car and into the passengers of the tram opposite. Heydrich and Klein leaped from the car and confronted the attackers. Heydrich then collapsed, and Klein was shot, while the assassins escaped.

Heydrich had been seriously wounded by shrapnel from the bomb. He seemed to be recovering at first, but died a week after the ambush when his wounds became septic, probably because they contained horsehair from the upholstery of his car. He wasn't treated with penicillin, which would probably have saved him, for Germany had none.

Doubtless glasses were raised in London and Buckinghamshire. Glasses were not raised in Prinz Albert Strasse, the SS headquarters in Berlin. Schellenberg tells us that there was incredulity there; fear even. How could this have happened? Who was behind it? The more suspicious speculated that it could have been an inside job, ordered by Himmler or Bormann maybe. Had the SS Obergruppenfuhrer fallen foul of the snake pit of Nazi power politics? The top ranks of the Nazi party – principally Bormann, Himmler, Heydrich, Goering and Goebbels – were always vying for their lord's attention; Heydrich, of late, had been speaking to Hitler in private. The others wouldn't have liked that; had they deemed him to be becoming too powerful, and snuffed him out, as Heydrich and Himmler had arranged the death of Ernst Rohm?

They were quite wrong in this; Heinrich Himmler, the head of the SS and Heydrich's nominal boss, is said to have cried on hearing the news. Then he ordered the murder of 150 Jewish inmates of Ravensbruck concentration camp. More mature reflection made him turn his attention to Czechoslovakia.

British plastic explosive, British fuses, British detonators and a British sub–machine gun littered the scene of the attack. There was no doubt where the assassination had been organised; the next task was to kill the perpetrators.

Aftermath

The Germans turned Prague upside down. Colonel Ronald Littledale, an escaped British officer who was hiding in the city at the time, described 'the almost insane' brutality of the SS as they sought to revenge their fallen master.

On the evening of Heydrich's state funeral in Berlin, German and SS police surrounded the village of Lidice; which they believed (wrongly) was home to Czech resistance fighters. The 500 residents were rounded up and the boys and men separated and shot. The women were deported to Ravensbruck concentration camp where sixty of them died. The children were 'racially screened' in the Heydrich prescribed manner. Of the 91 children, nine were judged sufficiently German to be sent to Germany and raised there. The rest were murdered. German labourers razed the village to the ground.

A week after Lidice, Gabčík and Kubiš were betrayed and trapped with five other resistance fighters in the crypt of the Church of Saints Cyril and Methodius, in Prague. After a long gun battle in which four hundred besieging German troops failed to overcome the 'terrorists', the SS forced the Prague fire brigade to flood the crypt, while simultaneously bombarding it with tear gas grenades. The remaining defenders killed themselves before they were drowned.

Church of Saints Cyril and Methodius, flooding the crypt

The Nazis still needed Czech weapon production, so 'only' five or ten thousand died for the killing of Heydrich. Were their deaths a justifiable price for his people to pay to be rid of Heydrich? It is hard to disagree with the words of František Moravec. He pointed out that Heydrich's job was:

'The eradication of the Czech nation and its amalgamation into the Reich …as Kubiš and Gabčík knew, freedom and, above all, liberation from slavery, have to be fought for, and this means losses in human lives.'

Had Heydrich survived, and had the Nazis not been defeated, what had happened to the people of Lidice would have probably have happened to most of the Czech population.

It would be wrong to say that the killing of Heydrich put the fear of God into the Nazi elite; the only gods they believed in were themselves. It did, however, show that they could be called to account by man: and it made crystal clear what the verdict would be for them. They were by now so steeped in blood that only two options awaited them; victory or death.

But victory did not seem to be getting nearer for the Nazis; they had invaded but not yet beaten Russia – worse, perhaps, they had declared war on America. Soon the United States would begin to pour arms and armies into Britain to act as a launching point for an assault on Nazi Europe. That could not be allowed to happen; the island must be defeated.

The Nazis could not engage the British army on land and they had tried and failed to defeat the 'Tommies' by air and on the surface of the sea. The island must be brought to ruin, then, by submarines. It couldn't be long until that happened, either. In the month Heydrich died (June 1942) , Germany sank more British ships – 135 – than ever before. The shipping lanes between the old world and the new would be cut. Britain would starve....

3: The Siege of Britain:
Defeating the U-boats

This precious stone set in a silver sea
Which serves it in the office of a wall
Or as a moat defensive to a house
Against the envy of less happier lands.
William Shakespeare - Richard II

The Siege of Britain

In June 1942 things had never been worse for the convoys coming to Britain. They were engaged in what Churchill called the Battle of the Atlantic. For once the old master did not do his subject justice. It was not one battle but many. Indeed it was the longest action in the Second World War. It started on the first day of the war and it finished on the day Germany surrendered; for while the enemy could not cross the moat it could starve the fortress into surrender. This was the Siege of Britain.

In 1939, Britain's Empire and Dominions were spread across the world in every continent. The island-seat of Empire not only traded by sea, its very survival depended on its enormous Merchant Navy. Britain was importing over two thirds of its fruit, sugar, cereals, cheese and fats. The country also imported over half of its meat and relied on imported feed to raise its own cattle. This amounted to around 20,000,000 tons of food a year. And it annually imported 10,000,000 tons of oil. At any one time, 2,500 ships were at sea carrying these goods. With the Mediterranean closed to British shipping, most of this came from the Americas, mostly to Liverpool and Glasgow.

Without these supplies, Britain would starve – as Germany had as a result of the British naval blockade in World War One. And she would lose the ability to defend or attack. Rationing and growing food at home would help somewhat, but it would not produce petrol or aviation fuel.

Churchill was to write: 'The only thing that ever really frightened me during the war was the U-boat peril.' Having been through much the same threat during the first war (I shall come to this in more detail when I talk about Dönitz), the question immediately arises as to why Britain wasn't better prepared.

The Royal Navy

In 1939, the British Royal Navy was the most powerful in the world. By mid-1941 it had disposed of or marginalised the Italian and German surface navies. 'The Andrew' (Royal Navy) was far bigger than the German surface fleet. Even if the best German battleships out-gunned the best British ones – which the battle between HMS *Hood* and the *Bismarck* showed to be the case - the Royal Navy could call so many units into play that they could pummel any enemy ship until it sank: which is precisely what had happened to the *Bismarck*. Only a couple of major German ships, holed up in Norwegian fjords, still posed a threat. Although these were a danger to the enormous convoys of supplies that Britain was sending to Russia, Hitler thought so little of them that he had to be persuaded not to scrap them and send their crews to the Russian Front. The RAF would get them in the end.

But Britain was not winning its war against the submarines. The Royal Navy had ASDIC – (known in America as sonar) a pulse which 'pinged' back from a solid object - to spot submerged submarines: but the range wasn't great, and it also 'pinged' off whales, fish and sea currents. Also it had to be used when the searching vessel was travelling at a fairly slow speed. Nor could it spot surfaced submarines – a major problem as that is what the German U-boats generally did (at dusk or night) to approach and attack convoys.

The Royal Navy started the war controlling their defences against submarines from the basement of the Admiralty buildings, in London. As this was not bomb-proof, they dug a 30 foot hole in nearby Horse Guards Parade – linking it underground with Churchill's War Rooms, Downing Street and lord knows where else – and built a new headquarters there which they called The Citadel. It's still there. A windowless monster, thankfully largely softened by Virginia creeper now. The frontline headquarters were in Liverpool, at Derby House, where there was a massive wall map of the Atlantic and a control room similar to the one at Fighter Command.

RAF Coastal command

The other part of the British defence was RAF Coastal Command, headquartered at Northwood, near Watford. The headquarters had been moved from Lee-on-Solent, on the south coast, in 1937, as part of RAF command centralisation. Now, Fighter, Bomber and Coastal commands were all within a few miles of each other and their political masters in London. They were also astride the communications lines which fed from the capital up Watling Street through Leighton Buzzard, and on to Bletchley Park and Whaddon Hall. That way they had immediate access to intercepts, radar and intelligence.

RAF Coastal Command badge

If the communications serving Northwood were up to date, Coastal's aircraft were not. Known as 'The Cinderella Service' it came a long way behind Bomber and Fighter commands in the RAF hierarchy. It started the war with around 450 aircraft – mostly obsolete – and around 10,000 personnel.

The early patrol planes were mostly Tiger Moths. As Chaz Bowyer, in his *Coastal Command at war* recounts, these were:

'Open-cockpit, fabric and wood-structured biplanes, bereft of radio, armament or any other warlike impedimenta and barely capable of achieving 85 mph (75 knots). Sole armament was a signal pistol, while communication could only be gained by use of two homing pigeons, carried in a wicker basket in the spare cockpit. Personal flying clothing for the solitary pilot was a Sidcot Suit (invented by Sidney Cotton), fur lined jacket, or any other type of privately supplied clothing available: and the only concession to personal preservation in the event of ditching was a part-inflated motor car inner tube, with a 30 foot length of string attached to a marine distress signal.'

De Havilland Tiger Moth

They flew in pairs. If any U-boat was sighted, one Tiger Moth could return to base and summon armed help, while the other circled the enemy. In the winter of 1939-40 (the coldest winter in living memory), the Tiger crews plodded round Britain's coasts, enduring severe icing, fiendishly cold temperatures, and hours of fruitless search. At least two pilots are on record as falling asleep, one woke as his wheels hit the sea, the other returned with seaweed trailing from his tail. Doubtless many others nodded off and simply disappeared. Coastal's weapons were ineffective. The bomb they used against the U-boats, for example, required a direct hit to do any damage.

Nor, it is to be feared, was the quality of its command quite as high as it should have been at the outbreak of war. Robert Hanbury-Brown, the prodigy who worked for 'Taffy' Bowen in radar development (see *The Intelligence Zone*), tells a revealing tale on the subject. Admiral Somerville, of the Royal Navy, had asked Bowen a key question: was it possible to spot submarines using aerial radar? Bawdsey had already spotted ships – the fleet – but what about something as small as a sub? Bowen and Hanbury-Brown answered the admiral's question by flying a plane from Royal Naval Air Station (RNAS) Gosport, in Hampshire. They spotted the L27 – the first submarine ever to be detected by radar - in November 1939.

Hanbury-Brown had just turned 23. He was already working with Fighter Command. He had, with Stuffy Dowding's backing (and urgent insistence), fitted radar to some and IFF transmitters to all of Fighter Command's aircraft. IFF (Identification Friend or Foe) told the radar stations that the aircraft were friendly. Without that, the operators had no way of knowing whether the planes that they were plotting were 'ours' or 'theirs'. Before it was properly installed this had led to 'The Battle of Barking Creek' – when the RAF shot down two of its own Hurricanes. Hardly surprising, then, that IFF transmitters (transponders) were manufactured and sent out to all commands to be fitted to all aircraft with the highest priority.

When Hanbury-Brown went to RAF Leuchars, the main Coastal Command base in Scotland, in January 1940, he expected, as the man who could spot submarines, to be greeted as the Second Messiah. He was rapidly disabused by the Signals Officer, who waved the annoying youth aside with the words:

"'I haven't got time right now to look at your radar, I am too busy doing tests on carrier pigeons." You could have knocked me down with a feather; but there was more to come: "Oh," he added, "before you go – can you tell me if the boxes which keep on arriving here are something to do with your radar? They are marked SECRET and so we have to lock them up and we are running out of cupboards with locks." He unlocked one of the cupboards and there were row on row of IFF radar transponders …I couldn't imagine anyone at Northolt telling Stuffy Dowding that carrier pigeons should take priority over radar.'

That was the whole problem. Although the war in the Atlantic was as critical to Britain as the Battle of Britain, Coastal Command had no Dowding. And unfortunately they had an opponent rather more competent than Goering.

Coastal Command fought under the direction of the Royal Navy in the Atlantic battles and, as we shall see, both used weapons – radar, Huff-duff, decryption and the Hedgehog - developed in the Intelligence Zone. The great British command, communication, intelligence and development centres - the Citadel, Liverpool, Northolt, Leighton Buzzard, Bletchley Park and Whitchurch – worked hand-in-glove to win the longest and hardest sea war that Britain has ever fought.

How the three-hander – the Royal Navy, Coastal Command and the Intelligence Zone - worked together to win that battle can best be understood (and, perhaps, can only be understood) if seen from the standpoint of their main enemy, the German U-boat service.

The Lion and his cubs

The head of the U-boats was Admiral Karl Dönitz. Dönitz was an old sea dog (born in 1891) who had commanded a submarine in the first war, when he was captured by the Royal Navy and imprisoned, first in Malta and then in Yorkshire. The German U-boats of World War 1 had been very successful, sinking nearly 6,000 ships (mostly British) and killing 15,000 sailors. They had nearly brought Britain to her knees and were one of the reasons why America had entered the war in 1917. One German commander alone had sunk 189 ships.

It was while imprisoned that Dönitz began to mull over how the U-boats could have been better used. He would use the ideas he formulated with devastating effect in his second war with Britain. The fact that he was considering these matters while still a prisoner tells us something about the single-mindedness of the man his future troops would call "Der Löwe" (The Lion). His drive, hard work and attention to detail took him to the leadership of the German U-boat fleet. He specified the design of the boats, their size, armament, where and how they would strike and how he would control them. Karl Dönitz had every intention of winning the rematch.

Until France surrendered, he had little control over where he could station his submarines – only on Germany's narrow coast around Kiel and Hamburg. That meant that they had to sail through the North Sea, bordered by the British coast and round Britain's northern waters, to reach the Atlantic. However, France's surrender opened up a much better possibility. Sailing his U-boats directly into the Atlantic was much less risky than the North Sea.

To make his plans possible, the German surrender terms specified that the whole west coast of France would be part of

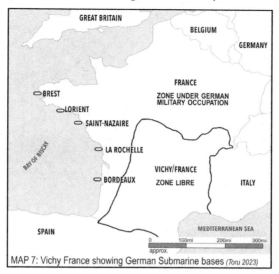

MAP 7: Vichy France showing German Submarine bases *(Toru 2023)*

the Occupied Zone - under direct German control. Dönitz arrived at Lorient, on the coast of Brittany, the day after the surrender was signed.

In his twenty years of planning Dönitz had allowed for, among many other possibilities, the fall of France. He knew exactly where his French submarine bases would be. His fleet would be at Brest, Lorient, Saint Nazaire, La Rochelle and Bordeaux. The headquarters would be at Lorient: which is why he was there on the 23rd of June, 1940. He found himself a nice house on the seafront across the inlet from Keroman - the new base he was having constructed - and installed himself and his staff. He commanded his submarines to be moved from Germany and, when they had arrived, sent them out across the Bay of Biscay and into the Atlantic. It was quite a small fleet. The Germans started the war with a mere 56 U-boats.

In 1940, while Fighter Command was fighting the Battle of Britain, the German U-boats were, thanks to Dönitz's French bases, sinking many British ships in the Atlantic. To add to the navy's woes, the German cypher arm, B-Dienst ('observation service' in English), had broken some of the Royal Navy's cyphers – and so knew where the British warships were.

The U-boats would space themselves in a line across the convoy routes and he who spotted a convoy would then, using his Enigma cypher machine, signal headquarters and the other boats. Together they would attack in a group: the 'Wolf Pack' Dönitz had dreamed up when in British captivity in 1918. The U-boat crews called this period of 1940 'the

Dönitz HQ, Kerneval, Lorient

first happy time' as the Wolf Packs sank ship after ship with virtually no loss. Convoy SC7, out of Newfoundland, in October, was the worst that year for Britain, with 20 ships (out of 35) being sunk, carrying steel, grain and trucks. The escorts were uncoordinated and five U-boats got into the convoy lines, on the surface, sinking one ship after another. No U-boats were sunk.

And so it went on. Over 500 Allied ships were sunk in 1940. Food and petrol rationing were introduced into Britain.

As I've described, RAF Coastal Command did not have the aircraft or weapons to do much about this carnage. By the end of 1940, they had yet to sink a submarine, though they had shared two with the navy. Apart from a couple of mines and a couple of accidents, the rest of the thirty-three which had been sunk since the start of the war were down to the navy. The Admiralty was not very happy about this and complained to the Air Ministry. As a result, extra aircraft were allocated and, in February 1941, the Admiralty was given operational control of Coastal Command.

At about the same time, in Germany, something went wrong with the National Socialist dream. Until then, things had gone pretty much Dönitz's way. Constantly lauded by press and newsreels, worshipped by small boys and big girls alike, his U-boat aces had replaced the (somewhat-discredited) Luftwaffe pilots as the pin-up boys of Nazi Germany. In March 1941, however, and all in the space of a couple of days, his three top aces, Prien (over 30 ships sunk, including the battleship *Royal Oak* at Scapa Flow), Kretschmer (35 ships) and Schepke (30 ships) were sunk by the Royal Navy. The three had sailed together from Lorient. The German press kept Prien's death quiet at first, but Churchill announced it to the House of Commons and the BBC repeatedly broadcast to Germany his taunt: "Where is Prien?" until Goebbels was forced to acknowledge the loss.

One of the three was spotted by ASDIC, one by eye and the third (the U-100, Schepke's) by shipborne radar – the first of a very long line for the technology. It was from this moment that the Intelligence Zone entered into the Atlantic siege.

Of the three captains, only Kretschmer survived. When his crew was brought ashore at Liverpool, the police who escorted them from the docks to the station had trouble holding back the screaming women who pelted them with missiles and wanted to tear them apart. Liverpool had been heavily bombed by the Luftwaffe and some of the crowd had been widowed by the U-boats, some perhaps by the very sailors who they wanted to get their hands on. Kretschmer had sunk seven of the ships in convoy SC7.

The RAF had been carrying out many (mainly small) air raids against the French U-boat bases in France, prompting Dönitz to decide that his boats must be protected when in port. The work at Lorient started in February 1942 and would result in the massive bunkers of Keroman, roofed in 7 metre thick

Keroman 1, U-boat base Lorient

Bundesarchiv, Bild 101II-MW-3936-06A
Foto: Dietrich | April 1942

reinforced concrete. These would prove impervious to bombing, even by the heaviest 'block-buster' bombs of later years.

I will hang my account of the U-boat war between May 1941 and May 1943 mainly on the experiences of two German submariners, Herbert Werner and Hans Goebeler; so perfectly do their stories fit into the wider picture.....

Werner cruise 1:
U-557, May–July 1941. North Atlantic. 6 pennants

In July 1941, while the permanent base was still being built, the U-557 arrived from Kiel, northern Germany. One of the officers on board was Ensign Herbert Werner. Werner had just finished his first – very successful - voyage: the U-557 hoisted six pennants, each representing a ship they had sunk on the voyage. Although she had been depth-charged more than once, she had escaped. Herbert Werner knew what his aim was:

'It seemed to me one thing remained to be done: intensify the U-boat war against England, starve the British and force them to surrender. Once we held the British Isles, the war would end.'

The Nazi star was in the ascendant. Germany's invasion of Russia was less than a month old. Werner didn't expect the gullible communists to last long:

'As everyone knew, the non-aggression pact we had signed with Stalin in August 1939 was but a temporary measure, a clever delaying tactic. Now that our Eastern armies were on the march, the fall of Russia could be expected soon and our Thousand-Year Reich would be assured.'

A military band awaited the U-557 as they sailed proudly into Lorient,:

'Many girls – nurses from our military hospital – were waiting for us ...with a smile, a kiss and a bouquet of flowers for each man. Now we knew that we had jumped off the devil's shovel, that life was sweet and rewarding... if the days were long, so were the nights. Our crews had inherited the local *établissements*; they enjoyed the girls who had served many a sailor before them, including comrades who now lay on the ocean floor... special bulletins informed us of the dramatic progress in Russia and U-boat triumphs.'

Werner cruise 2:
U-557, Aug – Sep 1941. N. Atlantic. 4 pennants

Werner's submarine sailed from Lorient in August. It was a peaceful run, they saw no aircraft over the Bay of Biscay. They played records in the submarine to pass the time - one of them a British hit of the era: 'We'll be hanging out the washing on the Siegfried line.' The shellac disc had been abandoned by retreating British troops along with a lot of other material. Indeed, so fast had the German advance been, that, having no spare uniforms of their own, some of the U-boat men were wearing British uniforms also abandoned at the time.

There were rich pickings for the hunters in the North Atlantic. On this cruise they sank four ships. They were pursued by an escort and depth-charged – but escaped. On crossing the Bay back to Lorient, they were again undisturbed by aircraft.

Coastal Command was flying many patrols over the Bay - they had 200 available aircraft for anti-submarine work - but there weren't many U-boats to find – about 40 on patrol throughout all oceans on an average day in 1941. The Atlantic is a vast area – finding a needle in a haystack would be child's play in comparison. The patrols were up to 15 hours long. The Sunderland flying boat and the American Hudson were Coastal's main long-range aircraft.

Short of Rochester Sunderland flying boat

Lockheed Hudson

Coastal Command's search aircraft were increasingly being fitted with radar. That radar was ASV2 – which had been developed at Bawdsey, principally by 'Taffy' Bowen, Gerald Touch and Robert Hanbury-Brown. 'ASV' was an acronym for 'Air to Surface Vessel.' The mark 2 – ASV2 – was the first version that worked well enough to be of much practical use. Even that wasn't giving particularly good results yet. New technology always takes time to be fitted, trained-up in, accepted and bed down. In the 5 months until the end of July 1941, Coastal Command had spotted just 4 U-boats using radar compared with 61 without it.

They didn't see Herbert Werner's U-577; it returned to Lorient in safety.

Lorient was like a different world to the returning crew; a respite from the fear, constriction, stinks, repetition – and sometimes plain boredom - of U-boat life. The first part of the new U-boat pens (Keroman 1) was now finished. Their beloved boat was now safe. Then there was the social life:

'A night filled with warm embraces made a pleasant prospect for our crewmen, but even this had become just another routine part of the sailor's life.'

Admiral Dönitz visited them when they paraded for a ceremony in front of the préfecture (county hall) and: 'showered us with iron crosses and took time to pin a medal on my chest.'

Werner cruise 3:
U-557, October 1941. N. Atlantic. 6 pennants

U-557's next cruise from Lorient was again to the North Atlantic. Once again, they did not see aircraft over the Bay of Biscay and once out of the Bay, into the Atlantic, they were too far from land for aircraft to track them. This was what U-boat crews called 'the black pit' and the British, more prosaically, the mid-Atlantic air gap.

Coastal Command hadn't spotted them and nor had Bletchley Park, the Germans being then ahead in the to-and-fro of the intelligence war.

Bletchley Park had earlier broken the Enigma U-boat code that they called 'Dolphin'. That had led to German suspicions so, on the 5th of October 1941, they had introduced a new one, known to Bletchley Park as 'Shark'. Bletchley could not read Shark yet.

The timely reading of the U-boats' Enigma coded messages by Bletchley Park was made possible by the development of an electro-mechanical device called the Bombe. This was the work of Alan Turing and Gordon Welchman. This subject is too complex for simple explanation in the space I have here. For more on the subject, please refer to the reading list pertaining to this chapter, go online, or - best of all - visit the Museum at Bletchley Park. I give an overview of when Bletchley Park broke the German Enigma naval cyphers in appendix A, at the end of this chapter.

The German codebreakers of B-Dienst had, however, begun to break into the Allied cypher used for communicating with the convoys, British Naval Cypher No. 3 (the Royal Navy had declined to take up the 'unbreakable' system that Oswyn Lywood had developed at RAF Leighton Buzzard). The Germans could, on a good day (for them), estimate where and when a convoy could be expected.

Herbert Werner's U-557 came upon a convoy on the 15th of October and attacked. The description in Werner's superb book *Iron Coffins* takes one straight to the North Atlantic in late autumn. The passage is in the first part of the book, which is called '*Years of Glory.*'

'The wind howled and the waves thundered above the clatter of our engines as we raced past the shadows and out-manoeuvred two escorts with ease. The sea swallowed our small steel drum; only the top of the bridge protruded. Now we stood in the horseshoe up to our necks in water, tied to the boat with wide steel belts. The phantoms rocked in several columns westward, their broad flanks exposed temptingly ..the final moment had come for some of the giants, and for those who manned them... "Fire!" Shouted the Exec... a blast, a fireball... large chunks of steel hurled into the illuminated clouds.'

They sank 6 ships on this cruise, then returned to Lorient. Lorient, home from home, was much as before: 'A good portion of the men found their French girls holding open house in the downtown bordellos. Most of the men were not seen on the base before reveille the next morning.' Once more 'Der Löwe', Admiral Dönitz, handed out the medals.

After the ceremony Herbert Werner was transferred briefly to Brest, just along the coast. He was warned that 'Brest was a hotbed of resistance and sabotage... occasionally members of the French resistance abducted or murdered our men.' He didn't need to worry, though. He was immediately posted to Germany to be trained up as an Executive Officer (Exec), the second in command of a submarine. The timing was providential for him. His U-boat, U-577, was lost with all hands on her next cruise (ironically run down by an ally – an Italian destroyer, who rammed her, thinking her to be a British submarine).

The year 1941 had not been a good one for Britain at sea. Four hundred and sixty-one of her life-line ships were sunk. It was even worse for Coastal Command – at least as far as that part of its task which was devoted to submarine hunting was concerned. Although it spotted and attacked well over a hundred U-boats, Coastal Command could claim only one sinking (U-452) and that shared with an armed trawler. However, Coastal did *capture* one, the U-570, the only U-boat ever to surrender to an aircraft in the war. It was captured by Squadron Leader James Herbert Thompson, a Hull man, flying a Hudson from Iceland (Britain had invaded Iceland 'for the duration' in 1940 to forestall Nazi occupation). U-570 was afterwards used as a Royal Navy submarine, HMS *Graph*. But that's a story in its own right. Of the thirty five U-boats Britain had sunk, Coastal Command had accounted for just two. The rest were, except for a couple of accidents and a mine, down to The Andrew.

Coastal were, however, keeping the U-boats' heads down. A U-boat would submerge when it saw a plane. And, indeed, that was the problem. Coastal Command was finding the needles in the haystacks and attacking them but their ASV2 radar - even at best - meant they could see a submarine at 6 or 7 miles, which was only a couple of miles before the submarine saw them. The plane took a minute or two to cover that distance while a submarine could crash dive in between 40 and 60 seconds. The depth charges the aircraft dropped had problems too, not detonating consistently in the right place or depth – and not delivering enough punch when they did go off.

On the credit side for Britain, America came into the war in December 1941. Now, as well as providing passive help – such as ships, supplies, the excellent Lockheed Hudson and Liberator aircraft, and convoy protection part way across the Atlantic – Uncle Sam would help in fighting the submarines. Also, Bletchley Park had begun to read Shark, the new German code.

A few weeks after Herbert Werner left Brest for training in Germany, another German sailor, of similar sexual voracity as Werner but of a lower rank, arrived in Lorient. His name was Hans Goebeler.

Goebeler cruise 1:
U-505, Feb – May 1942. Africa. 4 pennants

Hans Goebeler was a dyed-in-the-wool Nazi. He had lived through the economic horrors of the 1930's when his father was out of work for five years, the German currency became worthless and famine was rampant. Hitler had solved those problems. Goebeler was an enthusiastic follower of the Führer and a keen member of the Hitler Youth – priding himself on having been its youngest patrol leader:

'The Hitler Youth's emphasis on patriotism, loyalty and sacrifice fitted in perfectly with the values my father instilled in me. Little did we suspect that these same qualities would compel our nation to follow Hitler over the precipice to disaster.'

Having served the tough basic training of the navy, Goebeler was proud to be in the top ten percent that were offered the chance to serve in the U-boat arm. He was just 18 years old (the average age of a U-boat crewman was 20) when the ship he joined, his beloved U-505 (a ship he would serve until the end) backed through the oily water and out of the dimly-lit bunker of Keroman, Lorient, to the triumphal strains of a full navy band.

It was February the 11th 1942. That same month, (obviously) unknown to Hans, two things happened in the secret world of intelligence that were to have a profound significance in the Siege of Britain. The first of these was that a further rotor

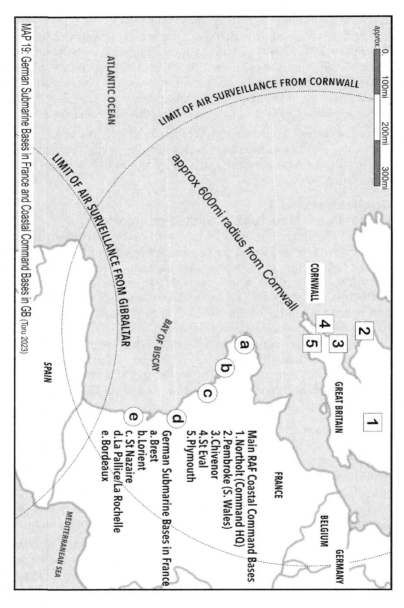

MAP 19: German Submarine Bases in France and Coastal Command Bases in GB (Toru 2023)

ATLANTIC OCEAN

LIMIT OF AIR SURVEILLANCE FROM CORNWALL

approx 600mi radius from Cornwall

LIMIT OF AIR SURVEILLANCE FROM GIBRALTAR

BAY OF BISCAY

CORNWALL

GREAT BRITAIN

SPAIN

MEDITERRANEAN SEA

FRANCE

BELGIUM

GERMANY

approx 0. 100mi 200mi 300mi

Main RAF Coastal Command Bases
1.Northolt (Command HQ)
2.Pembroke (S. Wales)
3.Chivenor
4.St Eval
5.Plymouth

German Submarine Bases in France
a. Brest
b.Lorient
c. St Nazaire
d.La Pallice/La Rochelle
e. Bordeaux

was added to the Enigma machines that the U-boats used to scramble the messages they sent back to base. This was Dönitz's riposte to his - perfectly justified - suspicions that his signals were being read. He had been losing his supply tankers. The tankers were stationed at sea to replenish the U-boats and cut down the number of journeys across the Bay of Biscay to and from port.

It was all very odd. Though the tankers and U-boats met-up in the most out-of-the-way places, the Royal Navy would still appear and sink them – as if by magic. Dönitz didn't believe in magic, so a fourth rotor was added to the Enigma machines and Bletchley Park couldn't read U-boat signals anymore. The blackout was to last until December.

To make life even rosier for the German sub-mariners, at the same time as Bletchley Park went dark, the German equivalent of Bletchley – B-Dienst – broke ever further into the convoy code, Royal Naval Cypher 3, giving them an even better idea when and where the convoys would sail 'across the pond.'

All this was, of course, unknown to Goebeler as the U-505 inched into the Bay of Biscay. The passage across the Bay was getting hotter for the submariners now. Coastal Command was concentrating on it – for it was the pinch point for the German U-boats between the French ports and the Atlantic. Patrols were flown over the Bay from Britain – principally RAF St Eval in Cornwall and Pembroke Dock, in West Wales – and from the British colony of Gibraltar, at the tip of Spain. The planes would fly several hundred miles before even starting the search – and then stooge back and forth; subject to the tender mercies of the Luftwaffe of course.

The RAF aircraft over the Bay were a mix but principally the American Hudson and the Sunderland flying boat with its crew of eleven. Their airborne radar (ASV2) was becoming increasingly useful but It would need further modifications and more training before it became a serious threat to the U-boats. On this trip, the U-505 saw several aircraft. However, by diving when they saw an airplane approaching and surfacing at night for air, they were not seriously inconvenienced.

Goebeler's first cruise was off the coast of Africa. The main problems he recorded was the suffocating conditions in the boat, which didn't do the eggs much good. In Europe they would keep for a month or two, off Africa they began to rot after a couple of weeks:

'Some of the boys began eating literally dozens daily. After a few days, though, no one could stand the sight of the little white devils.'

They sank a ship out of convoy and later an oil tanker (the victim of choice), the *Sydhav* headed for the British armies in North Africa:

'A sharp explosion was followed immediately by a deafening roar. A moment later a giant shock wave hit us, knocking us off our feet and rocking the boat like a baby's cradle. Huge waves blocked the periscope's vision for almost two minutes.'

Twelve men and a mess boy died on the *Sydhav*. Twenty three survived. In these southern seas, the chances of survival were much higher than in the North Atlantic.

Even so far from base the U-505 was spotted by RAF Coastal Command planes, operating from Freetown in Africa. Sunderland flying boats forced them to crash dive. When they surfaced again, they discovered a problem with their boat: 'A faulty upper deck plate built in Lorient, our first experience with sabotage by the shipyard workers of Lorient, a problem that would become much more frequent and serious as the war progressed.'

The Leigh Light

The U-505 may have been the first German submarine to see a Leigh Light. They had surfaced at night: 'when suddenly an aircraft appeared, illuminating our general vicinity with blindingly bright searchlights. A moment later, another aircraft appeared 300 metres to our starboard.'

The Leigh Light was the RAF's answer to a major problem. Early airborne radar would lose contact when they had got to about half a mile from a surfaced submarine, meaning, at night, they were attacking blind (in the day, the submarine would probably already have dived). An RAF officer, Wing Commander Humphrey Leigh, acting entirely on his own,

Wellington with Leigh Light

designed and developed a searchlight to be mounted beneath an aeroplane and pointing forward, which could be switched on just as the submarine disappeared from the radar screen. By then it was too late for the U-Boat to dive while the bomber had a clear view of the target.

However, the aircraft which was lighting up the U-505 was not attacking but signalling. Shortly after diving, Goebeler heard the 'ping' of a warship's ASDIC and they were depth-charged. They escaped. Although the aircraft had not damaged them, the radar/Leigh Light combination was ominous for Dönitz's fleet. Night was no longer a protection from air attack.

After sinking two more ships (the *West Irmo* and the *Alphacca*), the U-505 sailed back through the Bay - where they were bombed twice but not damaged - to a heroes' welcome in Lorient. As they inched into the massive protection of Keroman 1, with its 7 metre thick roof, they proudly flew four pennants, one for each vessel they had sunk:

'After our long ordeal at sea, we had only four thoughts in mind: a hot bath, good food, mail from home, and... well, satisfying the all-too-human lust for female companionship that every sailor feels after a sea voyage.'

They were feted, banqueted:

'Best of all, there was the beer... not the ersatz beer that was normally available but real bottles of Becks and Falstaff. Some of the boys became sick, but as soon as they were able they were back at the table, enjoying what we all knew might be our last chance to enjoy such a feast.'

Admiral Dönitz met the boat, as he did all the returning boats. 'We U-boat men had unbounded confidence and respect in him. It was for good reason we called him 'Der Löwe'.

The Lion's lair, however, was not as safe as it could have been. That same month Dönitz had to relocate his HQ from Lorient to Paris. British commandos had raided St Nazaire, just down the coast, shortly before. In Churchill's war, being near the sea was no longer a wise option for the U-boat chief.

Then out on the town:

'Our favourite street was nicknamed *Der Strasse der Bewegung* (the street of movement). Music and laughter poured from almost every window... the sweet smell of perfumes filled the night with their hypnotic magic. There were certain houses renowned for the beautiful girls who for a small fee, gave comfort and entertainment to lonely sailors ... "Come in sailor. Good music, beaucoup dance, good drink, amour." Later, perhaps, we would beat up some rear-echelon troops, or have a fight with the military police.'

While Goebeler was enjoying his leave, all hell was taking place off the American seaboard and in the Caribbean. One hundred and twenty six ships went down in May for the loss of 4 U-boats. Allied ships were being sunk faster than they could be built. Fuel tankers especially – essential for Britain's survival - were going to the bottom. No plane could fly, no ship run, no car drive without fuel from the Americas.

This period was called by the U-boat men the Second Happy Time (the first had been in 1940). It was called this because, with America at war, Dönitz's sent some of his submarines to cruise the Caribbean and along the east coast of America, picking off unescorted tankers (142 of them) sailing from the oil refineries in Central America to the north. It only ended when the American Commander-in-chief, Admiral King, belatedly learned the advisability of convoys. Five thousand American sailors lost their lives in this period, twice as many as at Pearl Harbour. It was the greatest naval defeat the USA had ever – and has ever – suffered. For those who are interested in this little known (in Britain) subject I can heartily recommend the excellent book *Operation Drumbeat* by the American author, Michael Gannon.

Goebeler cruise 2:
U-505, June- Aug 1942. Caribbean. 3 pennants

Goebeler's second cruise was, not surprisingly given the rich pickings on offer there, to the Caribbean. June 1942 (the month when Heydrich died) was the month in which the most Allied ships – 135 of them – were sunk by the U-boats.

The U-505's trip across the Bay was uneventful. Arriving in the Caribbean, she sank two large unescorted American freighters, the *Seathrush* and the *Thomas McKean,* both laden with (in all about 50) aircraft bound for Britain for transhipment by British convoy to Russia. Then she sank a third; a sailing ship – not a tanker or merchantman. The ship was a neutral, and its sinking wasn't appreciated by its owners; indeed it caused Colombia to declare war on Germany. That's just an aside. Remarkable things were the norm on a Goebeler cruise.

It was not all plain-sailing for the submariners. American aircraft, fitted with ASV2 radar, surprised the U-505 at night with flares. Britain had handed over the secrets of her radar development (along with much else) to America in the Tizard Mission and America was now using her enormous resources to manufacture radar sets. Although they were bombed and depth-charged, U-505 escaped.

Huff-duff

All in all, they didn't see much shipping. Hans Goebeler suspected that they were being monitored and shipping routed round them. With the benefit of what he learned post-war, Goebeler mistakenly says that they were being tracked by Bletchley Park. He was wrong there, Bletchley was still locked out because of the addition of the fourth rotor to the submarines' Enigma cypher machines. He also says that they were being tracked by Huff-Duff, radar's bedfellow. In this he was correct.

I have mentioned Huff-duff before (in *The Intelligence Zone*), and its role in tracking the Bismarck. The technology behind direction finding was fairly simple and well understood by both sides. Huff-duff used the Adcock aerial. Sir Frank Adcock was a professor of Ancient History at Cambridge University who was seconded to the Admiralty's Room 40 (the forerunner to MI6) as a cryptographer during WW1. He developed the aerial to track German signals. After the first war the responsibility for its further development went to RRS Slough (at Ditton Park, Datchet) under, of course, Robert Watson-Watt. They used it to detect weather fronts. The section at Slough which wasn't working on radar was working on Huff-duff. Watson-Watt says that (in finding submarines): 'At a rough count, radar led over Huff-duff by nearly two to one, with Huff-duff leading over sonar (ASDIC) again by two to one or a little more.' Huff-duff let an operator determine the direction of a radio signal, regardless of whether the content could be read.

There were a lot of messages from the U-boats, partly because the U-boat war was controlled by Dönitz from his somewhat nomadic operational headquarters in Europe, partly because, as I've mentioned, the Wolf Pack tactic meant that the U-boat who spotted a convoy called in the others. Dönitz had suspected that signals were being monitored and ordered a limit on transmission times. It was not enough. British technology was more advanced than the Germans suspected.

Before the war Huff-duff used a manually-rotated aerial to fix the direction of the transmitter. RRS Slough improved on that. It produced sets with continuously motor-driven tuning to scan the likely frequencies and sound an automatic alarm the moment a radio operator touched his Morse key. The listener would then rapidly fine-tune the signal before it disappeared. It only needed 3 seconds for a signal to be plotted and then triangulated with other stations and the submarine's position identified.

Huff-duff detection stations were at first based only on shore in Britain – often at the radar stations. The information was fed mainly through the naval signals station at Scarborough then to Leighton Buzzard (the heart of the radar network) and to the Admiralty and Coastal Command. Huff-duff gave a pretty exact location of the submarines. That was fine for the none-urgent work of routeing convoys round submarines, but for immediate action - to chase down a U-boat and attack it at sea - it was also needed on escort ships.

By 1941, the sets were being made smaller and, as the availability of cathode ray tubes improved, more sets could be produced. These were installed on Royal Navy convoy escorts, enabling them to get fixes on U-boats transmitting from over the horizon, beyond the range of radar. This allowed hunter-killer ships to be dispatched at high speed in the direction of the U-boat, which could be located by ship-borne radar if still on the surface or ASDIC if submerged. A destroyer could then attack the U-boat, or at least force it to submerge, which might prevent an attack on the convoy. When two ships fitted with HF/DF accompanied a convoy, a fix on the transmitter's position, not just its direction, could be determined. Aircraft would also be summoned if they were within range.

Huff-duff on a ship

By the time of Hans Goebeler's 'Caribbean Cruise' in summer 1942, Huff-duff had been fitted on some British ships for over a year and on some American ships for a couple of months. The sets hadn't worked well at first, but they were working well by now. The first submarine detection by seaborne Huff-duff had been a month or two earlier, in March 1942. Now the equipment was being fitted on all Allied warships as a matter of great urgency. Huff-duff was coming to maturity at exactly the same time as airborne and ship radar, which would not do the U-boats much good. When U-505 sent a message to base, Huff-duff located them. When they surfaced at night, Allied aircraft, fitted with ASV2 radar, found and depth charged them time and again.

Out in the Atlantic, they were caught by surprise. The lookout had been inattentive. 'The big plane swooped so close we could hear the roar of the engines from inside the sub as we dived.' The 'big plane' would have probably been a Sunderland flying boat (wingspan 112 feet) flying out of Gibraltar. These giant aircraft were in the air for so long that they had two – sometimes three - pilots. The crew ate onboard. They took off and landed on the sea – and the crew did not have parachutes, but dinghies.

The U-505 escaped.

Milch-cow

Goebeler's 'Caribbean Cruise' lasted for ten weeks, so the U-505 rendezvoused with a 'Milch-cow' – a resupply submarine. There were several of these large craft which restocked other submarines with food, torpedoes and fuel. They had been sailing just a couple of months and were Dönitz's answer to the supply boats he had lost due to Bletchley Park. Given that the time to get to the mid-Atlantic and back was around 20 days, the Milch-cows enhanced his available strike force enormously. Bletchley Park would pay special attention to them when it did finally come back on air.

Milch-cow or not, U-505's current cruise was ending. Her captain, Axel Löewe, was ill, so they were forced to return to Lorient. In August 1942, the crossing of the Bay of Biscay was not pleasant for them: 'Air-dropped depth charge attacks became so frequent that we were forced to run the entire length of the

Rearming with torpedoes from a Milch-cow

Bay underwater, surfacing only long enough to recharge our air and batteries.'

In the spring and summer of 1942, Coastal Command was getting more long-range aircraft. Several squadrons of Wellington bombers were loaned from a reluctant Bomber Command and further aircraft came from America: more of the excellent Hudsons and the first of the long-range Liberators, which were to become the most successful 'sub-busting' planes of the war. These were then fitted with British technology – ASV2 radar and the Leigh Light - and sent on patrol.

A couple of weeks earlier, on the 5th of July, an air attack using the combination of ASV2 radar and the Leigh Light had sunk its first submarine. It was, of course, at night and it was in the Bay. The submarine which went down was the U-502, sunk by a Wellington bomber of 172 Squadron from Chivenor in Devon. The squadron was less than three months old and had been formed specifically to use radar and the Leigh Light. The pilot was an American, Pilot Officer Wiley B. Howell. Howell was a volunteer who had joined the RAF before Pearl Harbour. He was given a Distinguished Flying Cross (DFC) for his work. When he was given it at the Palace, he told King George that "the Folks back home will be tickled pink," that he'd been given it. The king was tickled pink, too. The U-502 was returning to Lorient from a cruise in which she had sunk 9 Allied ships. In all she had sunk 14.

Coastal Command were trying to stem a rising tide. On 8th Aug 1942, nearly 3 years after the war began, the number of U-boats at sea reached 100 for the first time. Dönitz finally had much of the striking power he considered that he needed to strangle Britain's lifeline with the new world.

The U-505 sailed into Lorient flying the three pennants which showed they had sunk three ships. The welcome was the same as ever – but the town itself was changed. The RAF had been hitting Lorient and Brest hard. The submarine pens were unaffected, the reinforced concrete was far too thick, but the dock area and many parts of the towns were now in ruins. Luckily Lorient's red light district had escaped.

Goebeler cruise 3:
U-505, Oct – Dec 1942. S. America. 1 pennant

Goebeler's third cruise was from October until December 1942. While in dock, the U-505 had been fitted with what the submariners called the 'the Biscay cross', an antenna which was fixed onto the bridge while surfaced and hurriedly taken down for submerging. By using it, the submarines would no longer have to worry about British radar, for it picked up the aircraft

ASV2 radar pulses, meaning that they could detect an approaching aircraft even before they were detected by it. This gave them plenty of time to dive. Germany was benefitting from French knowledge of passive radar, for the Biscay Cross, whose proper name was the Metox, was designed and manufactured in Paris. It would not be the only example of the Nazis benefitting from the technology of the countries they over-ran. Later in the war, the snorkel, a Dutch invention, would help them to keep their submarines underwater for longer periods.

U-boat with Biscay Cross

This time, the departure of U-505 from Lorient was somewhat undignified. Coastal and Bomber Commands had been sowing magnetic mines in the sea lanes outside the U-boat pens. These sank to the bottom and were activated when a submarine passed over them. Consequently, Hans Goebeler and all other crew not needed for boat steerage had to wear lifejackets and kneel on the outer casing of the submarine as they left port. This was to avoid their legs being driven into their backs if a mine went off. That's what had happened to a previous submarine. Only two men had survived.

The Biscay Cross quickly showed its worth and the U-505 crossed the Bay without serious problems, crash-diving when an aircraft approached.

On this cruise, they had to fix an engine failure, which Goebeler put down to sabotage in the workshops at Lorient. The work at the Lorient shipyards was nearly all carried out by *Volksdeutsche* – that is, ethnic Germans relocated from the conquered territories such as Poland. As Hans Goebeler had already said – and was to say again and again - the sabotage problem was to get considerably worse as the tide of war changed. It is a little known or considered matter but it had a real and significant effect on the U-boats.

His new captain (who Goebeler despised) opened his sealed orders. They had been sent south again, into the South Atlantic, where Britain and America was now routing more convoys to avoid the Wolf Packs in the north. They sank one ship, the *Ocean Justice*, but now they were being tracked: 'It was obvious the enemy's airborne radar was now effective enough to deny our traditional cover of night.' If they surfaced, they sailed in a zigzag... 'one thing was crystal clear: the 'Happy Time' for Germany's U-boats was over.'

U-505's cruise came to a sudden end. A Lockheed Hudson – a twin-engined bomber from RAF Coastal Command's 53 Squadron based in Trinidad - saw to that. Like many RAF Coastal Command flights, its crew was a mishmash of nationalities. It's captain was Flight Sergeant Ronald Sillcock, an Australian. His crew consisted of two British, a New Zealander and an American.

Ron Sillcock

Ron Sillcock was good. He had already heavily damaged two U-boats. He came in low and fast. The depth charge he dropped on U-505's aft deck was perfect. Too perfect. Instead of exploding a few feet below the sea's surface it landed on the submarine itself. The blast tore away the submarine's anti-aircraft gun and then went upwards, crippling the Hudson so that it crashed into the sea, killing all of the crew. Five more families that would never see their boys again. Just another incident in the U-boat war.

The U-505 limped away, two of her crew with shell splinters in their skulls: one of them with punctured lungs, suffering violent seizures. They met up with a refuelling ship – a Milch-cow – which took off the worst-wounded man who was operated on in another U-boat. They exchanged him for a sailor who had picked up a 'dose' from a French whore in Lorient and was being sent home in disgrace.

How the U-505 was coaxed home almost defies belief – but home to Lorient she went:

'We were especially wary when we passed through the flight path of the British planes flying shuttle patrols between Gibraltar in the south and Land's End, England, in the north – the infamous 'suicide stretch' ...I could hardly sleep that final night before our arrival home. After all the close calls with death during this patrol, I didn't want to die now, just a few miles from comfort and safety.'

The U-505 after Ronald Sillcock's attack

They made it. Lorient was even more bomb damaged now, courtesy of the RAF. Whole areas of the town were rubble. It wasn't much of a homecoming: 'A great number of the men received news of brothers and uncles killed or missing in action.' The feast they were expecting was sparse, There were food shortages even for heroes. Even worse, his special girl had left town. Many of the French girls – the ones that their countrymen were to wittily accuse of 'collaboration horizontal' – had gone.

While waiting for repairs (there was a great backlog of damaged U-boats in all ports), Hans Goebeler and his shipmates were bombed in their barracks. The building collapsed around them and he narrowly escaped with his life:

'The streets of Lorient looked like one of those medieval paintings of the underworld. Deep craters pockmarked the roads and there was burning all around. The air was filled with a hellish symphony of ambulance sirens and the frightened cries of woman and children... weeks ago the RAF had dropped leaflets on the city, warning the civilians to evacuate. It appeared now that these civilians were finally ready to heed the advice.'

Resistance was growing in Lorient and the surrounding area. A spy tried to board the U-505 and a fellow crewmate was approached by a French woman who said she could supply false identity papers so that he could desert. His crewmate was actually tempted. Goebeler talked him out of it.

Summary of 1942

The Germans were the clear victors in the U-boat battles of 1942.

They had done well in the intelligence war with their break into the British naval codes. For much of the year their own submarine communications had been secure. Bletchley Park had only managed to get back into 'Shark' in December, after a break since February.

In radar, the introduction of Metox - the Biscay Cross – meant that the U-boats could now 'see' approaching aircraft before they 'saw' them and dive.

The Milch-cows meant that the U-boats could be resupplied beyond the Bay of Biscay.

Dönitz now had more U-boats than ever – more than a hundred – operating in the North Atlantic.

The 'Second Happy Times' - the sinking of unescorted ships along the coast of America and in the Caribbean - had meant that the Allies were losing ships faster than they could build new ones. It was by far the worst year of the entire war for the Allies. 1165 ships had gone down, more than in the entirety of the first two and half years of the war. 86 U-boats had been sunk. That was good odds for the U-Boats.

Werner cruise 4:
U-230, Feb - March 1943. N. Atlantic. 4 pennants

The climax of the Atlantic battles came in 1943 and it can be best followed by leaving Hans Goebeler for a while (the U-505

was to take eight months to repair) and re-joining Herbert
Werner, who we last saw on his way to the Baltic to train as an
Executive Officer. Werner was now trained and ready for sea.
As he returned from his pre-sailing leave, he suffered air raids
and diversions through the growing rubble of a heavily-bombed
Berlin. He finally cast-off from Kiel, in the brand-new U-230,
on February the 1st 1943. The parting was workaday, the
farewell feasts of yesteryear but a memory; but that did not
matter in the least to Herbert Werner. Things were rolling
Germany's way:

'U-boat attacks had cost the Allies more than 6,000,000
tons in 1942. The ghost of starvation and a lost war was
marching across the United Kingdom and knocking at the
door of No. 10 Downing Street. We were convinced that
victory was only months away and that we had to hurry to
sink our score of enemy vessels.'

The conditions in the North Atlantic in the late winter of
1943 were often appalling. As U-230 surfaced the watchmen,
wearing rubber diving suits and eye masks, were tied to the
bridge by steel belts:

'Those hours of precarious existence on the bridge offered
us moments of fierce beauty. When the boat topped a
prodigious wave we could briefly see across the Alpine
mountain range of water, down into deep valleys 50 or 60
metres below... and when the walls of water surged to 70
metres high their crests collapsed and cascaded down upon
us, forcing us on the bridge to ride for long seconds far
below the surface, pressed to the deck by towering columns
of 30 and 40 metres of ocean ...our search for the convoy
became a mockery.'

If the hunter could feel the 'fierce beauty' of the elements, to
the hunted, on the great freighters, loaded with food, steel, tanks
and aircraft, yawing and pitching in the gale, clawing mile after
mile towards Liverpool, the sentiments were somewhat
different. The worst, perhaps, was to be aboard a tanker loaded
with aviation fuel, knowing that a single spark would vaporise
them, end all in an instant – if you were lucky. And, as I've said,
there were more U-boats than ever before in the Atlantic.

Wolf Packs ranged between the old world and the new: and in these bone-chilling winter days, they ran down three eastbound convoys bound for Liverpool. And so commenced the biggest convoy battle of the war.

SC121, HX229, and SC122

The assault started on convoy SC121 (SC signified a slow convoy from Halifax, Nova Scotia, HX a fast one) which had been scattered by nine consecutive days of north-westerly force ten gales and snow squalls. U-405 spotted the convoy and signalled its sisters. In all, 27 submarines joined the pack and sank 12 freighters with no loss to themselves.

As that one-sided battle came to an end, the submarines started using a new codebook for their Enigma messages. Bletchley Park, which had broken into 'Shark' again just a few weeks previously, was locked out again. Dönitz was again suspicious; too many U-boats were being pre-emptively attacked and too many convoys were escaping. Although Bletchley Park cracked the code in nine days, that was too late for convoy HX229 and convoy SC122.

Thirty eight U-boats were deployed against the two convoys as they made their way through the mid-Atlantic gap: the area beyond the reach of allied air patrols. Not that air patrols would have been likely, or useful, in the cyclonic winter weather. The curtain rose on a disaster of the scale of the tragedy of PQ17, the arms convoy from Britain to Russia which six months earlier had been scattered, mauled and smashed by German U-boats and aircraft. The positions of HX229 and SC122 was known to the Germans through their breaks into the convoy cypher, Royal Navy cypher 3. There were one hundred merchant vessels in the convoys.

Hugh Sebag-Montefiore describes what happened in his book *Enigma*:

'The human suffering caused by these attacks was terrible, as merchant ship after merchant ship was sunk by the pursuing U-boats' torpedoes. This was especially the case on board the British refrigerator ship *Canadian Star*, sailing in convoy HX229: she had civilian passengers on board when she was torpedoed. The women and children were ushered into the lifeboats first. A Royal Artillery colonel watched as his wife and young son were seated in one lifeboat. Then, to his horror, he saw a seaman, who was supposed to be holding onto the lifeboat as it swung above the sea, lose his grip after a sudden lurch. The lifeboat tipped up and fell into the sea, all its occupants were washed away.'

Many of the survivors found by convoy escorts were too weak to climb the scrambling nets thrown over the ship's side. Sailors who tried to help them were often washed away themselves in the raging seas.

In these two convoys, twenty-two ships were sunk. Three hundred and sixty men, women and children died. Only one submarine was sunk. The attack was only beaten off after very long-range aircraft flew out from Iceland to provide cover. An RAF Coastal Command Flying Fortress accounted for the one U-boat destroyed. A British Admiralty report stated:

'There seemed real danger that the enemy would sever the routes between America and Britain. In the first twenty days of March over 500,000 tons of shipping was lost... evasive routing was becoming more and more ineffective in face of the great increase of U-boats at sea ...the import programme was cut as low as it could be, and even then seemed hardly likely to be fulfilled.'

On the 19th of March, Menzies, head of Bletchley Park, cabled Churchill to say that they had broken the Shark code again. Churchill scrawled on the cable; 'Congratulate yr splendid hens.' And sent it back to Menzies. While this was too late for the three convoys, it was the last time Bletchley would be locked out of the U-boat messages.

Herbert Werner's book, *Iron Coffins*, is divided into two parts. The first part, *Years of Glory*, ends on the 25th of March 1943, while he still had two days to go before docking in Brest. His ship, the U-230, had sunk four of the ships in the convoys. It ends with the words: 'I was pleased by my prospects and overjoyed by our spectacular victories. Everything seemed to be right with the world.'

The final part of the book is called *Above us, hell.* The dividing point is largely down to a very specific development in the war between Coastal Command and the submarines – the fitting of ASV3 - centimetric radar, made possible by Randall and Boots' cavity magnetron - in the aircraft which patrolled the Bay of Biscay. Metox – the Biscay Cross – could not detect ASV3. This was wonderful for the Coastal Command aircraft who were used to flying hundreds of hours never seeing a thing. A lot of their aircraft had been shot down while they had never seen a submarine – for, of course, they were still fighting the Luftwaffe over the Bay.

The first 'blind' attack on U-230 came in the morning and was spotted by the lookout. They surfaced after half an hour. Another attack. They dived again. Four bombs followed them down, causing their diving-planes to jam and forcing them back to the surface to be attacked by a Sunderland. Four more bombs. Somehow they got out of that fix. They decided that they didn't want to be spotted by the 'Tommies', so decided to only surface at night. However, there were three more night attacks: 'The night was no different than the day.'

They ran submerged the next day at 3 knots (4 miles) an hour, listening to the propellers of a hunter-killer surface group, 'stationed in our front yard.' This was the first time they had come across Allied shipping in the Bay of Biscay. The Allied navies were strengthening at exactly the same time as the Allied air forces. U-230 surfaced at nightfall but was forced down by aircraft six more times during the night.

Coastal Command were over the Bay like a cloud of hornets. The Operational Research people at Northwood had looked at Coastal Command's captured U-boat, the U-570, now HMS *Graph*, and worked out that the average transit time of the 200 mile Bay crossing was 76 hours. Optimum average speed to conserve battery power was around 12 miles an hour on the surface, about 2 miles an hour when submerged. During that crossing, a U-boat would have to surface once for around 7 hours and a second time for an hour or two to charge its batteries.

That was the minimum for battery charging. The need of machines were immutable, the crew's less so. If a boat stayed under for longer than 24 hours, the air grew rank inside, pressure increased and conditions became worse and worse.

The crew would be ordered to remain motionless and eventually oxygen would be issued. The pressure could – and did - become so great that when the conning tower was opened, anyone in it would be blown out of the boat like a cork from a bottle.

To find the surfaced boats, Bomber Command had reluctantly loaned Coastal a couple more squadrons of bombers, mostly Wellingtons. Now Coastal had more planes, the Leigh Light, ASV3 radar that couldn't be detected and improved depth charges. This was why it was now hell above Werner in the Bay of Biscay.

After six more attacks, and having heard of a sister submarine being sunk close by, the U-230 entered Brest. Their reception was good – lots of kisses. Unfortunately Yvonne, (his special girl in the port), had fled; so he had to go to the red light district:

'We kissed the willing creatures as if we had never done so before and might never have another chance.'

The eager crew was given an educational film by the Madame:

'Janine was the first one to benefit from the lesson.'

Herbert Werner took solace in sex and alcohol but that did not weaken his resolve:

'The whole war hinged on our U-boat effort... we had to prevent American food and ammunition and airplanes piling up in Britain and Russia. We had to annihilate the enemy at sea before he could mass the material and manpower for an invasion of Europe. And we would do it.'

That was the size of it. If Britain and her allies America and Canada could break the Atlantic siege, supplies from America would make the invasion of Europe possible. That would mean the end of the Nazis.

Werner cruise 5:
U-230, April – May 1943. N. Atlantic. No pennants.

With these thoughts in mind, Werner sailed from Brest on April the 24th 1943. It took six days, under constant air attack: 'Thrown into shock, dismay, fear and anger by the British audacity,' to cross the Bay and reach the 'black pit' – that mid-

Atlantic gap which was out of range of shore-based aircraft. There they watched and waited. It was now May 1943. A bad time to be in a U-boat in the Atlantic. Werner's ship began to pick up a stream of terrifying signals telling where and why their fellows were going down. U-638 (Royal Navy), U-531 (RN), U-438 (RN), U-125 (RN), U-663 (RAF), U-528 (RN & RAF). Bletchley Park read the same signals.

Finally they saw a convoy approach. A big one. Almost on the heels of this came another. It might be expected that this would be a re-run of their earlier bonanza. But this was to be vastly different. As soon as they surfaced to approach the first convoy, aircraft appeared and depth-charged them. These were strange, ramshackle, single-engined planes that could never have flown from land. This was new. They were being targeted by a Royal Navy escort carrier - HMS *Biter* – an American merchant ship which had been given a flat top to convert it to take aircraft. The Royal and United States navies had closed the mid-Atlantic gap.

Time and again they were attacked from the air. If they surfaced they were spotted and attacked. If they broadcast, they were tracked and attacked. There was nowhere that the submarines could not be seen. Even as they avoided air attacks, messages continued to come through from other U-boats under attack and sinking. They shot down a single-engined biplane – a Swordfish - which sloughed past them: 'The pilot, thrown out of his cockpit, lifted his arm and waved for help, but then I saw him disintegrate in the explosion of the four depth charges.'

In protecting these convoys (HX237 and SC129), HMS *Biter* lost 5 aircraft, two of them with their crews (the others ditched). The Swordfish was not to be sneered at. Its pilots loved the 'Stringbag' and would sink 22 submarines with it during the war.

A 'hunter-killer' group of Royal Navy corvettes and destroyers then arrived and depth-charged the U-230 for hour after hour. With Huff-duff, radar and ASDIC for their eyes and ears, under commanders of the quality of Captains Walker and Macintyre, these convoy patrol groups had the measure of the U-boats.

They attacked with the Hedgehog launcher – the device which had been developed for the Royal Navy at 'Winston Churchill's Toyshop', The Firs, at Whitchurch, near Aylesbury. This was the weapon, you may recall that had so tickled Winston on his visit to The Firs that he demanded endless repeat demonstrations.

Hedgehog looked like a bundle of (24) firework rockets, slanting forward. Each rocket had a depth charge on top, and

The Hedgehog

the whole lot was launched as one. They hit the water ahead in a wide area – the wider the area, the more likely a hit. One in every five attacks made by Hedgehog resulted in a kill (compared to less than one in 80 with depth charges).

Hedgehog also had the advantage of not breaking ASDIC contact, as conventional depth charges had the habit of doing. Hedgehog, like all new technology, had taken a little while to bed-in but was now fully operational and, like HMS *Biter*, a nasty surprise for the submariners.

May the 13th, 1943, was Herbert Werner's 23rd birthday. He spent it submerged at 275 metres, breathing recycled air through potash cartridges with a mask over his face, sloshing around ankle deep in water, oil and piss – the bilge pumps would not work at this depth:

'Our nerves trembled. Our bodies were stiff from cold, stress and fear. Our washrooms were under lock and key; to use them could have meant instant death, for the tremendous outside pressure would have acted in reverse of the expected flow.'

The 'crush depth' on U-boats was thought (but no-one knew for sure) to be between 250 and 280 metres.

There was a brief lull, but it was only as the attacks were passed in relay from the giant convoy's front to its rear escort group. Then it began again, volley after volley of depth charges: 'The devil seemed to be knocking on our steel hull as it creaked and contracted under the enormous pressure.' The men choked in the poisonous atmosphere. 'I dragged myself through the aisle, forcing them to stay awake. Whoever fell asleep might never be awakened.' When the convoy was long passed, the hunters finally gave up and U-230 surfaced, the oxygen-rich air almost making Werner pass out: 'A minute ago, we could not believe that we were alive; now we could not believe that death had kept his finger on us for 35 gruesome hours.'

A couple of hours later, a second convoy approached. In a rerun of the previous day, they were spotted, bombed, chased down by a hunter-killer force of corvettes and destroyers and pinned down by endless depth charges (Werner counted 300). They were forced deeper, even deeper than the previous attack: 'A battery of canisters detonated, violently slamming into her starboard side, sending her down for her final crush.' U-230 levelled off near the 300 metre mark and:

> 'Vibrated in convulsive shakes... I did not know where our limit was, where the hull would finally crack. No-one knew. Those who had found out took the knowledge to the depths. We shivered and sweated; we were both hot and cold as we neared the limits of human endurance... deadly fumes escaped from the batteries. We were half poisoned and nearly unconscious... the men bit the mouthpieces of their rubber hoses, drawing hot air through the potash cartridges, incessantly coughing.'

Then, incredibly, silence from above. It lasted for an hour:

> 'We tempted the Tommies into a move with a hammer against the hull. There was no reaction.' They surfaced, he and his captain thrown up to the bridge by the pressure when they opened the hatch. Then they saw why the 'Tommies' had left. One of their oil bunkers had ruptured. The Royal Navy had taken the oil slick to be their death blood. The U-230 was so badly damaged that they could only return to port. They had not been able to fire a single torpedo.

Back in the Bay, U-230 was constantly depth-charged from the air by aircraft that their Metox could not detect. At night, these blinded them with powerful lights seconds before attacking. They had made the acquaintance of the coupling of centimetric radar and the Leigh Light.

The incoming messages piled up of their fellow submariners going down (and, of course, Bletchley read them too). Several were sunk in the Bay, including three by one pilot, Wing Commander Wilfrid Oulton, of 58 Squadron (recently transferred from an ever-reluctant Bomber Command), flying a Halifax. One of these was a Milch-cow.

Herbert Werner's account is like a tale from beyond the grave. Six of his Wolf Pack had been sunk and the seventh (his) was battered and unable to fight. All the crews had doubtless gone through the same hell from above in their 'iron coffins' but death had stayed his hand only for them.

Their group was not alone. At the start of May, there had been one hundred and eighteen German submarines at sea. By the end of the month, forty-one of them had been sunk – a quarter of Dönitz's total force. On the 24th of May, he called the survivors home. The Atlantic was cleared. He had lost the battle.

The U-230 limped into Brest on May the 28th. 'There was no band playing military tunes.'

***

May 1943 saw the lifting of the Siege of Britain. The Royal Navy and Coastal Command had already been fighting for three and a half years. Now, at last, had come victory. In the first years the navy had produced the results, now in 'Black May' for the U-boats, the honours were exactly even. Of the 30 U-boats they sank between them that month, fourteen were sunk by the Royal Navy, fourteen by RAF Coastal Command and two were shared. At last Coastal Command had come of age. Back in 1942, Dönitz had said: 'The U-boat has no more to fear from aircraft than a mole from a crow.' Now sea and air shared the laurels in the greatest British naval victory since the defeat of the Spanish Armada in 1588.

Nor were the Royal Navy and Coastal Command alone in their victory. The Americans had sunk six, the Canadians one, two had collided and two were lost through unknown causes. Unknown causes? What happened to the U-209 and U-381?

Sabotage? There was certainly a lot of that going on at Lorient, as I discuss in appendix B at the end of this chapter.

The Atlantic battles would go on – but the writing was on the wall for the U-boat arm. The hunters now had more and better planes, ships and tactics. Their eyes and ears: Huff-duff, centimetric radar, Bletchley Park, the Leigh Light and ASDIC, could no longer be avoided. Their weapons, which once had wounded, now killed. In 1942 the Germans had been sinking over 13 ships for every U-boat they lost. From now on they would sink fewer than one. Dönitz could no longer hold up supplies from across the Atlantic. Now Britain was no longer a beleaguered fortress but an ever stronger bridgehead, into which America poured myriads of troops, and thousands of aircraft, tanks and guns. Unless Hitler could come up with new tactics and weapons, Allied landings in northern Europe were a certainty.

Dönitz's had lost the battle in the bitterest way possible. Both his sons were in U-boats. His youngest boy, Peter, died aboard the U-954, sunk in a Hedgehog attack by the Royal Navy on the 19th of May. His other son, Klaus, was to be killed at sea within the year.

Looking at the Atlantic battles from the German side was the only way I could think of to show how British technical developments and intelligence were the key weapons which raised the siege. In doing so, I have only touched on the wartime story of Coastal Command, which at its peak had almost 90,000 personnel and thousands of aircraft, and fought many battles, ranging across the Atlantic and the Mediterranean and operating against surface vessels as well as U-boats. During the war, Coastal Command lost 2,060 aircraft to all causes (about a third of them in anti-submarine actions). It lost 5,863 men in battle and an astonishing 2,317 in accidents. It sank 155 U-boats (of 764 sunk in total), shared a few more with naval forces and damaged around 100. Coastal also ran the RAF air-sea rescue service. If you went into the sea, you had around a one in three chance of surviving. Given the distances from land, the sea conditions (a man could die within minutes) and visibility, even that proportion seems good: but not if you were an airman who had to ditch.

The other major players were, of course, the Royal, Merchant, United States and Canadian navies. The fact that I have hardly mentioned them is not through a lack of respect, but a lack of space.

I have though, I hope, shone a light on how *all* of the Allied forces were given the ears, eyes and some of the teeth to raise the siege of the Atlantic. Thus they won the sea war that Admiral Karl Dönitz, 'the Lion' had been planning for a quarter of a century and waging for nearly four years. 'Der Löwe' himself – perhaps the greatest of the commanders on either side of the Atlantic siege - said: 'The enemy has deprived the U-boat of its essential feature – namely the element of surprise – by means of radar. The scientists who have created radar have been called the saviours of their country.' Dönitz, of course, had never heard of Bletchley Park.

I started this chapter with a quote from England's greatest poet, William Shakespeare. I will finish it with a quote from one of Britain's greatest generals, Arthur Wellesley. Wellesley (Lord Wellington) famously remarked that the Battle of Waterloo was 'won on the playing fields of Eton' (then in Buckinghamshire). An exaggeration, of course. Wars are not won on playing fields but by fighting men. That said, three Buckinghamshire sites can be said to have been critical in the Atlantic war. They were RRS Slough in Datchet – just two miles from Eton (in the south of the county) - the Firs in Whitchurch half way up the county and Bletchley Park in the north.

As an aside, Hans Goebeler's boat, the U-505 still exists. It was tracked down by an American hunter-killer task force - using Huff-duff of course - and captured intact, along with Goebeler. After the war, the Americans very sensibly put the U-505 in the Museum of Science and Industry in Chicago. Hans Goebeler had been seen as a bit suspect by his fellow crew men in that he spent his spare time in the U-505 studying English (quietly). It came in useful in the end. He loved his ship so much that (to cut a long story short) he followed it to Chicago and became its curator.

It is a great pity that the British did not do as much with one of the many U-boats they captured – perhaps the U-570 which surrendered to the Yorkshireman, James Thompson?

Appendix A - when Bletchley Park broke the German naval cyphers

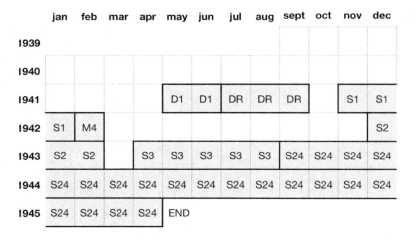

	jan	feb	mar	apr	may	jun	jul	aug	sept	oct	nov	dec
1939												
1940												
1941					D1	D1	DR	DR	DR		S1	S1
1942	S1	M4										S2
1943	S2	S2		S3	S3	S3	S3	S3	S24	S24	S24	S24
1944	S24	S24	S24	S24	S24	S24	S24	S24	S24	S24	S24	S24
1945	S24	S24	S24	S24	END							

D1 – first break into Dolphin (main German Enigma naval cipher)

DR – Dolphin being read

Shark introduced for U-boats 5th October 1941. Not read for several weeks

S1 – Shark being read (from 20th Nov 41 to Feb 42)

M4 – fourth rotor introduced (11th Feb 1942). BP unable to read Shark for 9 months

S2 – Shark being read again, followed by a break of several days

S3 – Shark being read again

S24 – Shark usually being read within 24 hours

Where the boxes are blank, this means that Bletchley Park could not read Naval Enigma

Appendix B - Sabotage at Lorient.

How much damage was the resistance doing? Back to Herbert Werner and Hans Goebeler. Herbert Werner, who finished the war as a skipper at Brest, tells of supply-chain sabotage. In order to stay underwater to avoid air attack, Snorkels were needed. Without a Snorkel the trips across the bay were semi-suicidal. 'I kept demanding a Snorkel but was repeatedly turned down. The explanation was that our supply trains were being sabotaged en route by the French underground.'

Hans Goebeler, at Lorient, talks of much more immediate and profound damage. He tells of putting out to sea and returning at once as 'nearly all the seals for our air relief valves, diving tanks, battery cells and fuel bunkers were totally corroded.' Someone had poured battery acid on them. When the U-505 was repaired and they put to sea again for diving trials, water seeped in. The deeper they went, the worse it became. They had to return to Keroman. The repair shop took a while to find out what was wrong. Oakum (rope) had been put between the plate joints and soldered over to disguise it:

'How could anyone expect us to win the war when our best weapons were suffering from a deliberate and pervasive program of sabotage by shipyard personnel. Almost every boat in the Flotilla was experiencing sabotage of some sort or another.'

Other boats found sugar in the lubricating oil and one a dead dog in the drinking water.

Who was behind the sabotage? Researching this subject is somewhat difficult. The Special Operations Executive – SOE – which Churchill tasked with 'setting Europe ablaze' would be where one would expect to find out more. That organisation was supplying the French resistance with men and women, money, weapons, radios and training, precisely to sabotage the Nazi war machine, as I have discussed in a previous chapter. The U-boat ports would have been a top – perhaps the top – target for them. And yet, in the bulky official history of the organisation *SOE in France* by M.R.D. Foot, who served with SOE - there is little more than a reference to adding itching powder to a shipment of

U-boat crew shirts. Low farce rather than high strategy. Foot says this was because: 'the five great German submarine bases on the Biscay coast were too carefully guarded.' Indeed they were, against direct attack. However, they were, in fact, infiltrated. Damage was being done in one at least – Lorient - on a grand scale. Not by SOE though.

The sabotage at Lorient was carried out by one of the many tentacles of the *Alliance* network, which was attached to SIS/MI6 (who dealt with intelligence gathering, not sabotage). *Alliance*, you may remember was run by that extraordinary French woman, Marie-Madeleine Fourcade. Her man on the ground at Lorient, who was primarily responsible for the sabotage, was Jacques Stosskopf, the deputy director of naval construction at the submarine base – the chief engineer. He was 'Volksdeutsch'; that is from a family which was ethnically German or from an area of France (in his case Alsace) which the Nazis considered to be a part of Germany. He spoke German fluently and had a degree from the prestigious École Polytechnique in marine engineering. He was on the best of terms with his Nazi masters.

Marie-Madeleine Fourcade talks about meeting an agent of hers, Joel Lemoigne, in early 1943. Monsieur Lemoigne had had a bit of a rough train journey, carrying, as he did, secret plans. He had been sitting comfortably in first class, doing his crossword, when he saw a man walking up and down the corridor, looking in. Lemoigne was wondering how to get rid of the papers when the man – Gestapo – entered the carriage and grabbed... the man next to him. The papers Lemoigne passed to Marie-Madeleine listed the U-boats currently at Lorient by number and emblem – 'a fish, a mermaid, an iron cross' - when they were to go to sea, their losses, their damage, when they had arrived and what they had sunk (the pennants they flew entering port showed the type of ship they had sunk – cargo, escort or warship – and how many). There were photographs of the U-boats. They had come from Jacques Stosskopf... 'the only Frenchman who is allowed into Keroman. He talks to the U-boat commanders when they arrive about the work needed. He is so far in with the Germans that he is hated by every Frenchman in Lorient.' He arranged and supervised all repairs.

Back went the information to Whaddon and thence to Coastal Command, the Admiralty, Churchill and Sefton Delmer – who, of course, we have also met - who would broadcast propaganda on the 'Calais' radio network mentioning such details as which flotilla had won the latest soccer match – or, as when Goebeler's commander committed suicide at sea, play a funeral march and offer condolences. 'These days,' in the words of Herbert Werner, 'British intelligence had its eyes and ears on us everywhere – in the compound, in the shipyard, in the restaurants, even in the brothels.'

As well as supervising repairs to the U-boats and passing back information about them, Stosskopf also sabotaged them. He was betrayed by a captured member of the *Alliance* network (doubtless under torture). Stosskopf paid for his aid to France with his life. He died in Natzweiler-Struthof, the only Nazi concentration camp on French soil and the primary holding point for captured members of the French resistance. Medical experiments were carried out on some of them. Jacques Stosskopf was one of twenty-two thousand (mainly) resistance fighters – men and women – killed there (including four British women working for SOE). Stosskopf knew his enemy and his probable fate and yet he fought.

The Lorient base is still there, as are most of the other U-boat bases. They proved too well-built and useful to destroy. Now it is a museum, open to the public. When it was built, it was called 'Keroman'. Now it is the Jacques Stosskopf museum.

4: The birth of the Information Age
How Bletchley Park shortened the war and developed Colossus

The plot thickens: the teleprinter joins Enigma

In order to learn what the Nazis were saying over the airwaves, Bletchley Park had to decipher messages sent from two main types of machines.

One of these was Enigma; as used by the armed forces and some civilian organisations. It was to decipher messages generated by Enigma that Turing and Welchman developed the Bombe; the device that was a major factor in the war against the U-boats.

The other type of enciphered messages were those which came from teleprinters. The teleprinter messages, which began in 1941, were used by the enemy high command to direct the war. This chapter is about how BP deciphered those messages and the consequences. It would be presumptuous of me to think that I could properly précis the work of the thousands who achieved this breakthrough in a few pages. I can only give the barest outline of this world-changing tale and hope to persuade you that it is a subject worth further study.

German high command intercepts

In May 1941, British Y service (wireless intercept) monitoring staff began to pick up a new type of radio transmission from the continent of Europe. These messages posed apparently insuperable problems to the secret listeners who were, as I explained earlier in *The Intelligence Zone*, trained to take down messages sent using Morse code. The problems were threefold:

* The new messages were transmitted so quickly that the listeners could not transcribe them by hand.
* Even had they been slower, transcription would have been a challenge, as they were not in Morse.
* They were typically much longer than previous messages.

The Y services and their customer, Bletchley Park, did not know the import of the messages; but, having recognised them as teleprinter messages, they were keen to find out. BP gave these messages the generic name of 'Fish'; each newly discovered German network being named after a specific species; for example they called the line between Athens and Berlin 'Tunny'.

Although they did not at first realise it, the British were logging the first transmissions from the networks which Hitler would use to communicate with his generals at the battle front. Obviously if a general can read the orders of his opponent, he is well on the way to beating him. That is precisely what Bletchley Park would help British, American and Russian generals to do.

As I've said, the Fish networks operated using teleprinters. In some respects these devices looked like the Enigma machines; they too used rotors (wheels); a technology I have described in *The Intelligence Zone*. But the teleprinters were much more complex. I explain this in a little more detail in the appendix at the end of this chapter.

The job of recording the teleprinter messages was given to staff of the General Post Office (GPO); the government department which ran all Britain's postal and telephone services. The GPO Y service staff recorded the messages using a device of their own manufacture called the Undulator, which was activated by the electric current of the radio waves received. The output from this went to a needle which was connected to graph paper. The incoming digital strings of zeros and ones were then punched by hand onto 5 hole perforated paper tape for the code breakers to work on. There were few Undulators in the GPO and few who could read them, so new and faster devices had to be developed on the fly.

The Y services were already under strain picking up the huge volume of Enigma traffic sent out by the Axis armed forces. The handling of Fish traffic would call for extra resource.

It didn't take Bletchley Park long to realise the importance of Fish. Fish networks were broadcasting from German high command to the one front that the Nazis were then fighting on, in North Africa, against Britain; but they were also transmitting eastwards. Why this was so became crystal clear a couple of weeks after the first Fish messages were logged when, in June 1941, Germany invaded Russia.

If Bletchley could decipher this traffic, they would have the inner thoughts of Hitler – who held the reins of power and directed Axis strategy to a remarkably low level. Britain - and through them Russia - would know when and where the Nazis would strike next; the very direction of the war.

Tiltman and Tutte

At Bletchley Park, the job of breaking into Fish was given to the Research Section, which answered to the head of the Military Section, Colonel John Tiltman. Tiltman was not your average soldier. Born in London, he had been offered a place at Oxford university at the age of 13 (the normal entry age being 18). He joined the British Army in 1914, winning a Military Cross in France. From 1921 to 1929, he was a cryptanalyst with the British army in India. The army analysts were reading Russian diplomatic cyphers between Kabul in Afghanistan and Moscow. Tiltman, who learned Russian in order to do the job, was involved in directing interception and traffic analysis as well as working on cyphers. This was the perfect background for the work he later did when he was transferred to Bletchley Park.

Col. John Tiltman
(courtesy of GCHQ)

Bill Tutte

At BP he taught himself enough Japanese in six months to work on Japanese cyphers. Having done so, he visited the School of Oriental and African Studies (SOAS) in London and asked them to put together a course of the same length so that others could learn enough Japanese to help him. In the words of Paul Gannon, in his book *Colossus – Bletchley Park's greatest secret:*

'The august academics demurred, explaining that it normally took five years for a diplomat to reach the required standard; but six months was quite impractical. Tiltman refused to accept this denial of his own experience, so he set up his own training centre. The six month course focussed rigidly on the task in hand. One student recalls that when his course was finished he knew the Japanese for 'submarine' but not for 'I' and 'you'. But it successfully trained several codebreakers – despite being based at a rather uninspiring location; a former showroom for gas appliances (in Bedford). Indeed, the courses were so successful that SOAS was shamed into setting up its own parallel lessons.'

Tiltman was one of the greatest codebreakers at Bletchley Park, holding the title of Chief Cryptographer from 1942 on. It was he who first broke into Japanese army and navy codes; sharing the information with an American delegation to Bletchley Park, who had themselves much to bring to the table. In his later life, he would play a key part in setting up the intelligence accord between Britain and America, work extensively in America and would be the first non-American to be inducted into the National Security Agency Hall of Honor.

Working in Tiltman's department was Bill Tutte, a young Cambridge-educated mathematician. It was Tutte who was the key figure in breaking the German teleprinter codes. In the words of Kevin Murrell, from the National Museum of Computing (at Bletchley Park):

'What Bill was able to do, with just a couple of captured messages, was to sit down and work out what this machine in Berlin would have been doing. He did this without ever seeing the machine or reading anything about it. That's probably the single biggest intellectual achievement at Bletchley Park during World War Two.'

The story of how Tutte (primarily) broke into Fish is, as is often the case with Bletchley Park, extraordinarily complex and beyond the scope of most people's patience. It is certainly beyond my competence to describe. The definitive work on the subject is Paul Gannon's *Colossus*.

By April 1942, there were six separate Fish networks operating on the Eastern front prompting the head of BP (Edward Travis) to take; 'Rapid action on a bigger scale than has hitherto been contemplated.'

That rapid action included the opening of a new intercept station at Knockholt, in Kent, which was completely devoted to tracking and recording the messages.

At Bletchley Park and the GPO's workshops, it involved the building of ever-faster machines to record the incoming traffic and analyse it.

Machines at BP

Deciphering the (Lorenz) teleprinter messages at Bletchley quickly enough to make them useful, called for mechanisation; which is where another member of John Tiltman's team, Max Newman stepped up to the mark. He mechanised Tutte's mathematical techniques; leading to the development of faster and more complex machines. Many different machines (including the splendidly named Heath Robinson) were invented to help in the decryption process. At one point, over 200 different types of machine were in use at Bletchley Park. I will return to one of them, Colossus, later. I do not have the space to say much about the others.

Cairncross and Modin

Let me now fast-forward to May 1943. A lot has happened in the meantime. Britain has got itself a couple of allies – Russia and America. The receiving station at Knockholt has opened and is processing Fish messages. Bletchley Park has undergone an expansion, too, to deal with Fish and the bewildering array of machines needed to make sense of it. A new member of staff has just joined BP. His name is John Cairncross.

Cairncross was one of the five(?) 'Cambridge Spies' who were highly placed in the British secret services and for years passed British (and some American) secrets to Russia. The five had been recruited by the communists from Cambridge University in the mid nineteen-thirties. They had begun with the best of intentions; faith in the world revolution – the coming dawn of the equality of man. Sadly they never wavered in their faith. If the bloody history of the Twentieth Century has one key message it must be that knowledge is a greater virtue than faith; and knowledge is only reached by questioning.

Once the Cambridge spies had swallowed the good news message, they did not question it; even as it became ever more obvious that the messiah, (Stalin) that they were following was a murderer with the blood of millions on his hands. An example of this is the *Holdomor* (death by starvation) - the grain famine which he engineered to bring his vassal state of Ukraine to heel, so that it would never again contest Russian rule. In this genocide of 1932-1933, over three million Ukrainians starved to death.

Instead, the Cambridge spies worked to make 'the dark night of Stalin' (as Sir William Hayter, the British Ambassador to Moscow, termed it) even darker. These five(?) men were prime examples of what Lenin called 'useful idiots'. Their mistaken faith would cost Europe dear; not least (but not only) by their betrayal to their deaths of numerous men and women in the lands of eastern Europe who fought against Russian occupation.

Yuri Modin was one of the London-based Russian 'minders' of the Cambridge spies (his predecessors having been recalled to Moscow and murdered in Stalin's purges). Modin wrote a book about them 'My five Cambridge friends'. In it, he says that Cairncross was a vain, humourless and resentful man, whose treachery seems to have been motivated more by 'the sizeable chip on his shoulder' than for the cash and gifts he received. Alec Cairncross, John's brother, said of him that he was 'a prickly young man, who was difficult to argue with and resented things rather easily.' The two brothers are an interesting study in nature and nurture. Alec would go on to be knighted and become the Chancellor of Glasgow University; John to betray his country.

Modin's book gives several interesting insights into the Russian take on the alliance between the Allies and Russia. He mentions, for example, how shipments of ammunition from the west were vital to the Soviet armies. He says that the lack of 'explosives' delivered by the Allies in 1944 ('not a single consignment of powder arrived in Murmansk') meant that the Soviet armies could not attack. I have touched on the critical importance of Allied supplies to Russia elsewhere.

What is less well-known than the importance of British and American Lend-Lease to Russia is the part played by intelligence from Bletchley to Russian strategy and success. Yuri Modin gives an oblique insight into the subject when he talks about the part played by John Cairncross (whom the Russians rewarded for his treachery with a car, the Order of the Red Banner and 'a large amount of money'). Modin praises Cairncross's actions for 'saving countless Russian lives and being one of the key factors which allowed Russia to defeat the German armies in the east.'

Cairncross, too, says that the spying that he did at Bletchley Park was of a fundamental importance in the war in the east. The subtitle of his autobiography (*The Enigma Spy*) is '*The story of the man who changed the course of World War Two.*'

What both of them were referring to was the information that Cairncross passed to Russia about German preparations for their attack at Kursk, in 1943. This battle was indeed all that Modin and Cairncross claimed; a turning point of the war. Modin tells us that Cairncross's information allowed the Russians to launch a pre-emptive strike against the German air force (the Luftwaffe), destroying 600 aircraft.

The spy and his minder are in perfect accord then. Cairncross was a key factor in the Battle of Kursk. If one digs a little deeper into the timing of Cairncross's treachery, though, something doesn't smell quite right. If the information he gave about the build up to the battle of Kursk was so important, it seems very odd that he left Bletchley Park two months *before* the great battle began (for the somewhat unheroic reason that he didn't like shift work). It seems even odder that his Russian minder ('Henry') didn't put obstacles in his way *but actually suggested he would be more useful elsewhere.*

If Cairncross had been a more reflective man, he would have wondered at that. How *could* he be more usefully employed than in passing live and critically important intelligence to the defenders at the sticky end of the greatest armoured assault in history. But then, John Cairncross wasn't a very clear thinker. If he had been, he would have spent a good deal more time wondering why BP was going out of its way to gather all this information about the German attack plans on Russia in the first place – and what, apart from dumping it on the floor so that he could stuff it down his trousers, were they doing with it?

But then, clear thinking was not exactly John Cairncross's strong suit. In *The Enigma Spy*, his own account of what led him to treachery, he claims to have been recruited not through support for the proletariat (perish the thought!) but as an 'uncertain youth caught in a skilful trap' who was subsequently afraid to give up spying. Cairncross is, however (and perhaps unsurprisingly), not to be trusted, contradicting himself on several occasions even in this, his own – unrepentant - autobiography. His most remarkable statement in the work has to be his description of the joint Nazi and Soviet invasion of Poland as 'a territorial gain for the Allies'. As an example of casuistry, this is breath taking, even by his standards. While it cannot be said that John Cairncross was his own worst enemy (there being too many candidates for that title), he certainly carried a canker within him which would harm the cause of civilisation and humanity.

The reason why Stalin didn't need Cairncross's information from Bletchley Park was, of course, because BP was already giving it to him directly. That was why the vast new aerial farm (where 600 personnel were working round the clock to record messages) had been set up at Knockholt. That was why BP was frantically working to crack the Fish codes.

The passage of intelligence from Churchill to Stalin had begun in 1941, ten days before Germany's assault on Russia; and had been ignored by the Russian dictator as 'a provocation'. It continued throughout the war; In the words of Churchill's biographer, Sir Martin Gilbert:

'Stalin rarely bothered to reply, but his commanders-in chief took action on the basis of every… communication.'

There were many occasions when Russian commanders knew of German orders even before these had percolated down to front-line German officers in the field. As early as three weeks into the invasion, Bletchley had provided information about the unfolding Nazi attack on Moscow. As I've mentioned elsewhere, this dovetailed into other British and American aid.

In 1942, BP informed Stalin of the German dispositions for the attack on Stalingrad. In August 1942, Churchill flew to Moscow to personally brief the Russian leader; receiving later one of Stalin's rare expressions of gratitude: ('many thanks for your warnings').

To return to the battle of Kursk.

Kursk

The battle for Kursk, in the summer of 1943, was the third of the German summer campaigns against Russia. Its intention was to nip off a forward bulge in the Russian front line and

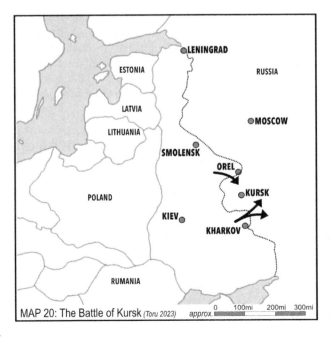

MAP 20: The Battle of Kursk *(Toru 2023)*

destroy the Russian armies there before resuming the drive on Moscow.

It was the largest tank battle in history. The Germans deployed 2,730 tanks and 900,000 men. The Russians had 3,440 tanks and self-propelled guns and 1,340,000 men. This was almost equal in terms of tank numbers. For opponents of German tank attacks, these were not good odds.

On average throughout the war, German armour destroyed around two tanks for every one they lost. Nor was the fact that there were more Russian troops than German as important as it might seem. Perhaps because Stalin had murdered many of his military high command in the Great Terror of 1938, (including 154 of the 186 divisional commanders); while the Russian armies fought with a bravery which could not be surpassed, their strategy and tactics were not as effective as those of their German opponents. And yet Kursk was a clear victory for the Russians and marked the end of major German attacks on the Eastern front. As John Cairncross said in the subtitle of his autobiography, the battle changed the course of World War Two.

BP had begun to inform Stalin of the impending attack two months before it started and continued to do so after Cairncross had quit Bletchley. It furnished the Soviets with a detailed breakdown of the strength and composition of the German divisions and the plans for the pincer movement. These were professionally presented appreciations of the whole German battle strength, drawn together from the thousands of decrypts at Bletchley – both from Enigma and from the Fish decrypts.

To put it in a nutshell, after Kursk, Germany could no longer win against Russia. From now on, Hitler faced only defeat and retreat in the east. The Soviets acknowledged Britain's part in their salvation when it awarded Cairncross the Order of the Red Banner. The medal should have gone to Bletchley Park.

Kursk was only one battle. Against the evidence of too many Nazi 'plans that had gone wrong', Hitler blamed his own signals staff who were:

"Absolute traitors …how does the enemy learn about our thinking? Why does he react to everything so quickly?"

The enemy he was looking for was not on his own staff, but in Buckinghamshire.

Intelligence from Bletchley Park was used to dictate strategy on all three of the fronts against the Nazis (North Africa/Italy, Russia and Normandy) and was a major factor in shortening the war. But it did not win the war. After America entered the fight it is doubtful whether anything that happened in Russia could have led to victory for the Nazis. Even in the worst case, it was only a matter of time until the atom bomb was developed by the west.

Still, shortening a war which was costing millions of lives a month is quite a battle honour for Bletchley Park. Astonishingly, it was surpassed by another; Tommy Flowers' invention of the electronic digital computer which opened the door to mankind's future.

Colossus: the door to the future

I mentioned earlier that Bletchley Park used and developed a bewildering array of machines to record and decipher the long and high-speed Lorenz teleprinter communications between the German high command and its battle fronts. The GPO was at the forefront in developing these machines. The key man in this process was the head of the telephone switching department at the GPO research site at Dollis Hill, in London, Tommy Flowers. Flowers was (along with his boss, Gordon Radley) one of the two GPO employees who were fully versed in the workings of Bletchley Park.

Flowers was asked to speed up the reading of paper tape. Early machines such as the Heath Robinson could process 2,000 characters a second, but they weren't always reliable; and they needed to be ten times faster (20,000 characters a second). Flowers believed that a new approach was needed. In the words of Paul Gannon:

'Instead of a few modifications needed to make the counting unit better, Flowers proposed a mammoth wholly electronic machine as the best approach to the brute force method with its need for lots of calculations in as short a time as possible.'

To achieve this, Tommy Flowers would use his unparalleled expertise in automating telephone exchanges.

The development of the telephone exchange dates back to the first telephones, in Connecticut, in 1878. The first automatic exchange was devised by Almon Strowger, an American undertaker a dozen years later. He was motivated to invent an automatic exchange after having difficulties with the local telephone operators, one of whom was the wife of a competitor. He was said to be convinced that she, as one of the manual telephone exchange operators, was sending calls "to the undertaker" to her husband.

By 1939, telephone exchanges and automatic switching technology had come a long way from Almon Strowger; and Tommy Flowers believed it to be the key to producing a machine fast enough to crack the Fish transmissions. If anyone was qualified to speak about switching technology, it was he; for he was perhaps the foremost authority in the world on the subject. But to get authority and resources to carry out the work was far from plain sailing. To Flower's frustration, not everyone at Bletchley Park believed that his approach was the right one. In his own words; 'No one else in the world was using this technology and that's what made it difficult to explain to Bletchley Park.'

But Flowers had the backing of two very important men at BP. One of them was the operational head of Bletchley Park, Edward Travis (Travis was the organisational brains behind BP and was largely responsible for its astonishing success). On the technical side, Flowers was supported by Alan Turing with whom he was closely involved in deciding the requirement for the machine. Turing understood what Flowers was doing better than most and his opinion carried a good deal of weight.

As an aside, you may have noticed that I do not talk much about Alan Turing in this book. That is not because I do not appreciate his massive, war changing, contribution. I don't talk much about this genius because I suspect that you already know about what he did and his tragic fate. If you don't, you can easily find out. In the limited space I have here, I would rather give some of it to things which, I suspect, will be new to you. History is the goldmine where all our stories are stashed. Its treasures enrich us, give us perspective and balance; sometimes even sanity. Its hidden veins are sometimes the richest.

Winning over the waverers took time; but Tommy Flowers could see the road ahead clearly and had no time to wait for the lights to change. With the Anglo-American D-day landings approaching, the need to read Hitler's mind became crucial to save Allied lives. Speed was key. In Paul Gannon's words:

'Flowers, his colleagues at Dollis Hill and the technicians at Birmingham worked in a frenzy to design, acquire, wire and, where necessary, manufacture components (made possible by) the prodigious efforts of the laboratory staff, many of whom did nothing but work, eat and sleep for weeks and months except for one half day a week... The US also contributed valves and an (IBM) electrical typewriter under lend-lease.'

Flowers got the electronic digital computer, Colossus, running in London (Dollis Hill) in December 1943. It was big, it was powerful and it was to be of help in winning the war. That was just a part of it, though. Colossus was a child of the military, born behind barbed wire; but computing soon grew too big to be constrained. Today it affects – and in some senses controls - each and every one of us.

I believe that something truly colossal happened when Tommy Flowers powered-up Colossus. I believe that at the moment of ignition a new age dawned for mankind.

The Information Age. Our Age.

Appendix. German teleprinter messages

Where Enigma used three or four rotors, and a substitution cipher, the teleprinters (manufactured by Lorenz) used an additional attachment with 12 rotors to encipher their messages. And the teleprinters did not use Morse code but the International Telegraph Alphabet number 2 (ITA2), a development of the Baudot code of the 1880s. ITA2 (which is still in use today) is digital – a string of zeroes and ones, rather than the dots and dashes of Morse. The teleprinter messages were generally much longer than Enigma messages. A typical Fish message of 15,000 characters was 30 times longer than a typical Enigma one. The enciphered teleprinter messages were not transmitted by an operator tapping a Morse key; but were typed in by hand. This produced a paper tape which was then transmitted.

5: Bomber Commands. The warlords of Wycombe

The Royal Air Force grew to employ over a million men and women during World War Two. Bomber Command was its largest component. The RAF was joined in Britain in 1942 by the United States Army Air Force (USAAF), which would itself grow to have half a million men in the British Isles. This massive joint Allied air force would spread over hundreds of bases, especially in the eastern counties of England and take up much of the flat lands there.

It would break Germany's ability to fight, and smash her cities and industry. With the Allied armies, it would finally lead to the end of the Nazi scourge.

With the arrival of American forces came a sharing of Allied power which led to a shift in the way the air war was waged. The characters of the commanders who moulded and led the air armadas were key to this. The stories of the troops who served the bomber warlords are sobering, absorbing and often frightening. So are the moral implications of unrestricted air war.

Bomber command moves to High Wycombe

The headquarters of Bomber Command, and the European USAAF, were at RAF High Wycombe, in Buckinghamshire. Unlike Fighter and Coastal Commands' headquarters, Bomber Command HQ was not easy to find. As befitted the Royal Air Force's holy of holies, it was buried deep in the woods and the folds of the hills. This was, and is, RAF High Wycombe, which opened in 1938. The camp lies in the beautiful beech woods of the Chiltern Hills. It is an ideal command post, since the trees and hills provide natural camouflage from the air.

The buildings were disguised; the Officers' Mess was built to look like a manor house and the fire station built with a tower to resemble a village church. Trees were preserved as much as possible to maintain the camouflage they provided. Tunnels were dug to connect each block on the station, all linked to an Operations Block built 55 feet (17 m) below ground. Needless to say, it was also linked into the communications web that I have described in *The Intelligence Zone*.

The site was suggested by an RAF officer, Alan Oakeshott, who grew up at Naphill, a mile down the road. His name is on the war memorial there. He is also commemorated at the powerfully moving RAF war memorial, which stands on a ridge above the River Thames at Runnymede, directly above the meadow where Magna Carta was signed. He is one of the 20,456 RAF service men and women listed on the seemingly endless tablets there. These are just the ones who have no known graves. Like so many of his companions, Alan Oakeshott died flying against Germany. He was shot down on July the 2nd 1942, after bombing submarine yards at Flensburg. He was 24 years old.

Bomber command pre–Harris

Although by far the richest of the main RAF commands (in the final pre–war expansion plan Bomber Command was allocated almost 4 times as much as Fighter Command), Bomber Command, like Coastal Command, did not start World War Two in a very good position. It was 'entirely unprepared for war, unable to operate except in fair weather, and extremely vulnerable both in the air and on the ground.' That was the assessment of Air Chief Marshal Sir Edgar Ludlow–Hewitt at any rate. His evidence can be relied on, one supposes, as he was the man in charge – the Commander in Chief of Bomber Command. He made the observation two years before war broke out. Just to make his feelings clear, he also said that: 'Our bombing force, judged from a war standard (is) practically useless.'

Training was dangerous (many men died from flying into hills and the ground), navigation being so poor that 'over 40% of a force of bombers were unable to find a target in a friendly city in broad daylight.' The city was the second largest in England, Birmingham. After sunset it was even worse. In a night exercise, two thirds of the bombers couldn't even find the city. This was in peacetime, with no blackout.

The Official History of the Royal Air Force is damning: 'When war came in 1939, Bomber Command was not trained or equipped either to penetrate into enemy territory by day or to find its target areas, let alone its targets, by night.' This, as the same definitive work states: 'seems a strange result after twenty years of devoted work.' Quite.

The RAF started the war with 536 bombers. The Luftwaffe had 2,130.

At the same time, in 1940, that Dowding and Park were sacked after (or for?) winning the Battle of Britain, the then head of Bomber Command, Charles Portal, was promoted to Air Chief Marshal, that is the military (as against political) head of the Royal Air Force. With a bomber man in charge, the Trenchard Doctrine remained unsullied.

Just to recap: the Trenchard Doctrine, the holy writ of the RAF, was that the 'bomber will always get through'. The key to victory was heavy bombing of the enemy. Minimal (or no) aid from fighter planes or land forces was needed. Given Dowding's victory over the German bombers, this might seem an odd conclusion. So it would prove to be. In the words of Max Hastings in *Bomber Command:*

'Seldom in the history of warfare has a force been so sure of the end it sought – fulfilment of the Trenchard Doctrine – and yet so ignorant of how this might be achieved, as the RAF between the wars.'

If the RAF's central doctrine was shaky, so was Bomber Command's equipment. Their aeroplanes were not good enough, nor were their explosives. The RAF's bombs were smaller than the Luftwaffe's and quite inadequate for destroying reinforced structures. Most importantly perhaps, the guns on the bombers – .303 machine guns (which were used by the whole RAF at the start of the war and by Bomber Command throughout it) – were no match for the heavy calibre automatic weapons used by German fighters.

As already stated, Bomber Command had difficulty in finding their targets. Not only was navigation poor, but Bomber

Command didn't seem to care. To cite just two examples: R.V. Jones, working in the Air Ministry in 1938, says; 'I was... astonished by the complacency that existed regarding our ability to navigate at long range at night... Bomber Command was confident that it could find targets in Germany at night, and that there was therefore no need for any such radio aids as I proposed. I was not popular for asking why, if this were true, so many bombers on practice flights in Britain flew into hills.' In the same year, Taffy Bowen, the radar man, proposed the use of radar to Bomber Command: 'only to have Bomber Command disclaim the need for it, saying the sextant was sufficient.' Shades of Coastal Command's pigeons.

By the summer of 1940 Bomber Command had, like the Luftwaffe, found that attacking the enemy's homeland during the day was suicidal – so the offensive on Germany was switched to the night. This did not help with accuracy.

Bombing accuracy was to remain problematical throughout the war. It improved as radar developed; and with the introduction of pathfinder squadrons – the best navigators and bomb aimers leading bomber fleets, marking the targets with coloured flares which the following bombers would bomb on – but these still only allowed the air fleets to be used on large areas, not for pinpoint bombing. That was confined to some specialist squadrons, such as 617 (the Dam Busters). This issue of accuracy, probably more than anything, would seal the fate of Germany's cities.

RAF Bomber Command losses during the early years of the war were catastrophic. In 1941, for example, 924 of its aircraft did not return from action and 260 crashed on return. Its total bomber fleet that year was never above 1,000. Not reassuring statistics for an aircrew member.

Nor was there any certainty that the objective – damaging the enemy – was being realised. By 1941, Churchill's scientific adviser, Professor Frederick Lindemann, suspected that Bomber Command was not having a major impact on Germany. He asked RAF Medmenham to look into the matter.

RAF Medmenham Photographic Interpretation Unit

In the opening chapter of *The Intelligence Zone*, I spoke about how Fred Winterbotham spied for SIS(MI6) in Germany before the war. It may be remembered that Winterbotham spent the First World War in the Royal Flying Corps (forerunner of the RAF), flying 'somewhat suicidal' reconnaissance flights over German lines, photographing their troops and guns. At the start of the second war Winterbotham, with equipment from the RAF and his 'spy in the sky', Sidney Cotton, had set up an aerial reconnaissance section which by 1942 had grown, having a headquarters at Medmenham (on the Thames near Henley) and an airfield at RAF Benson in Oxfordshire.

Benson flew spy planes and Medmenham dealt with the resultant photographs for all all of the RAF commands (Bomber Command had tried, and failed, to take it over: it was run by Coastal Command). As such, it was the obvious place for Professor Lindemann to look when he was distrustful of Bomber Command's rosy reports about its results.

Lindemann was a key player in the war and I have mentioned him several times already. He also gets mentioned in many of the memoirs of the time. Normally – indeed all–but universally – he gets a bad press. Dowding described him as a 'witch doctor', Bomber Harris called him 'a naive busybody', R V Jones talks of his 'technical incompetence'. Lieutenant Ted Briggs, one of the only 3 survivors of 'the day that broke the Andrew's heart' (the sinking of the Navy's flagship, HMS *Hood*), blames Lindemann's half–baked aerial mine device for the loss of the ship. And so it goes on. And on. But here, at least, Lindemann can be praised. He was quite right to be doubtful about Bomber Command. The man on the inside at Medmenham whom he asked to look into the matter was Glyn Davies.

Professor Glyn Davies was born in Pembrokeshire in 1914. By the outbreak of war he was teaching archaeology at Cambridge University. He then joined the RAF and was posted to Stonebridge, London as a photographic interpreter. He, like everyone else in London at the time, was on the receiving end of the Luftwaffe's 57–night blitz of bombs, incendiaries and booby–traps. He had a flat near Hyde Park and commuted. He worked nights. As he describes in his autobiography, the rather fine '*Some small harvest*', one night there were no trains because of the bombing and a bus was laid on into London:

'I walked from Paddington to Bayswater and turning into Queensborough Terrace passed the cheerful family who lived five or six doors away from my flat and waved to them as they breakfasted, as I always did after returning from my night shift. They waved back and there was a particularly cheerful wave from the young son... I climbed up to my flat, too tired to undress and have a bath. I had been asleep for half an hour or more when I was awoken by a strange noise and a rushing wind. The mirror on the wall was swinging to and fro and then crashed in pieces on the ground... I walked out down the street. A delayed–action bomb had exploded a few doors away. Police were arriving. There was a hideous gap in the buildings where my breakfast party had been. I climbed back to my flat and was sick.'

The continual bombing in London meant his section was moved, to Medmenham, Buckinghamshire, and he was billeted in a very fine house nearby. Davies was approached in the Hare and Hounds pub, in Marlow (it is remarkable how much of the wartime action in England took place in pubs) and taken to see Lindemann, who had a house nearby. Lindemann told him: "The Prime Minister and I want to know exactly what photo–intelligence is learning about the war."

So Davies told him. The evidence he provided – photographs from Bomber Command's bombing runs and pilots' logs for June and July 1941 – were passed by Lindemann to a Dr Butt, a statistician in the Admiralty, whom he had commissioned to compile a report on what was revealed. The evidence in the Butt Report was damning. Butt did not include the one–third of the aircraft which returned without having claimed to have found the target. Of the rest, he found that only one out of three planes got within five miles of the aiming point. Against the Ruhr (Germany's accessible and heavily defended industrial area), this fell to one out of ten. *On moonless nights only one in fifteen of Bomber Command's planes was within five miles of the target.* Not surprisingly the Butt report came as a seismic shock.

The Dehousing Paper

Churchill blew hot and cold on the issue of bombing, saying at one point: "it is very debatable whether bombing by itself will be a decisive in the present war." But it was something that Britain could do, something palpable and, importantly, something that would help Russia. Russia had started the war as Germany's friend, but in 1941, after the Luftwaffe had lost the Battle of Britain, Hitler had torn up his peace treaty with the soviets and invaded the country. Expansion to the east 'lebensraum' – room to breathe – was Hitler's main objective for Germany.

Since then Britain had been supplying Russia with arms through convoys from Liverpool and Glasgow; but Russia was on the ropes and needed more. Britain was in no position to land troops in Europe: it was too heavily defended and in any case the German armies were bigger and infinitely superior in weapons and leadership to Britain's. The bomber was just about the only weapon with which Britain could hurt Germany. If she were to continue to take the war to the Nazis, Britain's best option was to bomb at night. But, if night time bombing of industrial targets – oil, transport, shipyards and the like – was largely a waste of bombs, aircraft and men – then what could the bombers hit? The only thing that was too big to miss was the cities.

Largely as a result of the Butt Report, Lindemann (later Lord Cherwell) produced his Dehousing Paper. The paper said:

'In 1938 over 22 million Germans lived in fifty–eight towns of over 100,000 inhabitants which, with modern equipment, should be easy to find and hit. Our forecast output of heavy bombers between now and the middle of 1943 is about 10,000. If even half the total load of 10,000 bombers were dropped on the built–up areas of these fifty–eight German towns the great majority of their inhabitants (about one third of the German population) would be turned out of house and home. Investigation seems to show that having one's house demolished is most damaging to morale... There seems little doubt that this would break the spirit of the people.'

Morale was the key concept. Bombing would lead to a collapse in the will to resist. This belief was already a cornerstone of German strategy. They had pioneered city attacks in 1936, in Spain. After Guernica and Barcelona, they had targeted Amsterdam, Warsaw and London. The British air elite, too – not just Lindemann – believed that breaking morale was the key to success. At the heart of both Luftwaffe and RAF doctrine, then, was the belief that 'the bomber will always get through' and the bomber would decide the battle. This was law. This was holy writ. In the RAF, as I mentioned earlier, it was called the Trenchard Doctrine.

Lindemann's conclusion was based, he said, on 'careful analysis' of German air attacks on Hull and London. In summary, then, his Dehousing Paper recommended the bombing of Germany's cities. It seems strange that the fate of Germany's cities was decided by a man (Lindemann) who was born and schooled in Germany (although he had since been granted British nationality) – but so it was.

After a heated debate in Cabinet, the Dehousing Paper was accepted. It was then issued to Bomber Command as a directive – their future policy. Its stated objective was: 'to focus attacks on the morale of the enemy civil population, in particular of industrial workers.' In a follow–up letter Air Chief Marshal Sir Charles Portal, the head of the RAF, stressed that: 'the aiming points are to be in the built–up areas, not, for instance, the dockyards or aircraft factories.'

In 1940, Charles Portal had written with regard to SOE: 'The dropping of men dressed in civilian clothes for the purpose of attempting to kill members of the opposing forces is not an operation with which the RAF should be associated... there is a vast difference, in ethics, between the time–honoured operation of dropping a spy from the air and this entirely new scheme for what one can only call assassins.' The war had become bloodier since then.

While the head of the German Luftwaffe, Hermann Goering, would hardly have approved of the Dehousing Paper, he would certainly have understood it. Area bombing at night was, as I have mentioned in my chapter about Fighter Command, German policy too. They had used it with most concentrated effect on Coventry in November 1940. The Germans had even invented a new verb for the process '*coventrieren*' – to devastate or raze a city. Portal wasn't playing by Queensbury rules any more, he was playing by Coventry rules. The man his directive was given to was Arthur Harris, the new head of Bomber Command. Harris was the fifth Commander Bomber Command had had since the start of the war.

Sir Arthur Harris took over Bomber Command in February 1942. Air Marshal Harris was – and is – known to the wider public as Bomber Harris. This, too, was his nickname within the RAF, although in that service he was more generally (and affectionately) referred to as 'Butch'. This was known by all to be short for butcher, although the full word was not generally used.

Over there – the Yanks arrive at High Wycombe

On the same day that Arthur Harris took over Bomber Command, a delegation from the 8th United States Army Air Force (USAAF) arrived at High Wycombe. They were given the keys of RAF Daws Hill. This had previously been Wycombe Abbey Girl's School and its grounds. It is said that beside each bed was a bell labelled: 'if you need a mistress in the night, ring twice.' The 8th's commanding officer, General Ira Eaker, would never get to ring the bell (if the story was true) because he was to stay with Bomber Harris himself, in his house, Springfield.

Harris knew America and Americans. He had recently spent time in the United States as head of the permanent RAF delegation there. Although, as I've mentioned earlier, he believed that America should have joined the fight a good deal earlier, that didn't lessen his welcome for his new brother-in-arms. He liked Americans and generally got on well with them, especially with Eaker. They thought along the same lines as far as bombing went; Ira Eaker being part of what in America was called 'the bomber mafia' – which shared more or less the same beliefs as the Trenchard Doctrine.

It would take time – nearly a year – before American aircraft were flying over Germany. That was not down to the men on the ground (Eaker and his boss General Spaatz) but was a result of other priorities – that is, building up an American air force in the Pacific and in North Africa. In the meantime, many of the RAF stations in East Anglia were turned over to the USAAF.

The USAAF differed from the RAF in that it was part of the army and not an independent force. The quip in the USAAF was that there was 'one A too many'. That is, they wanted for their force what Trenchard had achieved for the RAF in 1918 – independence from the army. I will come back to the Americans a little later.

Bomber Harris

Arthur Harris was a forceful man who seemed to fear neither man nor God, his dry, vulgar, caustic wit was legendary in the RAF. For example, he said that the army would never understand tanks 'until they can eat hay and shit.'

And he was uncompromising. Like Churchill, he put into words what most thought but were unable, or afraid, to utter:

'The Nazis entered this war under the rather childish delusion that they were going to bomb everyone else, and nobody was going to bomb them. At Rotterdam, London, Warsaw, and half a hundred other places, they put their rather naive theory into operation. They sowed the wind, and now they are going to reap the whirlwind.'

There is no doubt of the almost universal support he got for these sentiments, from the highest in the land to his own aircrews. Of many similar opinions on Harris, let me quote that of Don Bennett – the man who would later set up the elite Pathfinder Squadrons, which would revolutionise bombing accuracy:

'He was full of fire and dash, was not easily baulked, and was also remarkably intelligent without trying to show it. He was, I knew, a real man, and my hopes for the bomber offensive and its ultimate destruction of Germany were revitalised.'

The public backed him too. After the blitz on London and other cities in 1940/41 and the barbaric behaviour of the Nazis in Occupied Europe, why on earth should Britain forbear to "dish it out"?

Harris was a leader. He didn't often shout – he didn't need to, he was obeyed – but he had a sharp tongue. His first wife, Barbara, divorced him: "not over the other women, it was the very rude way he spoke to me." He was also a bit of a joker, putting whoopee cushions under the cushions of his sofas and playing drinking games on occasion. He was irritable in the mornings and his staff trod warily then. Whether it was his ulcer, or the tot or two of whisky, or his chain smoking, or maybe all three, he was not good to be around first thing. He self–medicated with Collis–Browne's cough mixture, but it didn't seem to cure his ills.

Harris was not given to self–doubt. It took a lot to convince him when he was mistaken. Nor did he welcome the advice or opinions of others. Churchill, although broadly in agreement with Harris's brief, thought 'there was a certain coarseness' about the man himself. In the words of his army liaison officer, Charles Carrington: 'He enjoyed shocking the pedants... he never played for popularity, never wasted words or time on mere civilities... Bomber Command knew it had a master and the whole machine tightened up.'

Harris had his directive and his objective. About half his force would be used for what he called 'panacea targets' – i.e. ones he considered more or less a waste of time – the U–boat ports, some targeted daytime attacks on the French factories producing armaments for Germany, some mine laying, some shipping. The rest of the bombing raids were on what he thought to be the real war winner – night attacks on German cities. In his opinion an Allied invasion of Europe would be worse than pointless: 'a continental land campaign, except to mop up, would play into enemy hands.'

Sometimes Harris's barbs have drawn later criticism. For instance he called Coastal Command 'an obstacle to victory' – which, on the face of it seems not so much controversial as plain stupid. If Britain and her allies had not won the Siege of the Atlantic the country would have starved and his planes would have had no fuel. But he made the comment in June 1942, when Coastal Command, after nearly three years of war, had sunk just 7 U–boats at a loss of hundreds of aircraft and men. Coastal was, as we have seen, to come good. But Harris didn't know that at the time, nor could he have done.

He also objected to bombing the U–boat ports. The civilian casualties didn't bother Harris greatly: 'The French packed up at the start of the war, they should have fought for themselves. Except for the Maquis (resistance), they didn't.' What he did object to was that the destruction of Lorient, Brest and the other channel ports didn't affect the U–boats much, they were buried too deep in their bunkers (although dropping mines did sink a couple).

History has proved Harris to have been right in this. So many planes were shot down over the French ports – principally Brittany – that MI9's James Langley and the French resistance set up an escape line from the Breton beaches to Dartmouth, Devon. I will talk more about MI9 in a page or two.

Lancaster Bomber

Harris was just the man to carry out the directives of the Area Bombing Directive. To some extent he was lucky in that the tools he needed arrived at Bomber Command at about the same time as he did. Two heavy bombers the Halifax (introduced March 1941) and above all the Lancaster bomber (March 1942), with a heavier payload than any other aircraft of the war, at last made mass bombing a practicality.

Cologne; the first 1000 bomber raid

Bomber Harris knew the value of publicity. His large home, Springfield, at High Wycombe, was open house not just to his own deputy, Robert Saundby (who acted as a sort of buffer between 'Butch' and the world), and the American commander, Ira Eaker – both of whom lived there; the press were regular visitors, too and reported enthusiastically on the first 1000 bomber raid on a German city, Cologne, in May 1942. Harris had had to scrape a couple of hundred aeroplanes from training units (which was not necessarily a good idea) and 49 of the bombers had Polish crews (which definitely was a good idea; the Poles were first class). The raid was considered a success, with only one in twenty–five of the aircraft lost.

Radar was used in the Cologne raid – a triangulating system called Gee whereby the bomber pilots flew along the line of a radio frequency transmitted by a land station until they intersected that from a second station, at which point they released their bombs. It was a similar method to *knickebein* (dog–leg) which the Luftwaffe had used against Coventry. Cologne had been 'Coventrated'.

In Germany, Goering simply did not believe the scale of the damage. His armament minister, Albert Speer, in his book *Inside the third Reich* tells how the *Reichsmarschall* called the report from the police commissioner of Cologne 'a stinking lie' and told the commissioner to amend his report to Hitler. Speer took the matter up with Adolf Hitler, who was not amused but: 'The next day Goering was received as usual. The affair was never mentioned again.' The Nazi leadership was not yet ready to act in the way that the Trenchard Doctrine predicted – that is, surrender.

One of the RAF bomber pilots on that raid on Cologne was Leslie Manser. He won a posthumous Victoria Cross for refusing to leave the controls of his plane, allowing the rest of the crew to escape by parachute. His last words, to his co–pilot, Leslie Baveystock were 'For Christ's sake get out!! We're going in!' He died when the plane hit the ground.

Baveystock and all but one of the rest of the crew evaded capture and returned to England. They could not have done so without being sheltered, fed and escorted through occupied Europe by civilians. Their helpers did so at the risk of imprisonment, torture and death not only for themselves but for their families. Many who helped allied airmen lost their lives, including many of those who helped Leslie Baveystock (as I will tell in more detail shortly).

The RAF themselves were the catalyst for resistance in the occupied countries of Europe. If Bomber Command was the only way that Britain could strike against Germany, it was also the only force to be seen doing so by the occupied countries. The RAF *were* freedom. A low level of resistance in occupied Europe was the chalking up of Churchill's famous 'V' and 'RAF' in public places but the escape–line women and men went far, far beyond that. The stories of these enslaved people who would not bow to their invaders but risked their all to help the men who flew to free them are among the most inspiring lessons that come out of the war. The RAF owe them as great a debt of gratitude as Europe owes the RAF.

I will leave the grand strategy of the warlords for a page or two to talk of some of these ordinary heroines and heroes – and MI9, the organisation in Britain who supported them.

MI9 escape, evasion and interrogation

If Bomber Command was not performing well (to put it charitably) prior to the Butt Report, MI9 certainly was. MI9 was not an RAF organisation. It was started by the War Office and was an army unit (under Major Norman Crockatt), having been set up after Dunkirk mainly to deal with army escapers. It quickly broadened its remit to deal not only with soldiers, but with prisoners of the Axis from all services. It also set up interrogation centres at Latimer in Buckinghamshire (MI9a) and Cockfosters (MI9b) in London to interrogate Axis prisoners. Information was fed back from them to Allied forces – about submarine dispositions for example – and to Sefton Delmer's Black Propaganda section. Delmer also recruited broadcasters from anti–Nazi prisoners.

The other side of the equation – helping Allied prisoners evade and escape – was run from Wilton Park, Beaconsfield, again in Buckinghamshire. Evasion is the avoidance of captivity, escape is getting away after being captured. The distinction may seem trifling, but in legal terms it made a big difference to a man trying to get into, or be repatriated from, a neutral country. From now on, I'll just say 'escape'.

MI9 had a number of departments dealing with, for example, codes by which prisoners could pass back information from the camps, escape equipment (maps, compasses, money, disguises) and so on. It also had strong links to prisoner of war camps, with representatives in many of them. The staff of MI9 were often escapers themselves. The higher officials went under code names based on the days of the week – so, for example, the official in the British embassy in Lisbon was 'Sunday' – the man who was in charge of debriefing of returned prisoners, Major Airey Neave (who had escaped from Colditz Castle), was 'Saturday' – hence the name of his book on his experiences *Saturday at MI9*.

Escape kit

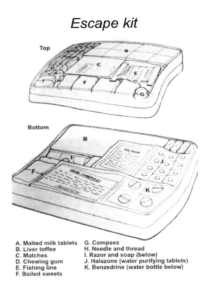

A. Malted milk tablets
B. Liver toffee
C. Matches
D. Chewing gum
E. Fishing line
F. Boiled sweets
G. Compass
H. Needle and thread
I. Razor and soap (below)
J. Halazone (water purifying tablets)
K. Benzedrine (water bottle below)

The European escape lines – some initiated from the continent, some set up by MI9 –were to become important operations. Mostly they passed back airmen shot down over Holland, France and Belgium. Obviously an airman took a lot of training and was very, very valuable. Apart from that, it was the duty of the armed forces to help their people escape; and it was very good for morale if an airman reappeared at his unit after being shot down over the continent. Each aircrew member was given an escape tin with matches, fishing line, a compass, water purifying tablets and sweets.

Aircrew were also given training in how to get away. For example, if captured the best time to escape was immediately, rather than trying to get away from a camp which was specifically designed to keep prisoners from doing so. And they were told who were their most likely helpers. Lucien Dumais who escaped from France and later went back to help set up the Breton escape route, says in his book *The man who went back* that they were told to approach:

'Not in the morning but at the end of the day. Women in preference to men. Old rather than young. Poor rather than rich. Country people rather than city. Priests and doctors rather than merchants or shopkeepers.'

There was more arcane instruction too. If being chased by dogs, urinate. The dogs will urinate too and lose the scent (this odd bit of advice actually worked on occasion).

Escape stories are often wonderful and amazing records of courage, perseverance and sometimes luck, love and tragedy. They are concentrated and powerful doses of the human condition at its best and worst. Leslie Baveystock's escape after being shot down over Cologne was no exception.

Leslie Baveystock on the run in occupied Europe

Baveystock, a Londoner from Finchley, was 24 years old when war broke out. He was in a reserved occupation (one exempt from military service) and also did three nights a week as an auxiliary fireman. A young man who loved his country, inspired by Churchill and angered by what was happening to his city, he joined the RAF. He trained in Canada and in England. While he was at RAF Cottesmore, in England, five of the 16 trainees in his intake died in accidents, confirming the danger of Bomber Command's training (especially, it would appear, in Handley Page Hampdens; which were phased out shortly afterwards and given to 'The Cinderella service', RAF Coastal Command).

He was stationed at RAF Swinderby, in Lincolnshire, in 50 Squadron, when he flew as co–pilot in the raid over Cologne. He tells in his book *Wavetops at my wingtips*, of how his aeroplane was shot down by flak, taking his pilot Leslie Manser to his lonely death. The crash was just inside Holland. Linking up with a fellow crew member, Stanley King, he knocked on a farmhouse door and they were both given shelter by a Dutch farmer. Thousands of airmen who bailed out over occupied Europe were helped in this way. The penalty for helping Allied airmen was death: but many civilians were prepared to risk it. Every airman who could be saved was one more soldier fighting the Nazis. Their Dutch hosts tuned into the BBC (a punishable offence) and Baveystock and King heard the news of the air raid on Cologne.

A third member of the crew, Bob Horsley, was bought to them, along with a Dutch couple who would guide them onwards. Their first stop was a windmill, as the guests of the Bruels. Gertrude Bruel, then in her mid-twenties, was arrested by the Gestapo a year later and died in Ravensbruck Concentration Camp.

From there, they were passed onto Brussels, where they were lodged in two flats. The two families who sheltered them were later arrested by the Gestapo, one shot on the spot and the rest sent to concentration camps where most of them died.

Then they were passed 'down the line' – taken by train to Paris. Leslie Baveystock captures a surreal moment when he was on a train:

'The strangeness and unexpected happenings of the ten days since I had walked in Lincoln with my wife bore the air of dreamland. To find myself sitting and cuddling, albeit in a brotherly manner, a pretty girl (the train was so crowded his guide was sitting on his knee) whom hours before I hadn't met, in a darkened train, in an enemy–occupied country, wearing another man's clothes was an unimaginable dream.'

The pretty girl on his lap, Andrée Dumon, would later be arrested along with her father Eugène and deported to the east. Eugène would die in a Concentration Camp. Andrée would be deported to Mauthausen, a Nazi death camp where she slaved in the quarries. When she was liberated she had typhoid. It would be two years before she could walk again. Andrée's sister took over her role as courier between Brussels and Paris.

In Paris, Leslie Baveystock was taken over by another Belgian girl. Dédée (Andrée) de Jongh. Dédée, then 25, was the founder of the Comet escape Line. She had begun the line the year before by sheltering and escorting escaped British soldiers after Dunkirk to the south of France and on into Spain. She continued the work for escaped airmen, setting up 'safe houses' for them in the south of France. From them, airmen were passed to a farmhouse on the slopes of the Pyrenees owned by a woman called Francia (Francoise Usandizanga). Baveystock and his crew (by now there were five of them) were gathered there. From the farmhouse they were taken over the mountains

Andrée (Dédée) de Jongh

Ami, si tu tombes,
un ami sort de l'ombre,
te remplacer
Friend, if you should fall,
another will will come from
the shadows to replace you.
Song of the Partisans

into Spain by Dédée and her guide, Florentino. Dédée and Florentino personally escorted fifty–four men over the Pyrenees. Less than a year after Baveystock's escape, Dédée and Francia were arrested in the farmhouse in the Pyrenees by ten German soldiers. They had been betrayed. Francia was sent to Ravensbruck where she was beaten to death by a guard. Dédée de Jongh was deported to Mauthausen. She was interrogated 19 times by the German army and twice by the Gestapo. Although she admitted to being the leader of the Comet Line, the Germans did not believe that this slight young woman was more than a minor helper; so they shot her father, Frederick. He was one of the thousand French resistance fighters shot by the Nazis at Mont–Valérien, in Paris. Dédée survived but was very ill. The Comet Line continued without her and helped over 700 allied soldiers to escape.

Leslie Baveystock and his crew got back to Britain just five weeks after being shot down. Baveystock was debriefed by Airey Neave and given his choice of where in the RAF he wanted to be posted next. He chose Coastal Command. Later in the war he sank two U–boats in the Bay of Biscay.

Britain owed a heavy debt to Comet and the other escape lines. MI9 also set up other escape routes and supplied them with money, revolvers, radios, tobacco, food, even bicycles. They used RAF Tempsford, the SOE/SIS base that I have already talked about in a previous chapter, to supply them. Foot and Langley, the authors of *MI9 escape and evasion* say that 3,600 British and Commonwealth servicemen and 3,400 Americans escaped in Western Europe during the Second World

War. The Royal Air Forces Escaping Society estimated that a total of 14,000 helpers worked with the many escape lines by 1945. I cannot find any figures for their casualties.

No German servicemen escaped from captivity in Britain (although one, Franz von Werra, did get away from Canada).

Singleton confirms area bombing

A further report to the British Cabinet (following on from the Butt Report) by Mr Justice Singleton (in May 1942) confirmed the area bombing policy: 'If Russia can hold Germany on land, I doubt whether Germany will stand 12 or 18 months' continuous, intensified and increased bombing, affecting, as it must, her war production, her power of resistance, her industries and her will to resist (by which I mean morale).' This conclusion was to prove rather optimistic.

Bomber Harris often visited the Prime Minister, Winston Churchill at Chequers and Ditchley. Chequers is about 6 miles from High Wycombe – once Harris rode there in a horse and trap (he was keen on horse carriages). Churchill backed his bomber chief. He was hitting Germany the only way that Britain could – and getting a lot of publicity for it.

Things were getting better for Bomber Command. There were a lot more Lancasters around. The Pathfinder squadrons and radar were now making bombing more accurate. The Pathfinders were set up by Don Bennett – another airman who had been shot down over Europe and escaped.

The USAAF in England gradually built up. Too gradually for Harris. He had handed over many of the RAF bases which were nearest to the continent (in East Anglia) to the USAAF – and yet the Americans weren't bombing Germany. He wrote to Portal: 'I cannot do it all by myself... Eaker is keen enough, but you know his army–navy troubles.'

General Ira Eaker's 'army–navy troubles' were that the Americans needed their aircraft to support Operation Torch – the Anglo-American landings in North Africa. Coming from a standing start a year earlier, even their vast resources could not simultaneously produce air armadas in Asia, Europe and Africa. Harris did not sympathise. He was not renowned for his breadth of vision.

For the RAF, the rest of 1942 passed with the same mix of raiding, but generally with smaller forces – generally two or three hundred aircraft.

May 1943 – ominous portents for the Axis

Two things happened in May 1943 that were to be of great significance to the Allied bombing assault on Europe.

First, as we have seen in a previous chapter, this was the month the U–boats were defeated as a critical threat. This meant that petrol, food and weapons could now come almost freely from the Americas, allowing an uninterrupted build–up in Britain for the assault on Europe. Secondly, twin attacks from west (Operation Torch) and east (the British army) forced the Axis armies in North Africa to surrender. One hundred and fifty thousand Axis soldiers were captured. Admiral Andrew Cunningham's fleet made certain that virtually none of them escaped. Also, the Americans were now able to supply more aircraft to their bases in England.

The RAF was experiencing great losses in aircrew and consequently training many more to take their place. Continuing my endeavour of trying to weave together the stories of the warlords and their warriors, I would like to show you what happened next through the eyes of one of the new pilots.

One of the bomber boys.
Jack Currie July 1943 – Jan 1944

Jack Currie came from Harrow, in greater London. He had spent almost two years learning to fly, mostly in the USA (There were many overseas flight training schools, mainly in Canada and the USA). By the time he began his first operational tour, Jack, like Leslie Baveystock, had seen many of his fellow recruits die in training.

Naturally enough there were incentives to fly against the enemy, so aircrew started on a higher rank and with better pay than the ground trades who serviced their aircraft. All aircrew were sergeants or above. Currie began flying operationally as a Sergeant–Pilot (he was commissioned a couple of months later). The average age of aircrew at that time was 21. Jack Currie was

22. His first tour of operations began from RAF Wickenby, near Lincoln.

Lincolnshire was known as 'bomber county' because of the density of airfields there. The joke was that one could cross the entire county by aircraft but never leave the ground. Lincoln Cathedral, that masterpiece atop Steep Hill which dominates the plains below, was a landmark for airmen.

Jack Currie was flying a Lancaster, 'the best of all bombers.' A dangerous occupation. He arrived at RAF Wickenby to news that 617 Squadron had breached the German dams which supplied power to the Ruhr . 'We thought they had done well to get eleven Lancasters back to Scampton out of the nineteen that had set out.' Eighty men had returned in the 11 planes which came back. Of the 8 planes which didn't come back, 3 of the crew were taken prisoner and 53 died. 'We had heard that crews who bailed out over the target... were liable to be summarily dispatched; by hanging from a lamp–post or by combustion in the nearest fire.'

One could have forgiven Currie if he had been nervous as he waited to go into action at RAF Wickenby. He was welcomed, he tells us, by an old timer at the airfield who said 'I give you two weeks.' It's hard to believe any airman would be so insensitive to a new pilot – or crew – but two weeks was, at that time indeed about the average lifespan for a new crew. Novice crews were killed in disproportionate numbers. That was why other crews didn't bother to make friends with the new boys until they'd done at least half a dozen flights of their tour. An RAF 'tour' (the period that an airman had to fly before he was taken off operational flying) was 30 flights. Given the odds, it is surprising that the number of crews who 'cracked up' and were charged with LMF (lack of moral fibre), demoted and ignominiously posted away to clean toilets or some such duty far away was tiny. All flying crew were volunteers, of course – but even so...

When the crews flew, they were ordered to leave their locker keys with an NCO. This was so that the lockers of those who didn't return could be cleared out quietly, with the minimum of fuss. Currie, a bit of a rebel, took his keys with him.

Jack Currie flew a mixture of operations, mine–laying (mostly against U–boats) and city–bombing. The most significant of them was the devastating attack on Hamburg which lasted for 8 days and 7 nights and was a joint RAF (at night) and USAAF (daytime) attack in July and August 1943.

The Hamburg firestorm and Berlin

Hamburg, the second largest city in Germany, was home to a lot of heavy and light industry, having shipyards, U–boat pens and oil refineries. In consequence, it was well protected. The Germans had made great advances in radar in the four years that the war had been fought. To get into Germany, the RAF had to cross the mighty Kammhuber line, a great belt of radar–directed guns and searchlights. The guns were the outstanding German 88 mm anti–aircraft and anti–tank gun; widely accepted to have been the best gun of the war. The line was supported by a large force of night fighter squadrons. Until now, the night fighters had had the best of it against the RAF. Wilhelm Johnen, a Luftwaffe night fighter ace, says in his book Duel under the stars:

'The civilians pitied the British bomber crews who were shot down. How could the RAF send their boys so irresponsibly to their certain deaths.'

This concern for the health of the RAF boys (if it were ever true) ceased abruptly at Hamburg. The RAF flew diversionary raids on several other cities to draw off the German night fighters. They also used Window for the first time – metallic strips dropped from the bombers which confused German radar so that they sent night fighters searching for none–existent bombers. Reg Jones (he of the wasted bathwater) was the champion who had won approval from Churchill for the use of Window, against much opposition; the opponents were afraid the Germans would simply use it back against British cities (they did).

When Window was used against Hamburg, the radar–guided German master searchlights wandered aimlessly across the sky. The anti–aircraft guns fired randomly or not at all and the night fighters, their radar displays swamped with false echoes, failed to find the bomber stream. The bombers dropped their loads almost without hindrance.

Up in his bomber, Jack Currie had been on the receiving end of night city attacks by massed bombers. He had been a fire fighter during the 57 nights of the first London Blitz. He knew nothing of the debates about Window; but he couldn't miss the grumbling of his bomb–aimer (Larry):

'Bloody hell, I drop the bombs, do the map reading, man the front–turret, and now I've got to push the Window out. If you stick a broom handle up my arse, I'll sweep the floor as well.'

It was mid–summer and hot. The Hamburg area had been suffering from a mini–drought for weeks and everything was very dry. Once the bombing started, houses and factories caught ablaze very, very quickly. Bombs and incendiaries created a tornado of swirling hot air that spread the fire rapidly. The heat of the tornado reached 1,500°F (820°C) causing the asphalt streets to burst into flames. During the week of raids about 35,000 civilians died in scenes reminiscent of Dante's *Inferno*. Many who sheltered died from lack of oxygen. On the streets, many were burned alive.

Arthur Harris had chillingly borrowed from the bible when he said of the Luftwaffe attacks on London that: 'They have sown the wind. They will reap the whirlwind.' This was the whirlwind.

In Germany, Wilhelm Johnen, the German night fighter ace (who had already shot down numerous RAF bombers), saw Hamburg as the writing on the wall:

'Everyone felt it was now high time to capitulate... but the High Command insisted that the 'total war' should proceed: The first doubts as to our war leadership began to rise and many people lost their faith in the Hitler regime.'

A friend told Johnen that in his opinion the enemy (the RAF and USAAF) had achieved its first objective, 'to destroy the morale of the home front.' There it was again, that word morale, the elusive quality that Bomber Harris aimed to break; so that the German people would rise against their rulers. The generals on both sides knew this was quite possible. It had happened in the first war, in 1918, when the German Navy had mutinied at Kiel, refusing to take to sea against the Royal Navy. This had led to other risings and forced Germany to surrender. The Trenchard Doctrine wasn't based on myth or forlorn hope but on precedent.

In the German high command Hamburg was seen as a watershed – by some. It reminded Albert Speer, the Armaments Minister, of a conversation he had had with Hitler, in 1940, when his fuhrer had said:

"Have you ever looked at a map of London? It is so closely built up that one source of fire alone would destroy the whole city as happened once before, two hundred years ago. Incendiaries, fires everywhere, what use will their fire department be when the fire starts?"

Now Hitler's dream for London had been visited on Hamburg. Speer said 'Hamburg put the fear of God in me... six more major cities... would bring Germany's armament production to a total halt.'

Goebbels, Hitler's propaganda minister was worried as well. He recorded in his diary:

'Our war in the east has lost us air supremacy in essential parts of Europe, and we are completely at the mercy of the English.'

Hitler was less concerned, dismissive even. He told Speer: 'You'll straighten all that out.' He didn't bother to go and see for himself what was happening to his people. He never did.

Another raid that Jack Currie took part in was on the 'V' weapon development centre at Peenemünde. That subject is so important that I will devote a whole chapter to it. He also took part in the Berlin attacks at the end of 1943. A by–product of one of these raids was that Albert Speer was bombed out of his office. He drove round Berlin to see how the factories (in Berlin as in Coventry, many of them were embedded in the city) had been affected:

'We drove over streets strewn with rubble, lined by burning houses. Bombed out families sat or stood in front of the ruins. A few pieces of rescued furniture and other possessions lay about on the sidewalks, There was a sinister atmosphere of biting smoke, soot and flames. ....above the city hung a cloud of smoke that probably reached twenty thousand feet in height. Even by day it made the macabre scene as dark as night. I kept trying to describe my impressions to Hitler. But he would interrupt me me every time, almost as soon as I began: "incidentally, Speer, how many tanks can you deliver next month?"'

Harris had predicted that: 'We can wreck Berlin from end to end if the USAAF come in with us. It will cost us between 400 and 500 aircraft. It will cost Germany the war.' The USAAF did not come in on the Berlin attacks; not yet. They were haemorrhaging elsewhere, as I will shortly tell. The RAF lost over 1,000 aircraft and 7,000 men before calling off the Berlin attacks in March 1944. These attacks were a defeat for Bomber Command. Wilhelm Johnen describes, on one foggy January night, shooting down four RAF bombers in forty five minutes. The chances of a man surviving being shot down in a Lancaster was slightly less than one in five. The German night fighters had won – with heavy losses and for the moment – the air battle over Berlin.

Jack Currie was an 'above average' pilot – he must have been that, and lucky, for he survived. Statistically, he should have died twice over. One last word from Jack. He has finished his first tour (he was to do a second). He is with his crew, in the back of a truck, leaving RAF Wickenby for good. The truck is bumping down Steep Hill in Lincoln. He is looking out of the back window:

'The cathedral loomed above us, beautiful and strong. It looked so balanced, so symmetrical and so permanent that our existence seemed the more precarious, out presence utterly transitory.'

Lincoln cathedral has seen and has been seen by many airmen. It was the last thing on this earth that many of them ever did see. If you visit it, please spare a thought for them.

1943: the USAAF builds up in England: oil and Schweinfurt

During 1943 the United States Army Air Force built up slowly in England. For the first half of the year they were a small force, sending out around 100 bombers at a time. Their tactics were radically different than RAF Bomber Command's. They attacked by day, generally attempting to hit specific military and industrial targets. When these were in cities – which they often were – the fires from the American bombs could be used as additional navigational targets for night bombing by the RAF.

Their main bomber was the B17 Flying Fortress. This was heavily armed so as to be able to take on and defeat fighters. As such it carried about half the bombload of a Lancaster – the extra weight being taken up by thicker armour and more powerful guns.

The 10 crew B17G – the standard Flying Fortress of the late war years

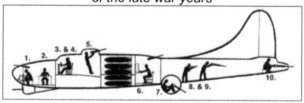

1. Bombardier	6. Radio Operator/Gunner
2. Navigator	7. Ball Turret Gunner
3. Pilot	8. Right Waist Gunner
4. Co-Pilot	9. Left Waist Gunner
5. Top Turret Gunner/Engineer	10. Tail Gunner

By the time that they reached Germany, the Flying Fortresses were beyond the range of fighter cover. Hence they flew in box formation, at regulated distances from each other, so that they could provide and be provided with covering fire. This called for a very high standard of formation flying. If an aircraft was forced out of the box – for example by an engine failure, or damage – they not only ran the danger of colliding with their neighbours, but could disrupt the formation and force others from it. Once out of the box, planes were much easier prey for German fighters. They suffered very heavy losses.

On the continent, the Comet Line and MI9's other escape networks were getting a lot of new customers. The best service, perhaps, was for an American airman who was actually hailed by a member of the resistance as he floated down to earth.

As they grew in power, the USAAF were launching attacks from two directions. From North Africa, with its Twelfth air force, it struck over the Alps at a group of Axis oil refineries at Ploesti, in Romania. Harris considered oil refineries, which had cost the RAF many aircraft earlier in the war, to be just another panacea target: 'a waste of time and effort.' The Americans sent 177 bombers against Ploiesti. The force was cut to pieces, 54 of the bombers being shot down and 53 more heavily damaged. 660 crewman died. It was proportionally the most costly major air strike of the war. It didn't stop or have a major effect on oil production – but it was, had Germany known it – a warning of things to come.

Whether the targets were military and industrial or not didn't make a lot of difference to those in the cities where the bombs fell. As I've said before, industry and housing were generally intermingled. Bomb aiming – in any air force – was nowhere near good enough to differentiate between the two. Then there was the weather.

'In the early days,' wrote James 'Jimmy' Doolittle, the phenomenally successful American air general, 'we were grounded (by poor visibility) four days out of five... when the German aircraft industry went underground, we were forced to bomb the areas where the factories were located. So the two philosophies (area and precision bombing) made little practical difference.'

The RAF provided part of the fighter escort from England (for as far as the Spitfire's fuel range allowed). Johnnie Johnson, who we have met before, was one of them. He confirms that the Americans weren't keen on European weather: 'Look for the biggest dirtiest cloud. England will be underneath it,' they grumbled.

In a major attack in October 1943, the USAAF bombed Munster from its English bases with all 236 of its Flying Fortresses and 216 covering fighters. The Luftwaffe sent up 350 fighters. 700 people died in the city below . The Munster raid was unusual for the Americans. This was no industrial target. The aiming point of the raid was the steps of Munster Cathedral, at midday on a Sunday. The Americans lost 30 bombers with another 105 badly damaged. Over 300 American airmen were dead or missing. Of the thirteen Flying Fortresses which set out from one USAAF base (RAF Thorpe Abbots, in Norfolk) that day, only one returned. Its pilot, Robert Rosenthal, whom we will meet again over Berlin, said that the Officers Mess was a lonely place that night.

The USAAF, as I've said, generally targeted specific industries – at that time factories producing fighter aircraft and ball–bearings. Ball bearings were vital to the armament and transport industries. Without them there would be no aircraft, submarines, tanks, lorries, artillery or trains. Repeated attacks on the ball–bearing factories at Schweinfurt cost the Americans dear. Two days after Munster the USAAF lost 60 bombers there, a fifth of their force. Seventeen more were scrapped and 121 damaged. After these attacks, the USAAF in Europe had to rebuild almost from scratch. This has been called 'the black week of the USAAF'.

As James Doolittle wrote in his autobiography *I could never be so lucky again*:

'Due to the small number of aircraft and crews made available to him, Ira (Eaker) was never able to overwhelm the enemy's defensive force. Short on bombers and without long range fighters, he had been forced in 1943 to absorb prohibitive losses of upwards of 20 percent against such targets as Regensburg (aircraft works) and Schweinfurt (ball–bearings). Rarely was he able to send out more than 200 to 300 bombers at a time.'

It is hard to imagine the courage of the American aircrew carrying on with such losses.

With night attacks from the RAF and day raids from the USAAF, the Luftwaffe was under growing pressure. But it was a war of attrition that threatened to cripple the Allied air forces too.

That was only part of the big picture. By the end of 1943 the war was entering a new phase. Allied armies and air forces were being picked up, shuffled and re-dealt in readiness for the greatest and most dangerous military undertaking in history. The 'A' team were called back from the Mediterranean to England to plan Operation Overlord.

1944: the men from the Med.

The war was going well for the Allies in the Mediterranean war theatre. They had defeated the Germans and Italians in Africa, then invaded Italy and occupied a large part of that country (although the Germans still fought a bitter rear–guard action there). Now it was time to prepare and carry out Operation Overlord, the liberation of Europe. A command shake–up meant that the American general, Dwight Eisenhower – 'Ike' – was brought from the Mediterranean to be the Supreme Commander for Overlord. The RAF's Air chief–marshal Arthur Tedder came with him as his second in command. With them came Solly Zuckerman and USAAF General James Doolittle.

Eisenhower, Tedder, Zuckerman and Doolittle all got on well. They were to be vital players in the Allies' complete victory in the air war over Europe. As such, it is worth looking at them a little more closely.

General 'Ike' – Dwight D. Eisenhower

Ike first. He had been in charge of the Allies in the Mediterranean. He was replaced there by the British General Alexander (to whom the Germans and Italians in Africa had surrendered). It is difficult to imagine a better man for running Overlord than Eisenhower. He was competent, open, persuadable, listened to others, had authority and was liked and respected by just about everyone. His was the job of marshalling, managing, coordinating and sending into northern Europe the Anglo–American armies, navies and air forces.

The invasion was to be across the fickle English Channel, where so many invasions had foundered over the centuries.

When it reached the far coast of Normandy it would face coastal defences built up over years by first–class German engineers with the labour of countless slaves. Behind these defences lay the finest army in the world – unbeatable on equal terms.

Eisenhower had the full support of President Roosevelt (indeed he would later become president himself) and Winston Churchill.

Air Chief Marshal Arthur Tedder

That Eisenhower's deputy was an airman shows the importance of control of the air over the battlefield. Tedder was the airman he entrusted with the job. Ike – and Europe – were not to be disappointed. Tedder had been the head of Allied air operations in the Mediterranean. That was a post which was sometimes underestimated back in England: Bomber Harris, for example, disapproved of sending 'his bombers' and airmen abroad to the Middle East. He saw their transfer as a constant drain, grumbling: 'What they used them for there, I don't know; every doorman in Cairo I expect.' Harris, as was his wont, was caustically witty but quite unable to see beyond his own bailiwick. Tedder had used the bombers – along with the fighters, and, later, the USAAF forces under his command – for the defeat of the German and Italian air forces in Africa and Italy. This included the aerial preparation for and the protection of the Allied seaborne invasions of Sicily and Italy. Those invasions were the template for Normandy. Their air commander was the obvious choice for Overlord.

Tedder brought with him a man he would rely on to make Overlord a success, Group Captain Solomon – Solly – Zuckerman.

Solly Zuckerman's Transport Plan

Zuckerman was the man who had designed the bomber offensive which had contributed so much to Allied success in the Mediterranean. His excellent book. *From Apes to Warlords* tells the story in more detail. The book, apart from being a first class work, giving insights into many things other than war, also has a title of such ironical perfection that I am in awe of it.

(Solly Zuckerman's 'day job' was as a professor of biology specialising in the study of primates at Oxford University).

We have already seen a little of Solly Zuckerman, offstage. It was he who (with Bernal) had produced the report on the bombing of Hull and Birmingham which 'Prof' Lindemann had used as the basis of his Dehousing Paper – the rules that Harris followed in his bombing war. Zuckerman points out that he and Bernal had concluded in their paper that civilian morale in Hull and Birmingham had *not* been adversely affected by the bombing, in fact it had been strengthened. Lindemann contradicted this finding in his own report. Zuckerman knew Lindemann well. They were both Professors at Trinity College, Oxford and both lived in the city (Lindemann in the college).

Early in the war, Zuckerman had been co–opted by the Research and Experiments Department (at Princes Risborough, near Chequers) which dealt with various aspects of enemy bombing. He had also worked on a defence plan for Oxford after the expected German invasion and been ordered: 'when we are driven out of Oxford, you are coming with us to hold out in the hills'. Zuckerman set up (on behalf of Princes Risborough) his own department, the confusingly named Oxford Extra–Mural unit, which researched the effects of air raids. Part of his research dealt with the quantity, type and distribution of German bombs and incendiaries. The RAF in North Africa was interested in this research, believing that it could give them an insight into what and how many bombs they themselves should use to do most damage.

As such, Zuckerman went to North Africa to look at Luftwaffe damage there. He was given a warm welcome by the top brass of both the RAF and USAAF. He met Tedder, Jimmy Doolittle (in charge of the USAAF bombing fleet) and Carl 'Tooey' Spaatz, the overall head of the USAAF in the Mediterranean. He was impressed with the openness of all of these 'warlords' – and their ability to use science (Operational Research) to more efficiently wage war. His relationship to them was not dissimilar to that of the radar men at Bawdsey to the top echelons of Fighter Command prior to the war.

Zuckerman drew up the bombing plan which led to the surrender of the heavily–defended Italian island of Pantelleria, a

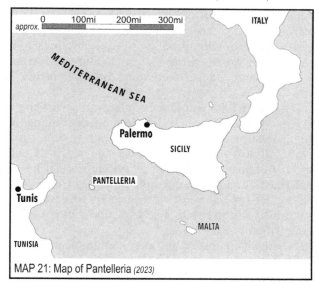

MAP 21: Map of Pantelleria *(2023)*

stepping stone between North Africa and Sicily. (The garrison of Pantelleria put out a white flag when the landing craft approached. The only casualty was a British soldier who was nipped by an irate mule.) His bombing plan also covered the destruction of rail and ferry facilities which made the conquest of Sicily and the landings in Italy relatively painless for the Allies. These achievements should not be underestimated. Attempts to invade enemy countries from the sea usually fail – as have numerous attacks on England between 1066 and the present day.

Zuckerman's air plan for Overlord laid out the attacks to be made by both the RAF and USAAF air fleets in Britain to support the D–day landings. Those landings, it will be remembered, were to be on five beach heads in Normandy (two American, two British and one Canadian).

The roads and railways which reinforcements would have to use to get to the beaches were, in Zuckerman's opinion, vulnerable points in the German defence. Therefore railways leading to the coast, as well as railway stations, marshalling yards, bridges and tunnels, would be heavily bombed. Coastal gun–emplacements, airfields and German coastal radar, were also, of course, targeted. The attacks would continue after D–day itself, targeting enemy build–ups and attempts to resupply as long as necessary to ensure that the landing and Allied build–up were a success. Zuckerman's plan was called the Transport Plan.

The Transport Plan would, of course, cut across the way that the RAF and USAAF were at that time conducting operations in Europe. Zuckerman was, therefore, sent to talk to Bomber Harris in High Wycombe. He spent the night of the 2nd of January 1944 there, dining alone with Harris and his wife. Air Marshal Harris was polite and welcoming (personally preparing Eggs Benedict for his guest). Zuckerman was 'much taken by his quiet sense of power and determination' but not by the scope of his questioning:

'He wasn't interested in what had happened in the Allied invasion of Italy. He asked only one question (about whether his bombers could be used to bomb coastal gun emplacements).'

Harris opposed Zuckerman's Transport Plan, arguing that Allied air support for D–day was yet another 'panacea target', like U–boats and oil. Eisenhower, Tedder and Zuckerman were to face heavier opposition than Harris – no less than Winston Churchill himself, as I shall describe in a little while.

General James Doolittle

General James Doolittle was Eisenhower's man to lead the American USAAF 8th (bomber) Air Force, based in England. He replaced Ira Eaker, who was transferred to the Mediterranean as second in command to General Alexander. Eaker was a little too deferential towards Bomber Harris for his masters' tastes.

Doolittle was a national hero in the States. Rightly so. After the Japanese attack on the American Pacific Fleet at Pearl Harbour, it was he who had personally led the first American bomber strike against Japan. He did it from the sea, from an aircraft carrier over 800 miles from their target, the Japanese capital, Tokyo. After the raid, with a round flight of over 2200 miles, he and most of his fellow flyers crash–landed or bailed out over China.

Latterly he had been in charge of the American Mediterranean bomber forces. He was a man of few preconceptions, as he wrote to his boss at the time: 'Conditions in air warfare are changing so rapidly that our very inexperience is often an asset – we have little to forget.' Solly Zuckerman got on well with him. On first meeting him he remarked that he was 'not prepared to find a two–star general who led his own bomber group in the air, and who was so open–minded and easy in his manner.'

On arriving in England, Doolittle got a frosty reception from Bomber Harris. Harris was not at all happy to see Ira Eaker go. Nevertheless, Doolittle installed himself at RAF Daws Hill, High Wycombe, and quickly put his stamp on his command.

Just to reiterate, then. In overall military charge of Overlord, the invasion of Europe, was Eisenhower. His deputy was Tedder. They were in charge of all the armed services, RAF and USAAF included, which would be used for Overlord.

Charles Portal was in overall charge of the RAF. Under him came Arthur Harris, who was in charge of Bomber Command.

The USAAF had two bomber fleets which it would use against Germany. The 8th in England, under Doolittle and the 15th in Italy. Carl Spaatz was Doolittle's line manager, in overall charge of all USAAF European air fleets.

A complex command structure, this.

If (and when) some of these over-lapping warlords decided not to pay too much attention to Zuckerman's Transport Plan, it would be down to Eisenhower to demand that Churchill and Roosevelt bring them into line.

February 1944 – Big Week

Like Harris with the Lancaster bomber, Doolittle had luck with an aeroplane. That plane was the Mustang. As I've mentioned earlier, a key reason for the USAAF's shocking losses when flying from England was that no fighter had the range to escort their bombers all the way into Germany. Recently, however, the Mustang had been arriving in quantity from America. The aeroplane was a happy mix of American and

British engineering. The airframe was American, the engine British. This marriage led to the greatest long–range fighter of the war.

Doolittle also made a vital change of emphasis. He tells of visiting his fighter commander (Major General William Kepner) and seeing a sign in his office which read: The first duty of the Eighth Air Force fighters is to bring the bombers back alive.' He had this replaced with one which read: 'The first duty of the Eighth Air Force fighters is to destroy German fighters.' The new order was that the Mustangs were not to fly with the bombers but ahead of them. This was music to Bill Kepner's ears. He had been urging Eaker and Spaatz for months that such was the best tactic. Now Doolittle had given him the authority – and the planes – to do it,

The Mustang

That changed the game radically. The Luftwaffe could no longer wait for the American bomber streams, they had to come up against the fighters flying in front. To ram the point home the Mustangs also strafed the German fighter airfields. The American fighter pilots were good. Thoroughly trained, in great numbers and with outstanding weapons, they overwhelmed the Luftwaffe. The result, in February 1944, was 'Big week' (Operation Argument). The Americans shot down almost a quarter of the Luftwaffe's fighters in the combat zone.

The Luftwaffe tried 'Big wing' attacks against the Americans – forming up all of their own fighters at altitude for a mass attack. The tactic – as when units of the RAF had tried it in the Battle of Britain – was a failure and was abandoned.

With American air emphasis shifting from the Mediterranean to Germany, there were now round the clock attacks from English bases by bomber forces that would would soon be as strong by day as by night. For the Luftwaffe – and German cities – it was a twenty–four hour war. Day after day and night after night, attacks took place on cities and on aircraft factories. The factory attacks had little effect – German aircraft production would continue to rise right until the last weeks of the war (Speer said the Allies were targeting the wrong factories. They bombed the airframe factories, they should have gone for the engine producers). However, the Luftwaffe was being worn down, many of the experienced pilots were now dead. Their replacements, as always with unblooded aircrew, were inexperienced and had disproportionately heavy losses.

In their daytime war of attrition, the Americans continued to suffer horrific losses. The American tour of duty, at that time, was twenty–five missions. Like their British counterparts, most of them didn't make it. Doolittle was to increase the number of missions to 30, then 35. This did not increase his popularity with his crews. 'Some bomber men didn't like me. Some still don't,' Doolittle wrote in his memoirs. Joseph Heller was an American who flew with the USAAF from North Africa. The ever greater demand of the generals on their aircrew is at the heart of his superb novel *Catch–22*.

Jimmy Doolittle liked to be present when his crews came back from combat. One day he was at an airfield to meet a group of Flying Fortresses returning from bombing Germany. He was with the ambulances as wounded crew members were taken out of one of the planes:

'The tail gun turret had been blown apart, and the tail gunner crawled out surprisingly unhurt, I couldn't believe it. I asked 'were you in that turret when it was blasted?' The lad looked at my three stars and replied, politely 'yes sir.' He didn't elaborate. As I walked away, the gunner said to a buddy of his standing nearby, 'where the hell did that bald–headed bastard think I was – out buying a ham sandwich?'

His buddy tried to shush him up, but I had heard. The airman was right. I had asked a stupid question.'

One has some difficulty imagining Bomber Harris being involved in a similar scenario.

Three warlords are a crowd: Ike – "I'll quit."

The aerial preparations for D-day did not run according to plan. That was because neither the RAF nor the USAAF showed much interest in complying with Zuckerman's Transport Plan.

Bomber Harris had said that the invasion was unnecessary. His prediction (of December 1943) that Bomber Command would force German to surrender by April 1944 might seem, like the earlier Singleton prediction, to have been over–optimistic, but it was, Harris believed, only a matter of time. Similarly General 'Tooey' Spaatz, the overall commander of the United States Army Air Forces in Europe, is said to have suggested that the idea of a Normandy landing was soon to be made redundant due to bombing success.

Germany's air defence problems were now insurmountable. Now that Italy was out of the war, American aircraft could come into her back yard. Spaatz, Doolittle's boss, was sending his English (8th) and Italian (15th) based air fleets against oil refineries, aircraft works and ball bearings. And they had begun full–scale daylight bombing of Berlin.

Eisenhower, however, didn't want Harris and Spaatz to follow their own stars. He wanted them to follow orders and get on with the Transport Plan. If no air support was given to Overlord, D–day could, and probably would, fail.

On March 22, Eisenhower dictated a memo that detailed the history of the dispute. By the time that he finished it, he was so irked that he bluntly stated that if his opponents didn't give in quickly, he planned 'to take drastic action and inform the Combined Chiefs of Staff that unless the matter is settled, at once I will request relief from this Command.' He put the threat more explicitly in a conversation with Tedder: "By God," Eisenhower told him: "You tell that bunch that if they can't get together and stop quarrelling like children, I will tell the Prime Minister to get someone else to run this damned war. I'll quit."

The argument was to go even higher and involve both Churchill and Roosevelt, as I will tell shortly. The warlords were not quite fighting between themselves yet, but they were beating their chests.

Johnen in Switzerland April 1944

In April came a double blow against the Schweinfurt ball–bearing factories. Bomber Command attacked with 734 aircraft, as did 266 American bombers from Italy. The American planes flew over the Alps.

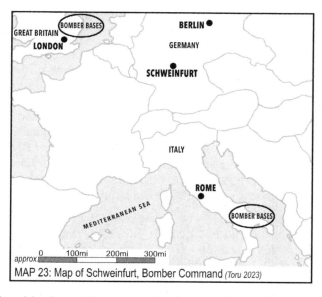

MAP 23: Map of Schweinfurt, Bomber Command *(Toru 2023)*

The ubiquitous German night–fighter pilot, Wilhelm Johnen, was there. When he lost an engine while fighting an RAF Halifax bomber over Switzerland, he had to make an emergency landing in the neutral country. Like all belligerents who crossed the Swiss border uninvited he was interned. His story is an illuminating one, showing the somewhat different standard of aftercare afforded by the Nazis to its downed aircrews compared to MI9's.

When Johnen landed in Switzerland there were six Flying Fortresses there too, crash–landed after the latest Schweinfurt raid. He exchanged cigarettes with an American pilot (he thought the American cigarettes excellent, the Americans called his "stinking weeds"). They also had a word of advice for him: "You damn Messerschmitt guys. Why are you fighting for Hitler? Hitler kaput!"

Back in Germany, Johnen's family and those of his two crew were arrested by the Gestapo, the houses closed up and sealed:

'On the same day,' Johnen tells us, 'two men in civilian clothes with diplomatic passports left Berlin for Zurich and Berne. One of them had been instructed to blow up my plane and the other to put an end to my earthly existence with a well–aimed bullet.'

Someone in the SS evidently suspected Johnen of desertion. Luckily his squadron heard of this and informed Goering, who called Himmler's dogs off. The executioner was stopped at the border, but the sabotage man was already in Switzerland:

'On the third day of my internment my aeroplane blew up in mysterious circumstances on the airfield of Zurich–Dubendorf. On the seventh day of internment my family was released, after giving their word in writing that they would never breathe a word of what had happened.'

Johnen and his crew were released by the Swiss, along with 3 RAF escapers who had made it into Switzerland. Johnen was returned to his squadron. 'That same evening we took off to attack the RAF bombers who were raiding Frankfurt.'

Tedder and Zuckerman fight their corner; April 1944

As Zuckerman (and many others) said: 'Under Churchill's protection, Harris had been almost a law to himself.' Now Harris tried to stop the Transport Plan. Lindemann, too, as the author of the Dehousing Paper, did not want to see Bomber Command diverted from the German cities in order to support Overlord. As a result, Eisenhower complained to Churchill that Bomber Command was not following his orders. This resulted in Tedder and Zuckerman being ordered to justify the Transport Plan in front of Churchill himself. They were called to a night-time conference in the underground command labyrinth under Whitehall in London which is now open to the public as 'Churchill's War rooms'. It was at night and Churchill was in the chair. His main objection was that there would be civilian casualties when the French railways were bombed; as there generally was, whatever the target. The chief of the RAF, Charles Portal, supporting Tedder and Zuckerman, said that the estimates of French casualties that Churchill had been given were far too high.

Zuckerman describes the meeting in *From apes to warlords*:

'By this time the temperature of the discussion had risen markedly.' Churchill angrily asked Zuckerman why he had given incorrect data. Zuckerman replied that the estimates that Churchill was looking at were not the ones that he (Zuckerman) had calculated. They had been arbitrarily increased by Bomber Command: 'It all seemed to depend on how Bomber Harris and his staff felt on the day.'

Bomber Harris, Zuckerman says, was using the fact that Churchill was extremely sensitive to French civilian casualties to try to stop the Transport Plan. (The Prime Minister's sentiment in this area is indisputable. In a filmed interview of 1977, now on Youtube, Harris says 'I was told by Winston "don't kill Frenchmen"'.)

It was a harrowing meeting. At the end of it, Tedder gave Zuckerman a lift back to his flat. Arthur Tedder had suffered from Churchill's wrath in the past, when he had disagreed with another of Winston's golden boys, Max Beaverbrook, on the subject of aircraft manufacturing priorities. Now he was afraid he might lose his job:

'He (Tedder) had clearly been shaken by the evening's proceedings, and particularly by the personal hostility which Winston had directed at him as the night went on. As I got out of the car, he said in his usual sardonic manner, "I suppose this might be the end, Zuck. I wonder how much it will cost to set up as a tomato grower."'

Thankfully he never found out. Luckily for Overlord and the Allied armies, Tedder stood firm, Ike backed him, Roosevelt backed Ike, Winston backed down.

Air Vice-Marshal Harris was told to report to General Eisenhower from 14th April 1944. He did, and obediently devoted Bomber Command to attacking coastal defences and rail targets.

Oil, May 1944

The boss of the United States European air forces, Carl Spaatz, was also bought to heel. However he insisted on two major oil attacks before D–day. On May the 12th 1944, Mission 353 struck at three groups of refineries in Germany. The effect on German oil production was severe. Albert Speer says: 'On that day the technological war was decided... the attack of 935 American bombers (and 735 fighters) meant the end of armament production.'

The Americans lost about 5% of their aircraft. Not bad compared to some of the catastrophes they had experienced in the past few months, but the damage was uneven. Twelve of the 26 aircraft from RAF Snetterton Heath in Norfolk – a USAAF base – were shot down. Ten had been lost 4 days earlier. After a week Snetterton had to rebuild its squadrons practically from scratch.

Bletchley Park intercepted and decoded the resultant German signal traffic. General orders told all units to expect less oil and to cut back consumption immediately. They also deciphered orders cancelling the movement of 9 anti–aircraft batteries to France. Eight other flak units were ordered to be moved from the protection of aircraft factories. All were reassigned to synthetic petroleum sites.

Albert Speer says that he warned Hitler:

'The enemy has struck us at one of our weakest points. If they persist at it this time, we will no longer have any fuel production worth mentioning. Our one hope is that the other side has an air force General Staff as scatter–brained as ours.'

Nevertheless, after 16 days, the Germans managed to bring oil production up to previous levels. (Speer must always be read with care; Germany also had nineteen months of oil reserves). Then the Americans struck the three refineries again (and also Ploesti, in Romania). This time they did twice as much damage as they had on the first attack. This reduced German fuel production by 50 percent.

On D–Day itself (June the 6th 1944), Bletchley Park passed along the following decrypted statement, restricted to Luftwaffe supply officers:

'As a result of renewed interference with production of aircraft fuel by Allied actions, most essential requirements for training and carrying out production plans can scarcely be covered by quantities of aircraft fuel available... allocations only to bombers, fighters and ground attack can be considered in June. To assure defence of Reich and to prevent gradual collapse of German air force in east, it has been necessary to break into OKW (German Armed Forces high command) reserves.'

By D–Day, of course, the USAAF and RAF had been taken off oil, ball–bearings and cities and were carrying out attacks in accordance with Zuckerman's Transport Plan.

Germany's military position was grim. In 1918, in the first world war, a similar situation had led to the naval mutiny at Kiel, when German sailors had refused to sail to fight against the Royal Navy. This had led swiftly to German revolution and military collapse. That victory, which all the current generation of warlords had either seen first–hand or learned of at Staff College, was largely what the Trenchard doctrine and its variants was based on. Hit them hard enough and morale – even German morale and that was as strong as Krupp's steel – would collapse.

But things had changed this time. In 1918 'Kaiser Bill' had only faced exile. Hitler, Goering and Himmler faced death. Besides, even if Germany did throw down her arms, who would pick up the pieces? Russia? Nobody wanted that, least of all the Nazis – their hands were far, far, too bloodstained for that. Nazi

Germany would fight on, counting on their 'V' weapons, all aimed at the heart of the megacity of London.

D–Day targets and Das Reich

In the run–up to D–Day, Bomber Command and the Eighth USAAF carried out attacks on railways, roads, tunnels and bridges across Northern France. German fighter airfields were also attacked, along with Atlantic Wall defences and radar installations. The Luftwaffe hardly intervened. They couldn't, they were short of aeroplanes and aviation fuel.

As far as railway traffic was concerned, the air attacks just about cut Normandy off from reinforcements. French and German rail records show that by D–Day the traffic was down to one seventh of what it had been before the bombing started.

German armoured columns sent to sweep the Allies back into the sea after the landings were delayed or destroyed en route. The RAF and USAAF had complete air dominance. Bombers attacked the main military concentrations, while fighters targeted anything that moved. Any traffic on any visible road was liable to be attacked at any time. The RAF even shot up Rommel, the German commander, and put him in hospital (it took Hitler to finally finish him off).

Perhaps the most militarily important of these attacks were those on the 2nd SS Panzer (tank) Division 'Das Reich', which attempted to move to Normandy from Southern France. The distance was 450 miles. The division consisted of 15,000 men with 1,400 vehicles. The armoured division was targeted both by the Allied air forces and the French Resistance, who had been sabotaging the railways for weeks and who sometimes attacked Das Reich directly, at bridges and cuttings.

The Das Reich Division arrived in Normandy piecemeal, It took them 5 weeks to be able to operate as an integral force. The consequences of this – and other reinforcement delays – on the Allied build up in Normandy was huge, perhaps decisive.

I will talk more about the French resistance risings in a future chapter.

After D–day, the air generals Spaatz and Harris sometimes attacked the railway systems (in accordance with Eisenhower's wishes) and sometimes they followed their own wishes (oil and cities). In Zuckerman's words:

'The two heavy bomber forces continued to pay lip service to the directive to attack communications targets. The Americans preferred... to attack oil plants, while Harris went on with his area bombing of German cities.'

One of the bomber boys. Harry Yates Aug – Dec 1944

I shall at this point hand the narrative back to one of our 'bomber boys', a pilot in RAF Bomber Command. Through his tale, I want, again, to come away from high strategy and give the faintest of tastes of what it was like to be one of the bomber aircrew. His name is Harry Yates and his book *Luck and a Lancaster* is of the highest order. Like all great memoirs, it contains the personal and the universal. I strongly recommend it.

Harry Yates was from Stony Stratford, a small town on Watling Street – the road which was, since at least Roman times, the main road between London and North Wales, and which lies at the heart of the Intelligence Zone.

Stony has its tales to tell. It is an old coaching town, with many large and old hostelries with their stables. From two of its rival inns comes the phrase 'a cock and bull story' (the Cock and the Bull are still there). Richard the Third kidnapped one of the two princes that he took to – and perhaps murdered in – the Tower of London from an inn there. That building is still there too (though no longer a pub). All in all, Stony is a typical small English market town where nothing, the locals will tell you, ever seems to happen.

Harry Yates left school at 14 and was 17 when war broke out. He was a junior clerk, living with his parents and his sister in a Victorian terraced house. His heroes – every British boy's heroes – were the pilots of the Battle of Britain, the tin–legged Douglas Bader, Stanford Tuck, Sailor Malan, Ginger Lacey. He joined the RAF as soon as he could. He wanted to be a pilot and started his training at the de Havilland School of Flying, a few miles down Watling Street, at Hatfield, the spot where British radar can be said to have been born. There Yates learned to fly, winging over Stony one exuberant day and 'beating up' his family's house until they appeared in the back garden, waving (he would have been thrown out of flying school if his instructors had caught him at it). Harry adored flying:

'To scream across the landscape at only the height of a man, with the ground reeling away under the nose of the aircraft, and everything coming at you too fast to think about... to wait and wait... and then astound even yourself with the audacity and precision of it all, that was flying. Absolutely nothing compared to it. I didn't know then how a twenty–year old in charge of a one hundred and fifty mph machine could be expected to resist it. And I don't know now.'

He was 76 years old when he wrote those words.

Harry Yates, like Jack Currie, went to North America (Canada) for advanced training. His troopship stopped in Iceland on the way, and he saw with amazement the U–570, the German submarine that Squadron Leader Thompson had captured. He welcomed the attacks on Germany: 'The German public... saw that real destruction could visit Hamburg, Essen or Berlin as readily as Guernica, Warsaw, Narvik, Rotterdam, London, Coventry or Southampton.'

He spent, against his will and because he was an above–average pilot, a year training others in Canada. He came back to England first to continue as a trainer and finally as a Lancaster bomber pilot. He had wanted to be a fighter pilot, but the RAF's need was to replace losses in Bomber Command. He formed his crew at RAF Westcott, near Aylesbury. This was one of the RAF's Operational Training Units, set well inland. The crew selection process was like none other in the RAF. The men of all the different trades were put together in a hanger and told to sort it out for themselves; make up their own crews. He teamed up with Bill Birnie, a navigator from New Zealand, Rob Bailey, a wireless operator from London. Then came Inia Maaka (Mac), a giant Maori bomb–aimer, Geoff Fallowfield an 18 year old gunner from London and Norrie Close, also 18, another gunner, a Yorkshire lad. The crew was completed by Denys Westell, an English flight engineer who everyone called Tubby: 'an affectionate reference to his undeniably rotund physique.'

Yates loved the Lanc. "Everything about it was just right. Its muscular, swept lines were beautiful to look at. It made the pilot's job easy. The standard bomb load was equivalent of two Flying Fortress B–17s.'

After crew selection, he and his men were posted to 75 Squadron, Royal New Zealand Air Force, at RAF Mepal, near Ely, in Cambridgeshire. Two other new crews arrived at the same time. They were replacements for lost crews, to bring the squadron back up to strength. His tour of operations started a couple of weeks after D–day.

Harry Yates would, in some respects, have felt quite at home in the U–boat service. He loved the luxuries given to aircrew: 'Save of course the impossible one that two hundred young males most desired.' He was a bit greedy there, as he had a girlfriend at home in Stony (she worked at Bletchley Park, a couple of miles along Watling Street from his home).

The Germans, notwithstanding their own appalling losses, were still putting up fighters, especially at night. Speer was to ensure that the number of aircraft produced actually increased all through 1944 and indeed continued to do so right until the last few weeks of the war.

Harry Yates was on a bombing run over the city of Bremen on a starry night:

'An open invitation to every German night–fighter... as we began our approach flak burst across the sky, not light anymore but a seemingly impenetrable wall of it. We'd seen nothing like this, nothing at all. The realisation came over me how very inexperienced and vulnerable we still were, really just a crew of six rookies and a veteran (himself) convinced he was going to die... From thousands of feet above us the night fighters released their own flares. They floated down on parachutes... I could see at least two dozen Lancasters, all as naked as at noon. We passed so close to some of the flares, they lit the cockpit with a brilliance that made me shield my eyes.'

Bremen was a sobering sight: 'Raging storms of fire engulfed vast areas... God knows what it was like to be down amongst that lot. It was no part of our job to think about it...

seconds later we were enveloped in a box–barrage of heavy flak. Two bombers were hit in front of us, one of them already a fireball.' There was an explosion under the aircraft. Yates' only option was to dive and weave. The radar–aided searchlights searched for and locked on them:

'The intensity of the master beam completely obliterated the instrument panel. There was no indication of attitude, altitude or airspeed. There was no Bremen below, no world beyond the Perspex. There was nothing but arching light and the convulsions from shellfire.'

Yates attempted to dive but the Lancaster did not respond well to the controls – she felt groggy. Mac, the bomb aimer, asked if he could release his bombs and Yates realised with horror what the problem was – the bomb doors had been open all the time. A flak splinter would have blown them to eternity. They dropped the bombs: "Skip, fighter coming from port. Corkscrew now." Harry Yates hurled P–Peter forward and away. Both his gunners opened up. An aircraft was going down in flames to starboard. Flame flicked over their starboard wing, then more:

'The flames were massively bellowed by a gale of over two hundred mph. Should I give the order now and get everyone out... or try and blow out the fire in a vertical dive? Bailing out truly terrified me... leaving the hatch offered... an excellent chance of being chopped in two by a tailfin.'

Some air crew who bailed out were machine gunned in the air: pilots on both sides did that to their enemy; why spare them so that they could fight again? Others bailed out in the path of their attacker. Wilhelm Johnen tells of a Lancaster rear gunner who jumped straight into the propeller of a comrade (Oberleutnant Reinhold Knacke, a 24 year old fighter ace who shot down forty–three bombers before himself being shot down and killed).

Or they might be thrown into the fires they had started by an enraged populace on landing. Goebbels carried out an extensive campaign against 'terrorfliegers' and encouraged the populace to vent their anger against downed airmen.

Roughly one in six survived being shot down. Like playing Russian Roulette but with 5 bullets in the chambers.

With the bomb–doors closed, Yates managed to dive. The flames went out. He nursed the Lancaster home to Mepal on three engines. They landed at three in the morning. He inspected his plane later in the morning:

'My beautiful Lancaster had taken a fearful beating... I walked slowly around, counting each hit by rocket or flak. It took some time. There were sixty–four, many as big as a football. I climbed aboard. Daylight streamed through the fuselage in unexpected places. Debris littered the floor. How it was we all had come through without injury I just couldn't imagine. P–Peter was a write–off. One more towards the thirty.'

From the German side, for the night–fighters, the carnage was as great, or greater. The Mosquito was their most feared opponent, as Wilhelm Johnen records:

'The radar equipment of this wooden aircraft surpassed anything that had previously been seen. It was technically so perfect that at a distance of five miles they could pick the German night fighters out of the bomber stream like currants out of a cake. They were 140 mph faster than our aircraft, but in addition to this we were fighting against enormous odds. Against a formation of 600 to 800 four–engined bombers and 150–200 Mosquitoes we could put into the air 60 to 80 night fighters. It was incredibly difficult to get a bomber in our sights for the Mosquitoes sought us out and sped like rockets to the aid of the bomber.'

Both sides had airborne radar now, though the Allied (British) sets were by far the more advanced.

These massive air battles consumed vast amounts of resources. In Germany and across its conquered territories, upwards of a million men manned and serviced the flak batteries and searchlights. These men could not be used against Russia. Again, to Russia's benefit, the Luftwaffe was preoccupied with the west, leaving little air support for the eastern front. Then there were the guns themselves – the 88's, the best guns in the war, defending the Reich from the RAF and

USAAF rather than blunting or spear heading attacks against the Soviets. The bombing, of course, also damaged industry. Bremen, where Harry Yates met his first night fighter, was home to a giant Focke–Wulfe aircraft plant.

The German air force was outnumbered by the vast bomber and fighter fleets the RAF and USAAF now commanded. They were losing many planes and, worse still, pilots, to Mustangs and Mosquitoes. The Luftwaffe was much less of a threat now and Harry Yates and his companions flew by day as well as at night:

'Refineries and coking plants, marshalling yards and entire towns …together with the hardy perennial of mining sea areas, the duties placed upon 75 squadron over the next three weeks satisfied every official analysis and theory about the bomber offensive. Not that we gave much consideration to the respective merits of the Oil Plan of General Spaatz, the Transport Plan of Lord Tedder, or our own C–in–C's private obsession with area bombing. Grand strategy was something of which aircrew were sublimely and properly ignorant. We went out to do what we were told must be done for victory, and did so in the hope that each trip would bring the day nearer.'

Harry Yates's war nearly ended on a raid against Kamen, an oil refinery in Germany. It was a daylight raid. Harry was flying the lead Lancaster. This was a great honour accorded only to the best: but a somewhat dangerous one. Still, being the spearhead of hundreds of aircraft was quite something for a lad from Stony:

'"Half the RAF's on our tail." His radio operator told him. "Kites as far as I can see." Above us our escort shining like gems in the sunlight. They were incredibly distant and, indeed, were nigh on twice our altitude …but no more than thirty seconds away at diving speed.'

Kamen was heavily defended by anti–aircraft guns. As I mentioned earlier, Bletchley Park had picked up the messages that Speer had sent out, pulling flak guns away from the cities to defend these refineries. Yates had bombed his target when:

'A tremendous explosion ripped at the air... the entire nose section ahead of me disappeared, taking with it the front gun turret, then the Perspex windscreen disintegrated before my eyes into a thousand fragments... flung full into my face... I was in darkness, disorientated by shock and pain – what felt like dozens of blades slicing into my eyes... the eyes, dammit! I always hated fishing about in my eyes for dust and dirt and now this!'

In the gale, in the wreck of the cockpit, his flight–engineer, Flight–Sergeant 'Tubby' Westell helped Yates remove his flying helmet and dabbed at his eyes:

'More than once during this exchange Tubby addressed me by my Christian name. Only Bill, my fellow officer, generally made a habit of this. To the others I was never anything but 'skipper'. I had never dreamt that one day my Flight Engineer might feel obliged to extend his patronage to me in this way. I suppose that as my senior by twelve years he was fully entitled to do so.'

Somehow Flying Officer Yates continued to fly: 'I could see into the mid distance but short range was difficult and moving my eyes in their sockets impossible. Most of the instrument panel remained a blur.' Somehow he landed the noseless Lancaster back at base, to be told:

"I'm afraid Perspex doesn't show up on X–rays, Flying Officer Yates."

The largest splinter was embedded one sixteenth of an inch from the retina of the right eye. The splinters were dug out with a needle (Harry Yates was under anaesthetic, but conscious). He was back flying after 7 weeks – for his thirteenth operation. Now, there was virtually no fighter resistance:

'The series of attacks on synthetic oil tanks begun by the Americans in May 1944 had yielded dramatic dividends. By autumn only about one twentieth of coal–derived aviation fuel was reaching German fighter stations.'

Harry Yates and his men completed their tour at 4.22 pm on New Year's Eve 1944. Yates was 22. The other two crews who had joined 75 squadron at the same time as them were long dead.

1945: the triple assault continues:
oil, transport and cities

Harry Yates was slightly wrong in his assessment as to why he saw so few enemy fighters. Hitler's oil reserves were far from exhausted. Wilhelm Johnen, who was still flying, says:

'In addition to the enemy's air superiority, we now began to have the greatest difficulties in supply. Fuel was stored in great quantities at the depots but as a result of constant attacks on bridges, roads and railway lines, it no longer reached the airfields. We often pumped the fuel out of several machines to get at least one in the air.'

The bombing went on, its weight and significance discussed and disputed among the bomber lords. In Britain, Harris was ordered by Portal to shift more of his attacks from the cities to oil. He declined and offered his resignation, which Portal refused. It is an odd fact that Bomber Command were not cleared to receive Ultra – Bletchley Park communications – though the American 8th Air Force was. Anything of relevance that Bletchley Park learned went to Portal, who then briefed Harris.

If you want further details about the spats between the warlords, I suggest you start with the books in my bibliography. For my part, I will look at the result of a single bomb on Berlin, a strong contender for The Best Bomb of the War.

Berlin February 3rd 1945 – the hand of God?

The head of the USAAF Eighth Air Force, James Doolittle records: 'On February 3, 1945, I dispatched 1,000 B–17s (Flying Fortresses) to bomb transportation targets in and around Berlin.'

Leading the bombers was a man we have already briefly met: Colonel Robert Rosenthal, a Jewish lawyer from New York, flying from RAF Thorpe Abbots, in Norfolk. We saw him last over Munster, when his was the only one of thirteen bombers not to get shot down. He had, as you may recall, spent a lonely evening in the Officer's Mess.

170

Given that railways are often in the middle of cities, it is not surprising that bombs aimed for them often hit other buildings. This day was no exception, many bombs fell wide. One of them fell on the People's Court. Even though it was a Saturday, the president of the court was hard at work inside the imposing building. The president was a diligent man; there was more work than ever to be done if the Reich was to be cleansed. Today he was sitting in judgement on one of the German army officers who had tried to assassinate Hitler the previous summer. The bomb from the American raid rewarded his diligence with death.

The People's Court was the instrument that wreaked revenge on Germans who did not worship Hitler. Its president was, until the bomb fell on him, Roland Friesler. In 1938, as Reich Minister for Justice, Friesler had attended the infamous show trials of Germany's then ally, Russia. In Stalin's trials guilty and innocent alike freely admitted their guilt. They had been broken by torture and brain washing. Their families were imprisoned as hostage to their compliance. Friesler had watched and learned. These became Nazi methods too.

There would have been a certain ironic justice if the bomb that fell on Friesler was from Rosenthal's plane, as Rosenthal was a Jewish lawyer. Friesler, as the Reich Minister of Justice, had (at the Wannsee Conference), framed the laws that condemned all Jews in Nazi hands to death. Justice was not a frequent visitor to the People's Court, though. It is an insult to decency to call that place a 'court' at all. A kangaroo court, perhaps; but in truth it was more akin to a holy grove of yore where the high priest sacrificed the heretics. Nine times out of ten the sentence was death, either by hanging or guillotine. That sentence had been handed out by Friesler's 'court' five thousand times in the last three years.

In 1942, as the tide of war turned against Germany, an armament factory worker was up in front of the People's Court. Her name was Marianne Elise Kurchner. She was the twenty-one year old widow of a German soldier and had been arrested for telling the following joke:

"Hitler and Goering are standing on top of the Berlin Radio tower. Hitler says he wants to do something to put a

171

smile on Berliners' faces. So Goering says 'Why don't you jump?"

Standing in judgement was Roland Friesler. Marianne admitted making the joke, saying that she had been distraught at the time as her husband had recently been killed on the Russian front. Friesler sentenced her to death and she was guillotined. So perished all enemies of the state.

Roland Friesler (centre)

Friesler was a showman. He wore a scarlet robe. His courtroom was bedecked with swastikas, behind him stood a bust of Hitler. He opened his sessions with the Nazi salute and would bully, hector, humiliate, shout and scream at those in front of him. Sometimes the proceedings, especially in high focus trials such as those against the army's (belated) attempt to kill Hitler in July 1944, were filmed and shown in cinemas.

The White Rose Group came up before Friesler. They were young Germans whose leaders were medical students at Munich university. Some of them had been seconded to Russia and seen for themselves the atrocities and murders committed by troops against the Russians and Jews. They printed six leaflets describing this and distributed them in secret. The leaflets proclaimed that Hitler could not win the war, only prolong it, and appealed to their readers to denounce 'National Socialist (Nazi) sub–humanism' for all time. They stated that 'the day of reckoning has come for the most contemptible tyrant our country has ever endured.'

Hans and Sophie Scholl

Hans and Sophie Scholl (a brother and sister) and Christoph Probst were three of the leaders of the White Rose Group. When taken before Friesler, Sophie Scholl stood up to his hectoring attack saying: "You know as well as we do that the war is lost. Why are you so cowardly that you won't admit it?"

They were guillotined the same day. As the blade fell on Hans he cried out *"Es lebe die Freiheit."*

Friesler was perhaps the living embodiment of why carpet bombing of German cities could not work. British naval power in the first war had led to the Kiel mutiny and German surrender. Hitler's Nazi party had learned the lesson well. German morale would never fail again. Hitler's people were more afraid of their leaders than their enemy.

To Hans and Sophie Scholl and others like them who perished on Friesler's block, Germany owes her soul.

Friesler's corpse was taken to Lützow hospital. As it was laid out a worker commented: "It is God's verdict." The remark was met by silence. Friesler was buried in the grave of his wife's family. His name is not recorded on the gravestone.

A bit over a week later Colonel Robert Rosenthal took off again from RAF Thorpe Abbots in Norfolk. It was to be his final bombing raid on Germany. He was shot down near Berlin. Two of his crew died on board, another was lynched on landing, another had a leg amputated. Rosenthal ended up with the advancing Russians. He survived the war.

The same night that Robert Rosenthal was shot down, the RAF sent their bombers to Dresden.

Dresden

Harried by Mosquitoes, shot–up in the sky and bombed on their own airfields, low on fuel, the German night–fighter force still fought on. Wilhelm Johnen recounts:

'On the night of the destruction of Dresden, the 13th February 1945, the enemy bombers droned at low altitude over our heads but we were in reserve and I received no orders to go up.'

Dresden is a city in the east of Germany which, until then, had been spared much Allied bombing. The primary reason for bombing the city now was to help the Russian Advance; Stalin's troops being less than seventy miles from its suburbs. Dresden was a major rail hub and destruction of its railway yards would certainly stop supplies getting to the German army in the east. Colonel Harold Cook was an American prisoner of war who was held in the Friedrichstadt marshalling yards in Dresden on the night before the attack. He later wrote:

'I saw with my own eyes that Dresden was an armed camp: thousands of German troops, tanks and artillery and miles of freight cars loaded with supplies supporting and transporting German logistics towards the east to meet the Russians.'

For a night and two days, Dresden was bombed by the RAF and USAAF. The defence was light because the city's heavy flak batteries had been moved to the Russian Front a month earlier. The marshalling yards were destroyed. The city of Dresden (which was an architectural treasure), went too. It burned in a firestorm triggered by the relentless bombing. It is estimated that 25,000 people died.

Churchill wrote to Harris:

'It seems to me that the moment has come when the question of bombing of German cities simply for the sake of increasing the terror, though under other pretexts, should be reviewed. Otherwise we shall come into control of an utterly ruined land... The destruction of Dresden remains a serious query against the conduct of Allied bombing.'

Harris replied:

'In the past we were justified in attacking German cities. But to do so was always repugnant and now that the Germans are beaten anyway we can properly abstain from proceeding with these attacks. This is a doctrine to which I could never subscribe. Attacks on cities like any other act of war are intolerable unless they are strategically justified. But they are strategically justified in so far as they tend to shorten the war and preserve the lives of Allied soldiers. To my mind we have absolutely no right to give them up unless it is certain that they will not have this effect. I do not personally regard the whole of the remaining cities of Germany as worth the bones of one British Grenadier. The feeling, such as there is, over Dresden, could be easily explained by any psychiatrist. It is connected with German bands and Dresden shepherdesses. Actually Dresden was a mass of munitions works, an intact government centre, and a key transportation point to the East. It is now none of these things.'

In the light of this and other comments from senior Allied commanders, Churchill sent a revised letter to Harris:

'It seems to me that the moment has come when the question of the so called 'area–bombing' of German cities should be reviewed from the point of view of our own interests. If we come into control of an entirely ruined land, there will be a great shortage of accommodation for ourselves and our allies... we must see that our attacks do no more harm to ourselves than they do the enemy's war effort.'

The United States Strategic Bombing Survey's majority view on the Allies' bombing of German cities, concluded:

'The city area raids have left their mark on the German people as well as on their cities. Far more than any other military action that preceded the actual occupation of Germany itself, these attacks left the German people with a solid lesson in the disadvantages of war. It was a terrible lesson; conceivably that lesson, both in Germany and abroad, could be the most lasting single effect of the air war.'

Dresden – view from the city hall
(Rathaus)

Let us hope that the 'solid lesson in the disadvantages of war' has been learnt by all parties. So far it seems it has. There has been no multi-country war in Europe since 1945. But man forgets.

Es lebe die Freiheit.

I don't suppose the opinion of a former Senior Aircraftsman on Sir Arthur Harris is of any great significance; but nevertheless I feel I would be ducking the issue if I didn't give it.

Harris was a commander who knew that he was right and did not suffer from self–doubt. That can be a great strength – and it leads others to follow. However, it is also a weakness, for an inability to question one's beliefs – or decisions – means that errors do not get corrected. Harris believed that the methods used to destroy Kaiser Bill – breaking German morale – would also destroy Hitler. He was wrong. Hitler didn't give a damn about the German people. The Trenchard Doctrine was a war too late.

Most generals, perhaps, begin their wars by fighting the previous one: but the first class commanders such as Dowding, Rommel, Zhukov, Patton and the rest, learn, improvise and adapt. Harris could not, or would not do that. As such, I do not think him a great commander. The 'father of radar' Robert Watson Watt thought that 'Butch' (as an ex–RAF man, I claim the right to use the soubriquet) was a man 'who had greatness thrust upon him.' I think so too.

That said, I don't think Harris's actions need my, or anyone else's, apology. The Nazi party was democratically elected to power in Germany. That elected government then suppressed all opposition and waged a war in which eighty million men, women and children died. Most of the dead were innocent, millions dying in gas chambers and concentration camps. Each month of the war cost about a million lives. If razing German cities and industry – around 400,000 Germans are thought to have died under Allied bombing during the war – was believed to be the quickest way to get rid of the scourge of the swastika, then, in the terrible blood–logic of war, the justification is hardly arguable.

Harris's aim was without a shadow of doubt the right one: to bring the war to an end as quickly as possible. Death, of innocent and guilty alike, is one of the costs of war and the guilt lies with the aggressors, not with those who seek to stop them.

As for Bomber Command – had I been a brave young man in 1940 I would have been proud to serve in it. I would have been prouder still if I had ended up with a skipper such as Jack Currie or Harry Yates. Had I been an American, I couldn't have hoped for better than Robert Rosenthal.

For year after year, the people of Europe knew nothing of life outside their Nazi prison camp except the drone of the RAF at night and the BBC. Then came the silver armadas of the USAAF. For most of those looking upwards, the air fleets spelled hope. For some, especially the people of Germany, they meant fear.

Those who flew above them were often afraid, too. Of all the Allied services in the war, RAF Bomber Command and the United States Army Air Force aircrews had the highest proportion of fatalities. 55,000 died in RAF Bomber Command – nearly half of those who flew. Around 20,000 USAAF airmen flying from England also died in action.

As the guillotine blade fell on Hans Scholl's neck, he cried out "*Es lebe die Freiheit!*" (Long live freedom). Freedom lived. Without RAF Bomber Command and the USAAF it would have died. That is what Europe, Germany included, owes to the warlords of Wycombe and their warriors.

6: Technowar - the attack on London

Britain; the Fuhrer's unfinished business

This chapter is about Hitler's V weapons, the V1, V2 and V3; which were largely developed to knock Britain out of the war.

Hitler had dreamed of conquering Britain from the air from the very start of the war. This is graphically shown in an account written by Albert Speer. Speer was very close to Hitler; at that time he was the Fuhrer's architect, and in the process of designing Germania, which was to replace Berlin and be the capital of the Thousand Year Third Reich. Hitler planned it to be his world capital when he had won the war. Speer writes of being with Hitler and Goebbels, in 1939, at the showing of a brand-new film (a product of Goebbels' Propaganda Ministry), which showed Hitler's Luftwaffe bombing and strafing Warsaw, Poland's capital, more or less at will:

> 'The film ended with a montage showing a plane diving towards the outlines of the British Isles. A burst of flame followed, and the island flew into the air in tatters. Hitler's enthusiasm was unbounded. "That is what will happen to them!" he cried out, carried away, "that is how we will annihilate them."'

Warsaw, then, was a curtain-raiser for the assault on London. Unfortunately for Hitler, Hugh 'Stuffy' Dowding, the head of the Royal Air Force's Fighter Command, got in his way. The V weapons, in 1944, were intended to be round two, the death blow for the city on the Thames. In the interim, Hitler's attitude towards Britain had changed from anger to blind hate.

For the first year after Dunkirk, Britain was Hitler's Public Enemy Number One (in an admittedly small field, as no one else was fighting him). That changed in June 1941, when the Fuhrer launched his attack on Russia. But Britain was still 'unfinished business'. Hitler referred to the subject again in a speech he made in October 1941. Before getting into what a wonderful success his troops were having in Russia (although

179

winter clothing might come in useful), he listed his friends. His voice dropped in regret as he spoke of the one that got away: the country that he had 'wooed most strongly':

'We did not succeed in bringing about a link between Britain, especially the English people, with the German people as I had always hoped for... if it were impossible to gain the friendship of England it would be better if we experienced her enmity at a time when I was still the leader of Germany.'

Later in his speech, he said that the basis of his attack on Russian was: 'help yourself and God almighty will not deny you his assistance.'

There it was; Hitler's policy in a nutshell; God helps those who help themselves. This is where the British people – under Churchill's leadership – took issue with him. In their view, land–grab was land–grab; whether dressed up as a holy crusade or not. For the British, standing up against the Nazi aggression was both a practical necessity (else they'd probably be next) and an ethical one. That was why they were fighting Hitler. That is why, when their allies were broken by force of arms or surrendered, they fought him alone.

Churchill's message to Europe.....and to Hitler

Such an illogical stance was enough to exasperate any God–steering man; even one as patient as Hitler. The idea of 'do unto others as you would be done to' – decency – was an outmoded ethic of superstitious and gullible fools; why should Britain be prepared to sacrifice her empire – her very people even – to support it? When, in 1941, his deputy, Hess, parachuted into Scotland to make the point face to face, the ungrateful British imprisoned him. That goaded the Fuhrer to even greater paroxysms of rage. How many times did he have to declare his peaceful intentions before the war–monger Churchill stopped attacking him?

The thorn in the Fuhrer's side would only get thornier. For example, when Hitler sent his troops into Russia, the British sent convoys and trainloads of arms and supplies to the Soviets. Germany couldn't do much about it as Britain had largely destroyed their surface navy.

Worse still, Churchill persuaded America to abandon its isolationist policies and support his country more and more openly. When Britain ran out of money, the United States even began to give them free supplies. American aid amounted to undeclared war on the Reich. Hitler eventually got so fed up with this that, on the 11th of December 1941, he declared war on the United States. That was a bad move of the Fuhrer's.

The British were at the root of Hitler's problems. If Britain didn't want to be friends with him and, as friends do, leave him to his own devices – in his case treachery, mass murder, enslavement, genocide and world rule - then he would destroy her... but how?

The Fuhrer's armies were more than a match for any foe, Britain included. Very rarely did their infantry or tanks suffer more casualties than they inflicted. But they couldn't get over the Channel.

What about technology? At the start of the war, Britain had a considerable lead over every other country in several key scientific fields, such as radar, computing, communications and atomics. When America came into the war, they added their own ideas and developments in these areas.

Germany wasn't behind in every scientific field, though. In the development of guided missiles, the Nazis were years ahead of the rest of the world. These were their 'V' or vengeance weapons. Work began on these weapons in Germany in the 1930's; though they weren't called V weapons back then. They were only given that name as a cock–eyed compliment to

Britain and specifically to the BBC's Victory Campaign which had the angry people of Europe scrawling large 'V's across German notices across the continent – a campaign that Winston Churchill had taken to his heart.

In the years 1942 and 1943, Hitler was to be persuaded that the V weapons were the way to defeat Britain.

By 1943, Hitler had run out of other options. The Royal Navy, with the help of America, had denied him control of the sea. On neither of the land fronts on which Hitler's troops were fighting – North Africa and Russia – were things going well. He had lost an army of over half a million men in Russia, at Stalingrad. In North Africa his star general, Rommel, had been defeated by the British at El Alamein.

To add to that there had been a major landing of British and American troops in the French colonies of Morocco and Algeria in North Africa (Operation Torch).

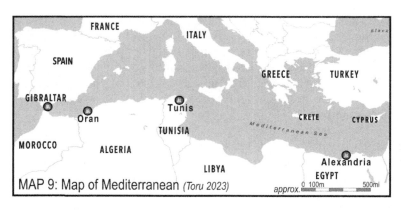

MAP 9: Map of Mediterranean *(Toru 2023)*

The idea behind the landings had been to enlist the support of the very sizeable French armies there to fight against the Nazis in the liberation of France. The operation had been under American flags – as it was thought (rightly) that to be liberated by British troops would hurt French feelings. Hundreds of ships had converged on North Africa from across the Atlantic and Scotland with little opposition. The Axis were no longer able to fight above the waves and the invasion fleets were too big and well protected for the U–boats to try their luck with.

Of the 543 British and American craft that took part in Operation Torch, none was lost in passage, though several were sunk in fighting to support the landings. That was because the French, who the Allies thought they were liberating, fought back. In the grand scheme of things this was a minor hiccup, a footnote in an action that is now long forgotten. It was important, though, for the 1,100 or so Allies (American and British in roughly equal numbers) who died. There were around the same number of deaths among the defenders. Those defenders, I stress, were not Germans or Italians but the French army, navy and air force. As well as being out of sorts with the British, it seemed that the Vichy generals did not want to be liberated by the Americans either. Having no stomach for fighting the Fuhrer; they fought their 'liberators' instead. This surprised the Americans somewhat – they had been expecting to be welcomed. The British rolled their eyes. The tiff was resolved when the French generals, not at all sheepish about their volte farce, decided magnanimously that it might, after all, be a more profitable option to fight the Nazis rather than *Les Anglo-Americaines*.

Defeat in North Africa to the pincer movement of British and American troops would cost Hitler a great number of captured soldiers; and the collaboration of his vassal French state. In November 1942, in response to the decision of the Vichy generals in Africa to join the Allies, the Germans moved their troops to take over the unoccupied (Vichy) area of France.

The Nazis quickly moved troops and armour to the French port of Toulon, to take over the main French fleet which was berthed there. This gave the French navy three options; to surrender to the Germans, flee to join the Allies, or scuttle their ships. The senior French Admiral ordered his fleet to sink their ships. Three French submarines and one surface ship disobeyed orders and sailed to join the Allies. The other 77 vessels, including 3 battleships, 7 cruisers and 15 destroyers were scuttled as ordered. This at a time when it was obvious that the Allies would at some time need to cross the English Channel to liberate France. Those ships could have been useful on D–day. A shame. And shameful.

A couple of weeks later, Churchill and Roosevelt met in one of the liberated(?) French colonial ports, Casablanca, and issued a statement – the Casablanca Agreement – demanding Germany's unconditional surrender. The first signature on the agreement was President Roosevelt's. The American giant had awakened. From now on, he would be calling the tune.

In the same month as the Casablanca Agreement, American bombers joined the RAF's attack on German cities. Also in that month (January 1943), the SIS(MI6) in Britain got its first hint of Hitler's V weapons. It was as well that they did, for the Fuhrer had decided that every last one of these would be deployed against England – and, above all, against London.

Doctor Jones sounds the alarm

The key man in the Allied fight against the V weapons was the Head of the Scientific Section in Britain's SIS, Doctor R.V. Jones.

We have met Reg Jones in *The Intelligence Zone*. He was the man who worked out how the Luftwaffe was pinpointing targets in England in what he called 'the war of the beams'. He and his wife Vera had, you may remember, been bombed out of their flat on Richmond Common and he had been pretty cross with her for throwing the bath water away. More significantly for the Allied war effort, he was the best informed man in the world on the subject of the European air war; for he sat at the centre of an intelligence web which had many strands. Anything relevant that Bletchley decoded ended up in his in-tray. Reports from Whaddon from the resistance movements were there too. He had a spy or two in the German armed forces. He only had to ask to be be shown aerial reconnaissance photos from RAF Medmenham – and he was on the circulation list for output from the extensive bugging operation of Axis officers which took place at Latimer.

Jones had been aware for years that the Nazis had a testing centre at Peenemünde, on the German Baltic coat, where they were developing aerial weapons. He had learned this from The Oslo Report; a multi–page overview of the German use of electronics in weapons development that the anti–Nazi German scientist, Hans Mayer, had passed to the British secret services back in 1939 (Mayer was later arrested for listening to the BBC and criticising the Nazi regime and was imprisoned in several concentration camps but survived the war). From the end of 1942, new intelligence came into England on how and where Nazi rocketry was being developed. The name Peenemünde again cropped up in these reports. The information came from several sources – and its implications were terrifying.

One of the sources of information was prisoners of war. The Axis defeat in North Africa would mean an influx of around a quarter of a million German and Italian prisoners to Britain. In March 1943, Jones received the transcripts of a conversation between two German generals captured in Africa. The recording was from the holding and interrogation centre for senior prisoners at Trent Park, on the northern edge of London. Trent Park was heavily bugged, both indoors and outdoors. The generals were having a conversation. One of them (Von Thoma), said to the other (Cruewell): 'This rocket business... these huge things... they've always said they would go to 15km into the stratosphere... there's no limit to their range.'

Von Thoma also said that he knew that their prison was somewhere near London and since they had heard no large explosions, there must have been a hold-up in the rocket programme.

The steps that Jones took to find out more are described in *Most Secret War,* which is, I reiterate, the most important (and superbly written) book ever written about the 'technowar' and the birth of scientific intelligence. If I had to recommend only one book on the subject, this would be it.

The vengeance weapons

In fact the Nazis were developing several V weapons at Peenemünde. The most Important of these were a flying bomb (the V1) and the world's first ballistic missile (the V2). The latter was a space rocket with an explosive warhead. Its terminal velocity was nearly 1800 miles an hour. Its speed meant that, given the technology of the time, it was more or less pointless to try and stop it after it had been launched.

V1 flying bomb | V2 rocket

Doctor Reginald Jones was worried and alerted the RAF, who commissioned spy flights to photograph Peenemünde and set up a section at RAF Medmenham to analyse the results.

Medmenham spies out the land

I briefly mentioned RAF photographic reconnaissance in the chapter about Bomber Command. By early 1941, the main British sites were at RAF Benson in Oxfordshire, home of the Photographic Reconnaissance Unit (PRU) and RAF Medmenham in Buckinghamshire the home of the Central Interpretation Unit (CIU).

To do any kind of justice to the story of Medmenham would take a volume; and volumes have been written about it. Yet again, in this book, I have to choose which story to tell. Should it be, perhaps, about how Sidney Cotton developed the first sophisticated 'spy in the sky', or maybe about Cotton himself, of whom Fred Winterbotham said:

'There were three things in Cotton's life. Flying, money, and women.'

The scale of the operation, too, is fascinating; as is the story of how aerial mapping has affected our modern world. I can only point the reader to the books and websites (which I list at the end of this book) which deal with this engrossing subject.

In brief, then, aircraft flew from Benson (and its satellites, St Eval and Wick) all across Europe to bring back photographs. These were studied at Medmenham by Photographic

Interpreters (PIs). The PIs could look down into factories and see what they were producing and how they were being extended. They could see shipyards and docks and know what ships were there. They could target bombing raids and assess damage afterwards. They could analyse the movement of goods, planes and army divisions.

Photographic reconnaissance of Europe by aircraft from RAF Benson (and its satellites) was extraordinarily widespread and detailed. This was the forerunner and prototype for all later spy–camera operations in the western world. Its importance can best be judged, perhaps, by the fact that one of Churchill's daughters (Sarah) worked there, as did one of Roosevelt's sons (Elliot). The latter would set up his own spy plane camp a few miles down the road – the genesis of American aerial reconnaissance.

Churchill visited Medmenham and was shown photographs of Peenemünde in early June 1943. A couple of days later, while poring over the same photographs, Doctor Jones spotted a rocket: 'I experienced the sense of elation that you get when after hours of casting you realise that a salmon has taken your line.'

This was information that could affect the course of the war. Because of his position as the head of the scientific section of the secret service, Jones was in a position to get something done about it. He set out his findings in a meeting of top politicians and military leaders, chaired by Churchill. By now, Jones had received yet more reports and drawings from agents on the continent. He presented all of this evidence, including his recommendation that Peenemünde be bombed. Churchill was convinced (he had dealt with Jones before and had plenty of reasons to trust him implicitly). Bomber Command was ordered to carry out a night raid on Peenemünde as soon as possible.

Over in Germany, a week after the British decision to bomb Peenemünde had been taken, Hitler, in the presence of top German scientists, was shown a film. Albert Speer, by now Hitler's Minister of Armament Production, was there too. The movie was in full colour and very impressive. The Fuhrer watched entranced what Speer describes as:

'The Magnificent spectacle of a great rocket rising from its pad and disappearing into the stratosphere'.

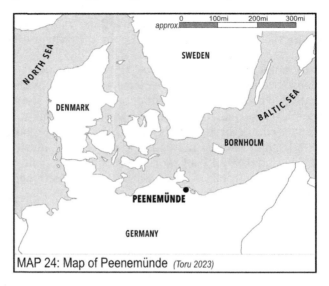

MAP 24: Map of Peenemünde *(Toru 2023)*

Speer tells us that Hitler was in raptures. Here was just the thing for England! The Fuhrer, Speer tells us, would have happily used an atom bomb on London, had he had one. He didn't need to. The V2 would do just as well:

'The (V2) is a measure that can decide the war. And what encouragement to the home front when we attack the English with it.'

Hitler ordered that the rocket be put to the top of the list for raw materials (thus delaying a lot of other things, including German jet aircraft development). He demanded that 2,000 V2s should be produced each month.

Six weeks after the Fuhrer had savoured his movie, 596 heavy RAF bombers pounded Peenemünde. The raid was a bloody battle. 700 workers on the ground were killed, as well as the chief engine designer. The RAF lost 40 aircraft and most of their 280 crewmen. The manufacture of the rocket is thought to have been set back by two or three months by this raid. It was one of the most important Allied aerial attack of the war; for it meant that the bombs and rockets which were being developed by the Nazis would not be ready for use until after the D–Day landings. The Nazis took it rather badly. The next day, the Chief of the German Air Staff, Major General Hans Jeschonekk, made it clear how he thought the Luftwaffe's duel with the RAF (and the recently arrived but already very active USAAF) was going. He took out his service revolver and killed himself.

The Allied air force's work was not at an end, however. The V1 and V2 production had only been delayed, not stopped. In London, many extra metal Morrison bomb shelters were ordered (it is said that the building of three battleships was shelved to provide the raw materials) to prepare for the expected onslaught.

Operation Crossbow: tackling the launch sites

When Hitler upped the priority of V weapon productions, he also ordered that the necessary storage and launching areas be built in France as soon as possible. Thanks to Reg Jones and his sources, the Allied top brass knew this. Allied bombers, which were already pounding the Nazi coastal defences, radar and transport in France in preparation for D–Day, were told to target the sites linked with the V weapons too. This was called Operation Crossbow and it began in December 1943.

Michel Hollard

The position of many of these sites were revealed by French resistance agents working for a man called Michel Hollard. Hollard, the head of a resistance network operating in France, followed the principle of keeping close to his enemy. Having already passed–on two items of information about the V1s, he blagged his way onto a construction site at Auffay, near Dieppe. He saw a ramp there and risked his life by taking a compass bearing along it. It aligned with London. He reported this to the British, who asked if he could look

189

for more sites. To do so, he recruited many young men, giving each of them a bike, a map of an area he was interested in and a description of what to look for; substantial building sites, each with firing ramps, curved fixed bunkers for storing the missiles (the sites were referred to as 'ski-sites' because of these) and other blast bunkers. By the end of October 1943, his recruits had found a hundred of these, lying in an arc between the Pas de Calais and the Cotentin Peninsula (where the D–Day landings would take place).

Later in the war, Michel Hollard was arrested by the gestapo, tortured, sent to a concentration camp but survived the war. Many of his men died.

Quite independently, the same information came through Marie–Madeleine Fourcade's *Alliance* resistance network, its source being a woman French resistance agent 'Amniarix' – the 24 year old Jeannie Rousseau – who was working for the Germans as a translator and interpreter. She gave detailed

Jeannie Rousseau

information about the V1s and V2s. Among the information she provided, she told of 108 sites in preparation along the Channel coast; which tallied nicely with the number of V1 sites that Hollard's men had found. She also said that technical problems had occurred with the flying bombs; but that they were on the point of being resolved. Like Hollard, Jeannie Rousseau, too, would end up in a concentration camp but survive the war.

From December 1943 onwards, the ski sites were visited by the USAAF and the RAF and mostly blasted out of existence.

As well as these fixed 'ski' sites, aerial reconnaissance and resistance workers had identified nine super-bunkers – the 'Heavy Sites', built underground or into hills. RAF Medmenham flew several aerial surveys over the whole of the Channel coast area in this period. British intelligence weren't certain about the exact purpose of these enormous structures – but knew they were connected to Hitler's V weapons; so the

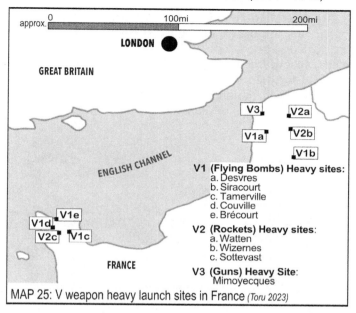

MAP 25: V weapon heavy launch sites in France *(Toru 2023)*

V1 (Flying Bombs) Heavy sites:
a. Desvres
b. Siracourt
c. Tamerville
d. Couville
e. Brécourt

V2 (Rockets) Heavy sites:
a. Watten
b. Wizernes
c. Sottevast

V3 (Guns) Heavy Site:
Mimoyecques

RAF and USAAF bombed them time and again in the run up to D–Day (6th of June 1944).

R.V. Jones' section continued to monitor German firing trials at Peenemünde (which was bombed again but still in use).

In early 1944, frustrated by the delays caused by the RAF to the V1 programme, the German Luftwaffe launched a conventional 'mini–blitz' on London. Jones remembers this as he and Vera and their 2 children (his son, Robert, was born on February the 11th) had to sleep with their heads under the dining table of their flat in Richmond during the air raids. Jones saw Churchill regularly during this time; as it was feared that should the Germans be able to launch flying bombs and/or rockets on the embarkation ports of Portsmouth and Southampton, the D-day assault could be disrupted or defeated. Jones' prediction was that the bombardments of England would start about a week after D–Day. He was right.

Apart from the couple of V1 'ski' sites that had escaped obliteration at the hands of the Allied air forces, the Germans had also been building modified V1 sites, which could be prepared pretty quickly and finished off by the addition of a prefabricated ramp. It only took two days for the ramp to be erected. Most of the bombs would be launched from these sites. These less–fortified sites were more dangerous to work from, having few fixed buildings. The flying bombs had to be held offsite, mostly in a trio of giant cave complexes.

V1 launching site 'lite'. Add ramp and rocket, light blue touch-paper and retire

A few of the new 'light' V1 launching sites were spotted by aerial reconnaissance; and this sparked off a major overflight of the whole of north western France, looking for more. This was Medmenham's fourth survey of the area. The Mosquitoes and Spitfires of aerial reconnaissance were working at break neck speed month after month, allowing the PIs at RAF Medmenham, aided by reports from the Resistance, to identify 180 sites.

On June 13th 1944 (a week after the D–Day landings), the first V1s landed on London. The V1 attacks caused extra Allied bombers to be switched away from the bomber offensive on Germany to the launch sites in France. The PIs at Medmenham developed a scoring system for the status of the V1 sites and they were normally only bombed when they were just about to be operational – best let the Germans use lots of resources before putting the site out of action.

The rapid breakout of the Americans from their D–Day beachheads to take Cherbourg captured a great swathe of sites in the north of the Cotentin Peninsula and mitigated the threat to the British ports of Southampton, Portsmouth, Bristol and Cardiff.

As well as the fixed V1 launch sites, the Heavy Sites were also targeted for destruction. That was not easy. The Heavy Sites had been designed by the same engineer who had constructed the U–boat pens on the French coast; which suggested that, once finished, they would be indestructible. The thousands of Allied bombers which had targeted the U-boat bases had succeed only in flattening the towns around them (such as Lorient and Brest), while themselves suffering catastrophic losses in planes and crews.

Labour was not skimped when building the Heavy Sites; the Germans shipped in tens of thousands of slave labourers from the east and the concentration camps. In addition, the Heavy Sites were well defended by anti–aircraft guns. The nine super–bunkers were attacked regularly by the American and British air forces. One of them, Desvres, was put out of action by the USAAF. That left eight. Four of those were on the Cotentin peninsula, in Normandy. No special priority was given to these, as they were expected to be over–run by General Patton's land army advance from the D–Day beaches (which they were). That left the four Heavy Sites in the Pas de Calais, a few short miles from the Kent coast. These were a tough nut to crack. Only the RAF had the type of bombs and planes needed to destroy them, and the pilots with the pinpoint target–marking ability to make sure that those bombs fell on the right place.

Crossbow the marksman: Leonard Cheshire

The man with probably the most target–marking ability in the Allied air forces was Leonard Cheshire of the Royal Air Force. I am not suggesting here that British pilots were inherently better than their American counterparts at bomb-aiming; but in 1944, perhaps because they had been at it twice as long, they were definitely in the lead.

Leonard Cheshire was the commanding officer of 617 Squadron, the Dam Busters; the cream of precision flyers. Cheshire, in training, had been marked as an 'exceptional' flyer; a natural. He was exceptional in many ways; for one thing he was still alive: of the 7 pilots he had been closest to in 102 Squadron (his first operational posting back in 1940), 6 were already dead and the other a prisoner of war. Since then, Cheshire had flown over fifty missions and been awarded the Distinguished Flying Cross (twice). Even among the pilots of the Royal Air Force, this man stood out.

He had been promoted to Group Captain at the age of 25; at that time the youngest man ever to reach that rank in the RAF. As a Group Captain, he was put in charge of an airfield of 2,000 men and 40 or 50 aircraft; but he wasn't allowed to fly. He hated being desk–bound, so, when the commanding officer of 617 Squadron, Guy Gibson, was rested from operations, Cheshire dropped a rank in order to take over his job. Cheshire believed in 'the eyeball mark one' – getting in low and close before releasing his marker flares, on which the high level Lancasters dropped their bombs.

The quality of 617's marking was recognised by British and Americans alike. The giants of American airmanship, Jimmy Doolittle and his boss Carl Spaatz, visited Cheshire's Squadron at RAF Woodhall Spa, in Lincolnshire to see what all the fuss was about. They liked what they saw and Cheshire got on well with them. Carl Spaatz was to prove a good friend to Leonard Cheshire.

The plane that Cheshire used for target marking was the 'Wooden Wonder', the Mosquito.

Crossbow the aircraft – The Mossie and the Lanc

The Mosquito was a true child of the Intelligence Zone; for it was born in the woods and valleys of the Chiltern Hills, just a few miles away from Chequers. If not all of the wood for the aircraft came from those hills (much of it was from Canada), the wood–working skills that made it certainly did. The Chilterns – especially around High Wycombe – had long been the centre of the English wooden furniture industry. Those same skills were used to make the Mosquito. Sub–contracted to many furniture makers, the Mosquito had many nicknames –the Wooden Wonder, the Mossie, Freeman's Folly (after the senior airman who championed it) and Termites' Dream, which it certainly was, especially initially in the far east where insects loved the milk–derived glue which held it together (the glue was subsequently changed).

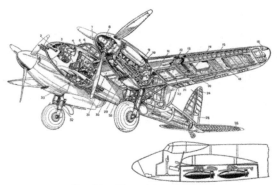

De Havilland Mosquito

The plane was designed by Geoffrey de Havilland and built at his aircraft work at Colney Hatch, in Hertfordshire; the same site, it may be remembered, where his aircraft had disturbed Post Office monitoring equipment and sparked off the development of British radar.

The Mosquito was a multi–role aircraft; a fighter, a bomber, a weather reconnaissance plane for the Metrological Flight, and a target marker. Its successes can be seen from its ratio of losses while serving with Bomber Command, which were a sixth of those of the Lancaster. The plane had speed (faster than the Spitfire), large bomb-bay capacity (more than the standard American bomber, the B17 Flying Fortress), a small radar signature, was agile and could fly at very high altitudes. It was the fastest fighter at high level over Europe until jets were developed, and it wreaked havoc on German night fighters. At the risk of annoying you, dear reader, I would like to repeat what the German night-fighter, Wilhelm Johnen, said of it:

'They were the night fighters' greatest plague and wreaked havoc among the German crews. The radar equipment of this wooden aircraft... was technically so perfect that at a distance of five miles they could pick the German night fighters out of the bomber stream like currants out of a cake. They were 140 mph faster than our aircraft.'

It was piloted by the elite of bomber pilots. One of them (Jack Currie) recorded:

'The Mosquito Mark 3 only needed touches to tell it what to do, but it really needed them... go dreamy in this high–strung animal and you might quickly find yourself upside down, with nothing on the clock except the maker's name.'

The Germans considered the de Havilland manufacturing plant to be so important that they parachuted a spy, Eddie Chapman, to blow it up. He didn't, but a team from nearby Denham studios, under the instructions of a professional magician, camouflaged the factory to look as if he had, and Chapman was awarded an Iron Cross for his (supposed) exploit; but that's another story (or two).

The planes that Cheshire would be marking for – the rest of 617 Squadron – were Lancaster bombers – which I have spoken about in an earlier chapter. The Lanc was the only plane on earth that had the capacity and power to lift the Tallboy.

Crossbow the arrow: The Tallboy

The Tallboy was a 6 ton bomb developed by the British engineer Barnes Wallis. Wallis had worked for three years – with little encouragement and much opposition – to develop a weapon which was effective against hardened structures. The bomb weighed 12,000 pounds; which was twelve times as heavy as the standard bomb that Bomber Command used. It was designed to spin, so as to reach a terminal velocity of 750mph. It was, until the atom bomb, by far the most powerful bomb on earth.

The Tallboy was cast in high tensile steel so that it would survive impact and bore through its target. The delay fuses it carried 'told' the bomb when to explode. Such was its strength that it could pierce nearly five meters (16 feet) of concrete. But

The Tallboy

Barnes Wallis would rather the bomb missed than hit. If it hit it might bounce. What he wanted was a deliberately contrived near–miss, so that the earth would be convulsed by an artificial earthquake which would shake the neighbouring buildings apart. Barnes Wallis explained all this personally to Cheshire, pointing to the drawings which he had made of the Heavy Sites and sticking in pins where he wanted the bombs to fall. Cheshire replied (not unreasonably):

"Of course, we can't guarantee to score near–misses from 20,000 feet as accurately as you can put pins into that drawing."

Barnes Wallis had had to fight tooth and nail to get the Tallboy commissioned. The fight had exhausted him and frayed his nerves. The 57 year inventor turned on the 26 year old chit of a boy (Cheshire) and snarled:

"These bombs are NOT meant to be flung about the French countryside like handfuls of seeds. I didn't invent them for fun."

Leonard Cheshire had been told.

The Crossbow bowmen: RAF 617 Squadron

The race between the Tallboy and the V1 was almost a dead heat. The first Tallboys fell on French soil just 4 days before the first V1 fell on London. Those first Tallboys – target marked by Cheshire in his Mosquito and dropped from the Lancasters of 617 squadron – were on the Saumur rail tunnel, 3 days after D–Day. The Saumur tunnel was the only operational rail tunnel under the river Loire. A Tallboy went through the roof of the tunnel, drilled 60 feet down, and destroyed it. This meant that

Panzer divisions could no longer use that rail route to move from Southwestern France to Normandy to contest the landings.

After this, Cheshire's 617 Squadron started on the giant 'V' structures. As I've said, Patton's troops over–ran those in Normandy. As for the four lying across the Straits of Dover; Watten, Wizerne, Siracourt, and Mimoyecques – 617 squadron finished them all off in six weeks, start to finish.

The British did not always know exactly what the Heavy Sites did – Mimoyecques was to come as quite a surprise – but they suspected that they were either launching, production or holding centres for the V weapons.

617 Squadron's most famous wartime exploit was breaching two major German dams. In terms of the effect that each operation had on the war, 617's achievement in nullifying the super–bunkers in the Pas de Calais, between 100 and 140 miles from London, dwarfs even the dam raids.

Watten/Éperleques – V2 launch site – Cheshire 19.6.44, Tait 25.6.44

Like the other Heavy Sites, Watten was constructed by thousands of slave labourers, many of them Russian prisoners of war. One exasperated German foreman described his workforce as being 'like a sack of fleas', so hard were they to control. Like fleas, they were rubbed out without compunction. The website for Watten (which is now a museum) says:

'A German commission that inspected the labour camps in the area in late 1943 commented: "The Eastern [European] worker is very tough. He works at his job until he falls flat on his face in the mire, and all that is left for the doctor to do is to issue the death certificate."'

This certainly accords with the Nazi killing factory of Dora, in the Harz mountain, where the weapons were produced. There the incoming slave labourers were told. "No one escapes from here. The only way out is up the chimney." Sixty thousand people were deported to Dora. Thirty thousand died there.

200,000 tons of concrete and 20,000 tons of steel went into building Watten. When Major–General Brereton of the US army visited the site after it had been overrun by the Allies, he

Watten/Éperleques – V2 launch site

Impression of a V2 in the assembly hall at Éperlecques

described the bunker as 'more extensive than any concrete constructions we have in the United States, with the possible exception of the Hoover Dam.'

Watten was designed to launch up to thirty-six V2 rockets a day. The site had a bomb proof railway station which would receive the rocket parts, which would then be taken into an assembly hall before being moved through 18 metre high revolving doors to the launch pads.

Watten had already been heavily bombed, and the Germans intended to convert it from a V2 launch plant to a liquid oxygen plant. It had been built by making a concrete plate 5 metres (16 feet) thick which weighed 37,000 tons. This was slowly raised by hydraulic jacks while walls were built beneath it. When Cheshire dropped his markers and the Tallboys began to fall, his navigator said to him: "God help the Germans."

It took 3 visits from the Dam Busters to finish off Watten. The first two raids were led by Cheshire. Wing Commander James Brian 'Willie' Tait – who took over 617 squadron when Cheshire was forcibly retired after fulfilling 100 missions - led the third.

Wizernes – V2 launch site –
Cheshire 22.6.44, Tait 17.7.44

Work began on Wizernes in November 1943. It was located in an old chalk quarry and roofed by a fifty–five thousand ton concrete dome. It was planned that rocket parts would be delivered to the site by rail where they would be safely assembled in the vast tunnel complex under and next to the dome. It was, in fact, planned to replace Watten.

Wizernes - V2 launch site

Although aware in November 1943 of the existence of this complex, the Allies were slow in targeting the bunker for air raids. Conventional bombing of the site began in March of 1944 with little effect, the dome being already complete. More than 3000 tons of bombs were dropped, damaging the nearby villages and upsetting the roads to the building site; but the dome remained intact. Work underground continued day and night, and as fast as the whip could drive the slaves, through 229 air–raid warnings.

Wizernes took two visits from the Dam Busters. On the second, decisive, attack, Lancasters dropped their bombs all around the dome. Three of the Tallboys exploded next to the tunnels, one burst just under the dome, and another burst in the mouth of one tunnel. The whole hillside collapsed, undermining the dome support, and covering up the two vertical rocket ways. Cheshire led the first raid, 'Willie' Tait the second.

Tait was later to be known in the RAF as 'Tirpitz Tate' when he led the attack on the German Battleship of that name (using a Tallboy bomb) which sunk her by blowing a hole in the seabed; into which she turned turtle.

Siracourt –V1 launch site – pas de Calais – Cheshire 25.6.44

The Siracourt bunker was for launching the V1 flying bomb. It is about 215 metres (705 ft) long, 36 metres (118 ft) wide and 10 metres (33 ft) high. About 55,000 cubic metres of steel–reinforced concrete were used in its construction. The roof had been built flat on the ground and then the area beneath it was excavated. When 617 Squadron hit it, about 90 per cent of the concrete had been completed, although the excavation of the interior had only just begun. Again, Siracourt had been bombed endlessly already before 617 Squadron arrived.

Siracourt - V1 launch site - pas de Calais

Cheshire was flying an American Mustang for this exercise. His Mosquitoes had been taken from him, and his American friends had obligingly – and, as usual, with astonishing efficiency – sent him a Mustang. It arrived, boxed up, on the day of the mission. Flying the Mustang posed a number of problems for Cheshire, as he had not flown a single–seat aircraft since his training days. His biggest issue was working out a course to the target. He had never flown without a navigator, and now he found himself in the position of having to ask for help. He asked the squadron's navigators to help him work out a course, while his ground crew put together the Mustang. His ground crew finished the job by late afternoon, some two hours after the bomber force had taken off. With no time for a test flight, off he went to chase down the Lancasters. The machine worked beautifully, with Cheshire arriving over the target just as the high illumination flares were ready to be dropped. He marked the target, and the Lancasters landed three Tallboys on it, destroying it utterly.

Mimoyecques – V3 – Cheshire 6.7.44

Mimoyecques was the V3 site. In some ways this was the most disturbing bunker of all; its repercussions going well beyond its destruction.

The complex consisted of a network of tunnels dug under a chalk hill, linked to five sloping 130 metre long shafts, each containing five gun barrels, all targeted on London. These twenty–five guns were by far the biggest in the world. They were designed to fire six hundred shells an hour, each containing 40 lbs of high explosive, into the British capital. One shell every six seconds, day and night. Endlessly. Winston Churchill later commented that this would have constituted "the most devastating attack of all."

Mimoyecques – V3 launch site

The reason why the allies had little inkling what the site was for was because it was reckoned so important by the Nazis that ninety percent of the workforce were German, with just 500 slave labourers to do the heaviest work. The firings of the guns had been delayed by design problems in the shells − but it had originally been planned that it be partly operational the month before D−Day and fully operational by October 1944.

The July the 6th attacks came in two waves. First, 100 planes carpet bombed the area; with little effect. Secondly came Cheshire and 617 Squadron. They dropped 16 Tallboys and destroyed enough of the underground passages to make the site useless.

The implications and repercussions of this site did not end with the Tallboys that caused it to be abandoned. Although the RAF had made the site unusable; there was no way of knowing that this was the case. Therefore the bombing continued. This included the USAAF's Operation Aphrodite, which took place from Norfolk. Two aircraft at a time set off, one packed with explosive, the other, the mother ship, steering it by radio remote control. The two man crew of the lead ship − the one packed with explosive − would bail out over England when the second plane had satisfactorily assumed control.

The crews were all volunteers; one of whom was Joseph Patrick Kennedy Jr. The explosives in his plane detonated prematurely, over Suffolk, and he and his crewmate Lt Wilford John Willy (who had designed the weapon system) were vaporised. Thus died Kennedy, a man who would probably have become a President of the United States, as his younger brother, John, would be.

And Mimoyecques has another tale to tell. When the site was captured (by Canadian troops) the British surveyed it and concluded that further action should be taken to make this gun pointing at the heart of their country inoperable. They didn't bother asking for anybody's permission to do this. As Churchill said: 'It would be intolerable if the French insisted on maintaining installations directly menacing our safety after we have shed so much blood in the liberation of their country.'

British troops filled the shafts with explosives and blew them up. This, it is said, infuriated the man Britain had raised to power, Charles de Gaulle. He considered it a violation of France's national sovereignty.

Mimoyecques is still there, a museum and a tomb; the last resting place for hundreds of labourers who were killed and entombed in the attack.

The defence of London

The Doodlebugs (V1s)

Even as the 'super–bunkers' were being dealt with, V1s from the 'light' launching sites were raining down on London. They were promptly christened 'Doodlebugs'. The motor of the flying–bomb was manually set to cut–out after the missile had flown for a pre–arranged distance, then it fell to earth, gliding in at an angle. This meant that when the explosion came, most of it was channelled outwards, rather than the downward explosion of a conventional bomb. The initial blast caused a vacuum, which was then followed by a counter–blast as the air came back. The blast stretched an average of 400 yards (a diameter of half a mile) and, in some cases – as was the case of the Lewisham Market bomb (which killed 56 people and injured 99 more) – as far as 600 yards. In the inner London suburbs, where terrace houses were packed together, a V1 could totally flatten up to twenty houses.

Beyond the zone of total destruction, roofs were ripped off and windows sucked out. Further out still, tiles were blown from roofs and windows smashed. The bomb was enormously destructive to property, which would lead to large sections of London being demolished after the war. It would have killed more people if the engine hadn't cut out when it dived, so that its final approach was in ominous silence. That gave those on the ground notice that in a few heartbeats they should expect to be torn limb from limb. They had 12, maybe 15, seconds to seek shelter; or crouch down, curl up, run or pray.

It should be noted that the warning silence was a design defect, not a humanitarian feature.

Tim Pile

The man in charge of the ground defences against the flying bomb was General Sir Frederick Pile, whom I mentioned briefly when I wrote about Fighter Command. In common with many of the British commanders (such as 'Stuffy' Downing, 'Straffer'

Gort and many others), he was more commonly known by his nickname; 'Tim'. He had picked up the soubriquet back in 1905, when he was based in South Africa. When his commanding officer's wife (Lady Crozier) asked him what his first names were, he had replied "Frederick Alfred". "Nonsense," she contradicted, "it's Tim from now on." And so it would be.

Frederick Alfred 'Tim' Pile

Tim Pile was a regular army man, who, like many of his breed, rode to hounds – he hunted with the Whaddon. He was nearly 60 years old when the V1 attacks started. Although an army man, Tim reported in the war to the RAF – initially to Stuffy Dowding; who he rated as the most outstanding airman of all (with the caveat that he was impossible to shut up).

Pile was based next door to Dowding's Fighter Command's headquarters, at Uxbridge. Much of his military career had been in tank design. He says that between 1928 and 1932 Britain was ahead of the world in the field; some of the designs at that time being better than the tanks with which Britain entered the war. The problem, of course, was money. The huge amounts that Britain pumped into the pre–war air force had caused cost cutting in other areas. His book 'Ack–Ack' is a wonderful work (like many of the finest books about the war long, of course, out of print). Ack–Ack is an abbreviation for anti–aircraft guns.

Pile is often mentioned in the war–time memoirs of the Allied high commanders. He is always recalled with affection as well as respect. He'd quaked under bombs himself in the London blitz, when his and his wife Hester's flat had been straddled by 500lb bombs: 'Never had I believed a building could sway so much without coming apart.'

He was appointed to head up air defence two years before war broke out and stayed in post until the end of hostilities –

being, in fact, the only British general to retain the same command throughout the war. He took control of Ack–Ack defences just as money started to become available. He had a lot of work to do after Dunkirk; the conditions at many of his sites being primitive,

Maunsell forts

without proper roads, electricity, buildings or water. At the height of his work, he was in charge of 87,000 men and women, including radar operators, gunners and ground staff and outposts on cliffs, around towns and cities; even in the sea – the Maunsell forts – in estuaries such as the Thames. For all of his elevated status, his wife, Hester, worked as a volunteer in the canteen at Euston Station. Churchill's youngest daughter, Mary, worked at one of Pile's Ack–Ack sites.

He was often in conferences with Churchill – and admired him greatly, especially at the darkest time:

'When things looked terribly grim and when everyone had related a most depressing account of their doings one could see a slight smile on his face, and then he would produce one of his classic remarks.'

Like others, he admired Churchill's openness:

'When you were at Chequers you could say what you thought, and it was never taken amiss. Not by Churchill, that is.'

Churchill himself visited the anti–aircraft gun sites; on one occasion, in October 1940, he invited Pile back, at half past four in the morning, to Number 10 for Bovril (Churchill rolled his pronunciation of the 'o') and sardines.

Tim Pile had lunch with Churchill and his entourage in October 1943 to discuss the V weapons. Characteristically, 'Prof' Frederick Lindemann pooh–poohed the idea of the rockets.

'Lindemann had an unfortunate manner when arguing; on more than one occasion he appeared to suggest that the papers... had been falsified.'

Tim Pile was not the first to note that Lindemann would use dirty tactics – including accusations of lying – to get his way. Luckily Churchill was quite capable of over-ruling his scientific adviser – and did so when evidence suggested the approach of the V1 attack. Well before the attacks started, he successfully persuaded America to put Britain at the top of their production list for their newly built SCR–584 radar sets and proximity–fused shells. The SCR–584 was a fire–control radar, leap frogging on the invention of the magnetron but also with an analogue gun–laying computer. It was developed by the recently–founded MIT Radiation Laboratory, in America. I will talk more about the proximity fuse in a moment. The shooting down of the V1s by Pile's guns was to owe a great deal to these American devices.

Guns against the Doodlebugs

The first V1 bomb to land in London hit a railway bridge at Bethnal Green, blocking all lines from Liverpool Street (serving East Anglia). To shoot these bombs down, Pile initially deployed almost 1000 anti–aircraft guns in a belt stretching to the south of London (from Maidstone to East Grinstead). The results were not that great: the guns hit around one in eight of the V1s they aimed at. The Doodlebugs were fast – and hard to lock onto. Then it was decided to move the entire Ack–Ack stock to the coast itself, from Dover to Beachy Head, so as to have a clear field of fire over the sea. The aircraft would now mainly intercept behind the guns.

The arrival of American SCR–584 fire control radar and American anti–aircraft batteries helped matters. The American batteries destroyed over 100 flying bombs. The arrival of large stocks of the proximity fuse, though, was a game changer for Pile's Anti–aircraft Command.

The proximity fuse

The proximity fuse had been developed at around the same time in both Germany, Britain and America. The British proximity fuse was included in the free gift of secrets that the Tizard mission gave to the Americans; but the British input does not seem to have made much, if any, difference to the American work. The winning fuse was very much the work of Mr. Merle Tuve and 'born in the USA'. The fuse was fitted into the anti–aircraft shells, sensed the target (in this case the V1) when it got within range of it, then blew up. It did not need to make contact with the Doodlebug.

The proximity fuse, along with the SCR–584 tracking radar, upped the kill rate of the anti–aircraft guns from one in 8 to over half and sometimes more. In one week towards the end of the first attack of the V1 bombs, only 4 of the 96 missiles released by the enemy reached London.

England was targeted by two waves of flying bomb attacks. When the flying bomb sites in Northern France were over run (in late August 1944), attacks began from V1 sites in Holland – and some from V1s launched from aircraft over the channel.

The RAF & USAAF

But it was not only Tim Pile's guns which helped to defeat the flying bombs. The Allied air forces shot down roughly the same number as the guns. Between June 1944 and March 1945, 3,957 V1s were claimed to have been destroyed. 1,979 of them fell to fighter aircraft, 1,866 to Ack–Ack guns and 232 to balloons.

The shooting down of V1s by aircraft was a difficult and dangerous procedure. If the aircraft got too near, it was quite possible it would blow itself up with the missile.

The most successful fighter was the Hawker Tempest (also manufactured in the Intelligence Zone, at Langley) with 638 confirmed kills, then the Mosquito with 428. The Spitfire came third with 303 and the American Mustang fourth with 232; although those numbers partly reflect on the number of squadrons of each types dedicated to the task rather than 'hits per aircraft'. Partly, as ever, it was 'down to the man'. One Hawker Tempest pilot, Squadron Leader Joseph Berry D.F.C. with 2 bars, was credited with downing 59 V1s, including 7 that he destroyed in one night. He was shot down and killed later in the war.

The Gloster Meteor, the only Allied jet fighter to fly in combat during the war, downed 13 V1s.

The V2 rockets

At about the same time as the second attack of the V1s began, the V2 rockets began to land on London. These carried about a ton of explosives. Unlike the drone–silence–explosion of the Doodlebugs, they gave no warning whatsoever. They, the first ballistic missiles, were launched from moveable continental launch sites; from which they powered 60 miles into the sky and re–entered the atmosphere above their target. A V2 falling in bare earth blows a crater 20 metres (65 feet) wide and 8 metres (25 feet) deep, ejecting approximately 3,000 tons of material.

Once they had left the earth, there was no protection against the V2 rocket. Reaching five times the speed of sound, it was far too fast to be intercepted by aircraft. Nor could ground fire at that time hit it, except by a fluke. The only way to catch a V2 was to destroy its launcher; and the Allied air forces put in a lot of work to do so.

London

In the cold light of analysis, it can be (and has been) said, that the V weapons were a failure. The same expenditure of effort in other directions – principally more jet fighters and the development of anti–aircraft missiles – would have served the Nazis better. None of this, though, would have saved them from the immense ground armies that crushed them from east and west. But what of England – and, in particular, London?

London had been severely bombed in 1940, 1941 and 1943. In 1944 and 1945 it was given the dubious privilege of being made the target for the world's first attack of flying bombs and ballistic missiles.

About 10,000 V1s were launched against England, of which about 4,000 were shot down and about 2,400 hit London, killing around 6,000 people and injuring about three times as many. About 1,400 V2s were launched at England, of which around 500 hit London, killing around 2,700 people and injuring about 6,500 more. From all causes, bombs, Doodlebugs and rockets, almost 30,000 people died in London as a result of aerial attacks. More than 70,000 buildings were completely demolished in the capital, and another 1.7 million were damaged. Great swathes of dangerous buildings had to be bulldozed and replaced post–war.

The deaths and the material damages were not, of course, all of the story. Millions of people ebbed back and forth from the city in mass evacuations. Many of London's children spent the whole war separated from their families. For those who stayed, life changed completely – with bombs, air raid alerts and mass air raid shelters – many of them in the London underground stations.

A boy called Bill

A thousand of this, ten thousand of that. Statistics; endless piles of sand, each of countless grains, simply shapes. But each grain has a story and each is profound; for in it we see the reflections of many others, atoms of the greater tale. I want, then, to look at the London Blitz as seen through the eyes of a bright boy who was not quite three years old when war broke out.

Bill lived in London, south of the river Thames, passing his childhood in the suburbs of Sydenham and Penge. Not far off is Southwark, from which centuries earlier Chaucer's fictional Pilgrims clopped down Watling Street on their way to Canterbury, telling tall tales to each other as they rode along to shorten the road. This may seem irrelevant but it isn't; for these are the approaches from Kent, Dover and France into London. Precisely the same route that the Luftwaffe took from its many French bases to its favourite target. And exactly under the flight path of the bombs and missiles the Germans would fling at central London… especially if for some reason they were to fall a little short.

At the time war broke out, even though he was still a month shy of his third birthday, Bill was the oldest of three children. Many of his first memories are, unsurprisingly, of the massive attacks that came from the direction of sunrise – the south east. Six months into the war Bill, along with his mother and two siblings (his sister just four months old) was evacuated to the

Welsh countryside. But his mother, like so many others, missed London; so she brought them back home. Home was a small terraced house in Sydenham. It, like most houses of the time, was pretty basic. Gas lighting, no hot water, outside lavatory. Because his mum was finding it hard to cope with three infants, Bill would be packed off from time to time by bus to his granny in nearby Penge. Bill adored his gran – and she adored him too. She had taught him to read at a very early age, and made the strange prediction, when he was just two weeks old, that 'this child is going to be world–famous'.

He remembers clearly the Battle of Britain:

'Everyone standing in the street, looking up to a sky completely filled with formations of German bombers. Among them were the white trails of our fighter planes. Everyone was cheering – it was great to be British.'

Bill's dad got a job up-country, building hangers for the RAF; so June 1941 saw another move for the family, to Nottingham. Bill was at school by now (having started at three and a half). The poor lad didn't take easily to his new school 'up north' where he was teased – and smacked by his teacher – because of his accent.

'I did what any five year old would do and often played truant with friends, hiding away in an old disused church, making bonfires to keep warm.'

Bill was sent back to London, to live with his granny in her two bedroomed terrace house in Penge. In the small garden was an air raid shelter (shared by several families). These shelters had been put up pre–war, by the government, who saw clearly which way the wind was blowing.

It was at Penge, in January 1943, that Bill lived through a fighter–bomber attack on a nearby school in which a Luftwaffe pilot, Hauptmann Heinz Schumann, killed 32 pupils and six staff. Sixty others were injured. Twelve year old Molly Linn had to have both her legs amputated. Schumann didn't just bomb the school, he machine–gunned it and the surrounding streets too:

'A German fighter–bomber roared towards us between the roof–tops, machine gunning the length of the road.'

Terrified, Bill ran for his gran's, who tried to shield him as they ran towards the air–raid shelter... 'but the plane returned before we could get there, and through the skylight window we saw it tearing past, very low... after the all–clear we went up and down the street collecting bullets, digging them out of the walls.'

Schumann was shot down and killed several months later.

Then Bill's mum and younger siblings (3 of them by now) came back to London and the lad joined them. He remembers a warning film about anti–personnel butterfly bombs. Attractive little things that should be ignored. If you picked them up, they blew you apart. A seven year old in South London needed to be aware of these things.

Butterfly bomb

Bill lived through the 'Baby–Blitz' of 1944 when Hitler sent the Luftwaffe against London in retaliation for the attacks on Berlin:

'During the frequent air–raids, trucks with pom–pom guns went up and down the road, firing shells at German planes ...I remember one night when we had no time to get to the shelter. Mum threw herself over us children, all sleeping in one bed, as she heard the bombs fall. I suddenly realised that she really cared for us.'

Death was too close, at that time, for even mothers to wear their hearts on their sleeves.

The Doodlebugs – the V1s – started to arrive in 1944:

'The few seconds of silence seemed to last for ever. Then a tremendous explosion made the ground shake. Dust and leaves and tree branches, were blown into the shelter. When the all–clear sounded we reappeared to a very different back garden, with bushes and trees smashed, debris everywhere. Looking back at our house, we saw our huge French windows lying in the garden. The flying bomb had glided down two streets away, flattening about twenty houses.

Inside, every piece of furniture we had had been flung to the walls nearest the explosion.'

When the rest of his family evacuated back to Nottinghamshire. Bill stayed with his grandparents. Another V1 fell;

'We rummaged through the rubble, picking up toys and books until we were chased off by air–raid personnel. It was only the next day at school that the harsh truth hit us; two girls in our class had been killed by that bomb.'

There were to be a dozen V1s in the immediate area, as well as one V2. Unknown to Bill, he was living near the epicentre of the attacks. The reason why many of these missiles did not hit central London was because SIS/MI6 fed back information via

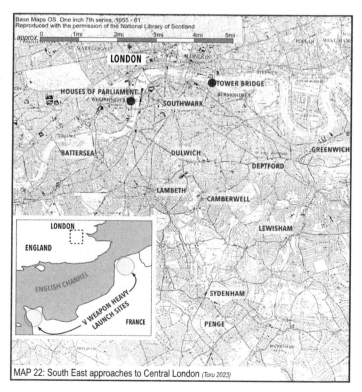

MAP 22: South East approaches to Central London *(Toru 2023)*

double agents which led the Germans to believe that their bombs and rockets were landing to the north of the capital. This led them to aim further south. Because of this, the epicentre of the damage was at Dulwich, four miles south of their target (which was Tower Bridge, which was hit once). Good news for central London – not quite so good for Dulwich, or nearby areas such as Penge and Sydenham.

Churchill toured the bombed area and made a speech; which impressed Bill. He was equally impressed by the chewing gum that American servicemen – everywhere in London as D–Day approached – handed out. His aunt Dorothy went out with some of them to dances and Bill would tag along. He'd watch them jitterbug; but it was the dance bands that he really loved.

The family returned to London and gradually Bill's life returned to – or at least became – normal.

I have spoken of a few children of the famous; the daughters of the Prime Minister, the son of a President and another who might well have been President himself. They show how the highest in the west were risking their all – their future – to win this war. Because of their parents, their offspring are automatically of interest. I mean those offspring no disrespect when I point out that they, the children of the elite, had history thrust upon them. Bill Perks wasn't one of them. His father was a bricklayer, his family was poor, sometimes hungry, especially in winter, when bricks couldn't be laid. Bill's mother and he and his siblings would do what they could to supplement the family income; once peeling sacks of onions for a bottling factory (their hands turned yellow and no one would come near them after a few weeks). The way his family moved about while he more or less stayed put is uncommon. Few children have recorded their war in such poignant detail. One sentence in particular moves me deeply and I will repeat it:

'Mum threw herself over us children, all sleeping in one bed, as she heard the bombs fall. I suddenly realised that she really cared for us.'

The wounds of war are not always visible, but they are there; and they are often lifelong. We poor grains of sand.

Bill himself would in time join the RAF, serving in the British occupation forces in Germany. It was there that he decided that his name, Perks, was not very exciting, so he borrowed one from a pal of his and became Bill Wyman. He was to join four other lads – all a bit younger – in a group called The Rolling Stones. Gran had been right. He, along with Jagger, Richards, Watts and Jones – all but one of them from South London – would become 'the greatest rock and roll band in the world'; and, with other English groups, explode out of the greyness of post war Britain. The Stones, Beatles, Who, Faces, Kinks and the rest would do much more than most politicians and soldiers to shape the modern world. Iron curtains would fall to their backbeat. These were the aristocracy of rock – the Sultans of Swing. Controversial, inspiring, imaginative, bawdy, humorous, hypnotic; above all, dynamic and alive; they would brighten the world. Fitting English heirs, perhaps, to Chaucer (and indeed Shakespeare) at Southwark.

History is an odd thing. If you follow its roots and branches, it will lead you everywhere. That – and the fact that it is pretty much all that we have to go on to understand ourselves – is what makes it interesting.

But I am leaping into the future. What of sleepy London town?

The guided missile attacks were only the last in a series of wounds that that old, old, city took in six years of war. Tens of thousands of her citizens were dead, tens of thousands more were physically or mentally maimed or scarred. What would be Britannia's reaction? What could Nazi Germany expect in return from her oldest enemy? Would the cycle of revenge and retribution continue? Could it ever be broken?

Fortunately for Germany, Europe and the world, Britain's leader, Winston Spencer Churchill had a wide world–view – his would be the moderating – and sometimes lonely – voice which would shape the future of Europe.

7: **Rites of passage**

Setting France ablaze

The D-Day landings of the 6th of June 1944 took place along a fifty mile stretch of coast. They were made into the teeth of strong, elaborate and inter-locked fixed defences, fortified and manned by the best army in the world. The attacks were on and behind five beachheads, two British, two American and one Canadian. One hundred and fifty five thousand American, British and Canadian troops landed on the first day. About a tenth went in by air, the rest from the sea. The latter were shipped in 7,000 vessels (80% of them British).

This gigantic assault (Operation Overlord) was the most complex military operation the world has ever seen. Its success was far from certain. As part of his planning, Eisenhower had prepared a statement to broadcast should it fail:

'Our landings in the Cherbourg-Havre area have failed to gain a satisfactory foothold and I have withdrawn the troops. My decision to attack at this time and place was based on the best information available. The troops, the air and the navy did all that bravery and devotion to duty could do. If any blame or fault attaches to the attempt it is mine alone.'

I have written about the clashes between the Allied and Axis armies in Normandy in a previous book (*A Normandy Tapestry*). For more about the critical part Bletchley Park played in the landings, I recommend *Bletchley Park and D-Day* by David Kenyon. What has received less coverage than the battles between the regular armies are the great French inland uprisings whose purpose was to stop the Germans from, in Hitler's words, 'throwing the enemy into the sea'. Those uprisings were orchestrated and supplied from Britain.

As I wrote in my chapter about SOE, guerrilla warfare was not a new concept for the British army. They had been worn down by it during the Boer War and defeated by it in 'the

216

Troubles' in Ireland. Spanish guerrillas had helped them win the Peninsular War and kick Napoleon out of Spain. One of Napoleon's officers recorded what it was like to be on the receiving end of the hit-and-run tactics:

'Wherever we arrived, they disappeared, whenever we left, they arrived — they were everywhere and nowhere, they had no tangible centre which could be attacked.'

In Normandy, too, the Allied troops were to benefit from civilian help; only this time the guerrillas would be French and the enemy Hitler.

By 1944 most of Europe had been under Nazi occupation for four years. SIS and SOE spies and saboteurs had been operating there for three years. The Americans, too, had set up their own sabotage organisation – the OSS.

The resistance fighters in France were sick of their terrifying war in the shadows; many of them wanted nothing more than to tackle their enemies head-on – win or lose, once and for all. After D-Day, their controllers in Britain gave them the go-ahead to wage open warfare. Among their most experienced warriors were Virginia Hall and Benjamin Cowburn.

Virginia Hall and Benjamin Cowburn

Hall and Cowburn had been sent to France by SOE back in 1941. They had arrived within three days of each other, though in different places. In the years that followed, they were to meet often and develop the highest regard for each other.

Virginia Hall's role was more organisational than hands-on. It could hardly have been otherwise, as one of her legs was made of wood below the knee. Virginia was an American, of wealthy New England stock; well educated (she spoke both French and German), intelligent and a Europhile. A beautiful blue-stocking with tom-boyish ways, she worked before the war in the American diplomatic services in Europe. She was ferociously intelligent (though her sex debarred her from the promotions she deserved). She lost her left leg in a hunting accident in Turkey. American surgeons in Istanbul sawed it off just below the knee on Christmas Day, 1933. She christened her replacement wooden leg 'Cuthbert'.

Virginia Hall

By virtue of her job (and her brains) Virginia was acutely aware of what was happening in Europe. When war broke out she volunteered to drive ambulances for the French army, escaping to Spain when France was defeated. There she met an agent in the British secret services called George Bellows. Mr Bellows was very interested in the glamorous and multi-lingual lady who was determined – against all the odds – to fight for Britain to free France. He told Virginia the name of his boss in London and strongly recommended that she contacted him when she got there. The boss (Nicolas Bodington: his wife and mother were both American), was glad indeed to meet Virginia. Bodington worked for the Special Operations Executive – SOE. With her fluency in French and German, her American citizenship and her intelligence and drive, he saw that Virginia could be very useful to British intelligence. He recruited her as the first female agent in SOE's 'F' (France) section.

After training, Virginia returned to France (via Spain). Working undercover for SOE, she got a job as a journalist for an American newspaper in Vichy. She didn't stay in Vichy long. In those first days she had no wireless operator; indeed no wireless; so she moved to Lyon, near the border with Switzerland – from where she could get in touch with England.

Back in those first months of the war and as the reality of defeat sunk in (more than a million French servicemen were held as prisoners in Germany) – French resistance began to coalesce. Both the Nazis and the collaborationist French government at Vichy were swift to crack down on such dissidents, with arrests, torture and imprisonments of anyone who showed opposition to German rule. SOE's fledgling organisation was hit hard. Within a month of her arrival, SOE in

France was left with, in the later words of SOE's historian; 'Little else in the field except Miss Virginia Hall.'

It was fortunate, then, that Hall was such a valuable and proactive agent. From the very start, she searched out those who were prepared to resist the Nazis and, crucially for their survival, set up an infrastructure to support them. Her key role in the resistance was to be the linchpin between the various *reseaux* (networks); organising, managing and overseeing contacts between them and London. This included finding and equipping 'safe houses', where the agents could work, live and hide when necessary. Virginia had begun the process by persuading the sisters of a nunnery to allow her to use part of their convent. Then she cultivated a new contact - Germaine Guerin – who was the part-owner of one of Lyon's most successful brothels. They were to become great friends. Guerin was 'a thirty-seven-year-old burning brunette with animal sexual magnetism.'

Germaine Guerin was a fiercely patriotic woman, who allowed Virginia Hall to take over part of her brothel and three flats. These premises would be used by agents going to ground when the heat became too much; and as staging posts for shot-down Allied airmen on their way to Spain. They were also places to stay for visiting agents from other parts of France, such as her colleague, Benjamin Cowburn.

Cowburn travelled largely in France 'on business.' His business was destruction. A Lancastrian who had been brought up in Paris, he had worked before the war in the oil industry. For SOE, he targeted oil refineries, engine works and electricity pylons (which he had been trained to wreck at Brickendonbury). When in Lyon, he was fed and housed by Virginia Hall.

Cowburn was, like Hall, one of the very few of the first wave of SOE agents to escape capture. That was because he was very, very careful. He was to become SOE's longest serving agent in France – lasting four years and through four passages back and forth to England. One of his jobs was training and leading French resistance workers (quite a few of whom were picked up by RAF Lysander aircraft and taken to England for specialist training). He came close to being discovered on a number of occasions. Once, when he was on his bike, going about his business (which on this occasion was blowing up railway lines with the plastic explosives he had stashed in his bag), he was pulled over:

'Two Feldgendarmes (German military police) popped out of a bush, one of them raising the stick with the red disc on the end which they used as a stop signal. I jammed the brakes on so hard that the wheels locked and skidded as I hopped off ready for trouble, but the stick was lowered, the helmets nodded and the two stood aside and waved me along …they were merely testing the brakes of all bicycles. Good for them!'

Cowburn, writing in 1960, thoroughly approved; telling his readers that the Feldgendarmes were: 'as strict about bicycles with no rear light as the present road-police ought to be.' Disapproving of young tearaways is not new; but tut-tutting at them is a bit strong, perhaps, from someone whose job was blowing-up trains.

The Lancastrian knew when to speak plainly and when to keep his thoughts to himself; and he knew the risks he ran:

'Security in France was nil, and 95 percent of the people arrested were caught simply because their friends had been incapable of keeping their mouths shut.'

Cowburn was often in Lyon. He said of Virginia Hall:

'If you sit in (her) kitchen long enough you will see most people pass through with one sort of trouble or another which (she) promptly deals with.'

Ben Cowburn speaks movingly of the terror and strain suffered by the undercover warriors, most of whom were operating from home: 'The comfortable home into which the Gestapo might burst any hour, the atmosphere of the invisible web being spun.'

All agents were scared; many of them suffered from insomnia. Many chain-smoked or drank. Danger was ever present and often fatal.

As the war went on, Virginia Hall's position became more and more dangerous. As members of her group were taken, she struck back. She organised a raid on a French prison which 'sprung' twelve resistants. In a striking parallel with the head of the *Alliance* spy network, Marie Fourcade, she was 'licensed to kill' traitors in her networks and arranged that it was done.

Sonia Purnell, in her book *A woman of no importance; the untold story of Virginia Hall* tells of the risks Hall took:

'The perennial shortage of safe houses caused most if not all operators in the Free Zone to end up at Virginia's apartment… indeed there were so many transmitting from her home that the hallway started to resemble a bird's nest of different aerials some up to seventy feet long tacked back and forth across the walls. Cowburn considered this arrangement extremely insecure for her.'

Virginia arranged supply drops from England of arms and explosives for attacks on factories and German transport. At the same time she continued her work in feeding and sheltering British airmen and organising their onward escape. The net gradually closed around her, but still she stayed. While the Vichy Zone was still unoccupied, sympathetic contacts in the French police allowed her at least some protection there; but the Gestapo knew where she was and what she was up to. When German troops marched into the Vichy Zone in November 1942, she was at the top of Klaus Barbie's list for arrest. Barbie, as head of the Gestapo in Lyon, would earn there the woeful title of 'the Butcher of Lyon'. Virginia Hall did not wait to meet him, but took one of the escape lines across the Pyrenees into Spain. Trekking across the mountains with a wooden leg wasn't easy. On the first night in the mountains she radioed back to England:

'Cuthbert is being tiresome but I can cope.'

The duty officer who took the message did not understand the intricacies of Virginia Hall's life and replied:

'If Cuthbert is tiresome, eliminate him.'

Back in London, Virginia went to Queen Mary's Hospital at Roehampton to have some new straps made for Cuthbert. Then she was sent to Thame Park in Buckinghamshire to learn how to code, send and receive radio messages. In the words of Sonia Purnell, Hall:

'almost alone had laid the foundations of discipline and hope for the great resistance battles to come.'

Hall was well known and, of course, easily recognisable because of her limp. SOE refused to send her back to France, considering that to do so would be tantamount to signing her death warrant. They wanted her to work in Spain instead. That was not at all to Virginia's taste. The impasse was broken when she was head-hunted by a new American sabotage service, the Office of Strategic Studies (OSS).

The OSS

The OSS was run by 'Wild Bill' Donovan (whom we met earlier, when he was having doubts about blowing up duck ponds at the SOE weapons factory at Aston House). Donovan modelled his OSS on SOE and the SIS. It was a bit of a revolution for America. In 1929, their Secretary of State for war had stated that 'gentlemen don't read each other's mail'. When the penny dropped in the USA that the Nazis were not gentlemen, they set up OSS.

Until its formation, the American intelligence services were disparate and had little inter-service co-ordination. It was Churchill's representative in Canada, Sir William Stephenson, who suggested to Donovan that America needed a new service to fill the gap. Wild Bill put forward a plan and President Roosevelt agreed (over the protests of the head of the FBI, J. Edgar Hoover) and put him in charge. Ian Fleming would travel to America on several occasions to help advise on the formation and procedures of OSS (which, after the war, would become the CIA). OSS could have had no better teacher in the black arts of British intelligence than the author of James Bond.

Virginia Hall was to be OSS's first female agent. She returned to occupied France in March 1944, when she was landed by night from a Royal Navy gun boat onto a secluded beach on the coast of Brittany. She had gone through the full SOE treatment of disguise (including having her teeth ground down). In Virginia's absence, the full force of Nazi fury had fallen on resistance networks in the now German-occupied area of Vichy France. For his part, Ben Cowburn was neither surprised by, nor even critical of, his opponents' actions. In his view: 'The Germans had every right to treat us as spies and put us to death.'

And it is true that Britain executed any captured German spy who they could not 'turn' to work for them. There was, however, a profound difference in what happened to the agents on opposite sides of the English Channel between their capture and execution.

In mainland Europe, the Gestapo were savage and ruthless. In the south of France, many captured resistance agents ended up in Lyon jail, delivered to the tender mercies of Klaus Barbie, who tortured and killed children and adults alike. He was directly responsible for thousands of murders, carrying out many of them with his own hands. He especially enjoyed torturing women. Lise Lesevre was arrested in 1944 and delivered to Barbie, who tortured her for nine days, beating her, nearly drowning her in a bathtub and finally breaking one of her vertebrae with a spiked ball.

Another woman, Ennat Leger, said that Barbie:

'Had the eyes of a monster. He was savage. My God, he was savage! It was unimaginable. He broke my teeth, he pulled my hair back. He put a bottle in my mouth and pushed it until the lips split from the pressure.'

It was Barbie who tortured the great French resistance leader, Jean Moulin, the man who had managed to pull all of the French resistance movements – including the Communists – into one group. Barbie broke his fingers and wrists in a door, ripped out his finger nails and beat him into a coma. He died soon afterwards. When Barbie killed him, France lost, perhaps, its greatest leader.

Barbie was, as I've previously mentioned, particularly interested in meeting Virginia Hall.

Virginia Hall, Benjamin Cowburn, Jeannie Rousseau, Jean Moulin, Marie-Madeleine Fourcade, Navarre, the Curies, Michel Hollard and countless others were not fighting the Nazis for obscure doctrinal points. They were fighting the system that gave the power of life, death, enslavement, rape and torture to Barbie, Heydrich and their like. While there is no conclusive proof that gods exist, devils certainly do. If you wish to know their form, look in the mirror.

Open French resistance begins

When she arrived back in France just before D-Day, Virginia Hall's brief was to coordinate and supply existing French resistance *reseaux* and set up new ones. Back to her old job, in fact. The difference was that these networks, which would be armed from England, were expected to rise and fight openly; to take pressure off the Normandy landings. Things were getting more and more bloody in France as resistance to the Germans grew. Field Marshal Gerd von Rundstedt, the German commander in chief in France spoke of general revolt. The lives of his troops were 'seriously menaced through shootings and bombings.'

Just a couple of days after Virginia Hall landed, the first full French resistance rising was finally crushed. It was at Gleiers and had been going on for two months. Originally it had been opposed by French forces – Vichy versus the resistance; but the Germans, finding the work was not being done properly, moved their own troops in and finished the guerrillas off. One hundred and fifty of the French resisters died in this battle – a sign of things to come.

Vichy not only put their own regular forces against their fellow countrymen, they recruited a force of French men – the Milice – to crush them. This force, of about 35,000, were renowned for their cruelty – and their efficiency. While a Frenchman – or woman – might be able to pull a fast one on the German forces (who were under instructions to be 'friendly'), they were less likely to get away with it against the Milice. Those whose French was good but whose accent was not perfect – like many of the SOE and OSS agents, ran a great risk from this Nazi-French force.

Miliciens

Shortly after arriving back in France, Virginia Hall moved base. She did so after seeing the severed heads of four anti-Vichy villagers which had been left by the side of the road as a warning to others. The Milice, Gestapo and regular German troops were taking their revenge with an increasing barbarity that echoed perfectly what Napoleonic troops had done to the Spanish guerrillas in the Peninsular War. So does history repeat itself.

When D-Day came, it was followed to the minute by a wave of sabotage across France which, co-ordinated with the Allied bombing raids, were designed to stop German reinforcements reaching the five beach heads in the Cotentin Peninsula, in Normandy.

The risings

Virginia Hall had moved to central France – the department of Nievre – to organise the fractured, poorly led and under-supplied resistance there. Working from *The Partisan Leader's Handbook*, Colin Gubbins' 29 page booklet about how to wage irregular warfare (which I have spoken about in my chapter about SOE), Hall instructed her resistance groups to: 'Shoot, burn, destroy, leave.'

She arranged weapon supply drops. Informers were shot, their bodies dumped in prominent places with notes left on them. While 'her' troops were cutting telephone lines, changing road signs and using SOE 'funnies' such as explosives disguised as horse or cow droppings, Hall was cycling (with her wooden leg) across the area, cajoling, instructing, arranging supplies. Under her direction, and acting from instructions from London and local knowledge, the resistance groups cut 16 railway lines, derailed trains and blew up a bridge across the Loire (this, like the Saumur bridge that Cheshire had destroyed with his Tallboys, was a key means for the Panzer divisions to reach Normandy).

Her friend, Ben Cowburn, was busy with similar work. He pulled off a spectacular attack on the railway yards at Troyes, the largest marshalling yards in eastern France; using lessons taught by SOE's sabotage schools in Hertfordshire. He struck at the turntable at the heart of the yards, destroying some locomotives and leaving others stranded. The turntable casting was a key piece of precision engineering which could not be replaced in time to allow trains to bring supplies to the hard-pressed German divisions.

As well as the SOE and OSS, significant sections of Britain's elite Special Air Services(SAS) were operating behind German lines. On top of that there were Jedburgh units, three men military sections (theoretically 1 British, 1 American and 1 French officer in each) who helped to co-ordinate and train the tidal wave (tens of thousands) of French civilian volunteers who joined the resistance. Large-scale supply drops came from the air. The resistance could even call down RAF and USAAF strike aircraft. The Allies put in a lot of effort to keep the Germans from reinforcing the Normandy landing beaches.

Some of the most militarily important of the resistance attacks were those launched against the Das Reich Panzer division while it was moving from the south of France to Normandy to repulse the landings. The 450 mile journey took the armoured division five weeks; and they arrived too late to 'push the enemy into the sea'. This joint action between the Allied air forces and the resistance resulted in savage reprisals by the German troops; the most vicious of them the mass-murder at, and destruction of, the village of Oradour-sur-Glane. I describe that atrocity in Appendix A, at the end of this chapter.

The disruption to the south of the invasion beaches was but one part of the French resistance uprising. In Brittany, to the west of Normandy, an even more active mini-war was being fought; again to stop German forces from coming from their garrisons to contest the landings (the private war here was very nasty indeed, the Germans using Cossack troops as well as front-line German soldiers).

To the east, towards Germany, similar teams directed Allied bombers onto German pinch-points. Nicolas Boddington, Virginia Hall's recruiter from SOE, was one of many who parachuted into this area.

The scale, importance and bitterness of these 'mini-wars' are all but forgotten now. To get a taste of them, I can recommend *No cloak no dagger* by Benjamin Cowburn and *The next moon* by Andre Hue – who was in charge of a large part of the Breton uprisings.

Another agent who wrote a book on the subject (*Maquis*) was George Millar. We've met him already; fleeing from France on the *Madura* and later training at Brickendonbury. Millar, too, landed in France shortly before D-Day. He too took part in the uprising. Once he used his training when he had to kill a German soldier, shooting him twice as he had been taught:

'The dead man, lying in a grotesque sprawl, twitched from time to time and bled profusely. He was soon in a cloud of flies. They swarmed on his contorted face and his smooth head, investigating his mouth and nostrils, Midges were biting him and us... as we went on to the village, I was remembering how much I had enjoyed the pistol range at Warnborough Manor (an SOE training camp in Sussex), thudding two rounds into each target. No thought of flies then, or faces. Or a wedding ring on a dead finger.'

The liberation of the Department of the Haute Loire before the arrival of Allied troops was largely down to Virginia Hall and her organisational genius and energy. Had she been a man, there can be little or no doubt that she would, in time, have been made the first director of the CIA.

Churl

Charles de Gaulle was disliked and distrusted by many Allied leaders, including President Roosevelt. The feeling was mutual. An indication of the Frenchman's feelings for the USA can most easily be had from studying his broadcast on the BBC on the afternoon of D-Day (see appendix B). De Gaulle started by namechecking England as being 'the last bastion of Europe'. The rest of his broadcast was about the French resistance (fair enough) and the 'reborn strength and glory' of French troops and how they would, 'tomorrow', as they had for the last fifteen hundred years, win victory. Given that 73,000 American, 61,000 British, 21,000 Canadian and 177 French troops landed in France on D-day, de Gaulle appears to have been slightly confused about whose troops were most likely to win that victory. It was not the only questionable aspect of de Gaulle's speech. Although he said 'France' seven times, the words 'America', Canada' and 'Britain' seem to have slipped his mind.

This amnesia on the part of the French leader was not an isolated instance. He would, from the off, go to amazing lengths to try and minimise the fact that foreign troops had freed his country. The process began when he ordered British SOE agents out of France and tried to suppress knowledge of what they had achieved (the definitive book on the subject *SOE in France* was banned from France for fifty years).

Charles de Gaulle's churlishness did not stop there. At the start of this work I mentioned Sir Edward Spears, the British officer who was sent by Churchill with an aeroplane to evacuate the French general before he was arrested by his own countrymen. In order to save de Gaulle, Spears had had to leave his own wife, Mary Borden, an American who worked for a French ambulance unit, in France. Mary and Edward adored France; and Mary continued to work for de Gaulle's Free French as an ambulance driver in the Middle East throughout the war.

In June 1945, the French held a victory parade in Paris. De Gaulle had forbidden any British participation(!). However, vehicles from Mary's Anglo-French ambulance unit took part – Union Jacks and Tricolours side by side as usual. When de Gaulle heard wounded French soldiers cheering, "Voilà Spears! Vive Spears!" he ordered that the ambulance unit be closed down immediately and its British members repatriated. Mary commented:

'A pitiful business when a great man suddenly becomes small.'

I will leave my last word on the general to another American, the distinguished journalist Ben Lucien Burman who passed the war with the Free French. Here he is speaking about de Gaulle's rejection of Britain when the latter wanted to join the European Union:

'Despite all his talk of grandeur, De Gaulle was and is suffering from a terrible inferiority complex. De Gaulle was created by Britain, nourished by Britain, sanctified by Britain. Without Britain in the war de Gaulle as we know him today would never have existed; with British aid withdrawn de Gaulle would not have lasted ten minutes. For one of his haughty nature to be a dependent for so many years (living in exile in England) must have been desperate humiliation. What a joy at last to kick his patron in the teeth.'

As ever where America and 'England' were concerned, de Gaulle acted as a graceless churl. That was not a capital offence – nor, given who he was, even a surprise. It is, however, profoundly important in Anglo-French, and hence European, history. De Gaulle believed himself to *be* France; many Britons and Americans thought he was too. They were bewildered by his actions and, because of who he was, felt contempt not only for him but towards France herself. Ingratitude is common enough – but actions as base as Charles de Gaulle's from one in an office as high as his can have profound effects. His betrayal would (and still does) poison Anglo-French relations.

Blow, winter winds, blow. Thou are not as sharp as man's ingratitude.

The spoils of war

Patrick Job

Guerrilla warfare wasn't the only unorthodox tactic that the Allies used against the Nazis. Another, which could have (and indeed did) come from the imagination of Ian Fleming, was 30 Assault Unit. One of its main actors was called Patrick Dalzel-Job.

Job had been in the forefront of combat right from the very first days of the war. He had evacuated the civilian population of Narvik (5,000 people) by sea in the Norwegian campaign of 1940 and in later years commanded a naval unit which carried out hit-and-run attacks on German coastal traffic around the coast of Norway. His unit of Motor Torpedo Boats had been based at Lerwick, in the Shetland Islands, roughly half way between Scotland and Norway. He and his men would take these small craft 200 miles across the North Sea in all seasons, steering through the channels and islands surrounding the

Patrick Dalzei-Job, Bond?   Ian Fleming

Norwegian coast then hitting German convoys. If they were caught, they could expect to be shot, whether in uniform or not.

On one occasion Job spent several days sleeping in the open air on a frozen island; radioing back to base the position of German ships, while German aircraft searched for him. This was in late autumn. He landed at night carrying a cripplingly heavy (80 pound) rucksack and then set off in the dark to climb the 2,000 foot summit. Finding the rucksack too heavy, he ditched some food and his sleeping bag. After several hours he got to the top of the hill. When he tried to sleep, the cold woke him, so he trekked downhill. He had made three compass bearings at the spot where he had left his sleeping bag and found it, in the dark, on his first attempt. That, to anyone who has ever worked with maps, compass, hills, bogs, cold, fatigue and darkness is astonishing.

Patrick Job's boss had warned him to 'temper his enthusiasm with a modicum of discretion.' It was advice he never really followed:

'It seems to me still that the fascination of pitting skill, endurance and wits against the enemy on equal terms in unknown country is the best game of all. Man is a fighting animal; the world would be a happier place, I think, if wars could be fought and won or lost by small groups of men moving silently with rifles.'

Job's unit sank 30 ships. The pressure on the German navy in Norway was one reason Hitler kept over 300,000 troops in that country.

In 1944, Patrick joined 30 Assault Unit (30 AU), a strike force commanded by Royal Navy officers (of which he was one) with covering troops provided by the Royal Navy's elite raiding force, the Royal Marines. The commanding officer of 30 AU was Commander Ian Fleming, who was the personal assistant to the Director of Naval Intelligence at the Admiralty, in London. We have met Fleming before; at Bordeaux, Whitchurch and working with Wild Bill Donovan to set up the OSS. He concerned himself with spying and sabotage as much as with naval matters. He was an imaginative and energetic man who supplied his department with a lot of their ideas.

Fleming had designed and organised 30 AU as a force to send ahead of the Allied advance to impound any technology (mainly naval) from the Germans which Britain might find useful. In Fleming's force of hard men, Lieutenant Commander Patrick Dalzel-Job was one of the hardest; he has been cited as being the inspiration for James Bond. In terms of dash and bravery, he may well have been – although he denied it, on the grounds that he didn't drink and only ever loved one woman; who would become his wife.

Both Fleming's and Job's fathers had fought as junior army officers in the First World War, when life expectancy for such men was measured in weeks. Both of them had been killed on the Western Front. Seeing his mother receiving the notification telegram was Job's earliest memory (he was then three years old). Putting themselves in the firing line seems to have been a family characteristic. The second war was to be even more bitter to Job's family than the first. Five of his six male cousins would die fighting in it.

Job's section of 30 AU consisted of eight vehicles and thirty men. They landed on Utah beach four days after D-Day. He enjoyed the following year or so:

'I am bound to say that I found it tremendous fun and it would not have been such fun had not one been aware that a German machine gun might open fire.'

Job was to fight in Normandy, Brittany and right through Germany. His autobiography *Arctic snow to dust of Normandy* is a classic.

He was helped more than once by the French resistance. On one occasion (at Caen) a resistance unit delivered to him a British glider pilot whom they had been hiding since D-Day. They, were, says Job: 'virtually bursting with enthusiasm and very anxious to help'. Here, though, in the front line, not being trained soldiers, they were not used. On another occasion the resistance offered him two women whose heads had been shaved for sleeping with German soldiers. They were poor, terrified, creatures. Job was asked if he wanted to shoot them. He declined. The two were lucky to escape so lightly from the bloodbath of retribution that went on as the fighting passed through France.

Patrick Job was also instrumental in saving a German officer who was on the point of being lynched. The officer was grateful, but bemused:

'When we first came in 1940, they were pleased to see us and said how glad they were that the Tommies had gone. We tried to treat them well, but they seemed to like us less and less each year. Now I think they hate us. I do not understand it.'

The German officer was a young fellow. The penny had not quite dropped with him that the reception that is given to a man with a gun in his hand is somewhat different than he can expect when he has his tail between his legs.

Dalzel-Job's crocodile of lightly-armed jeeps often operated in front of the American and British forces, searching out naval blueprints and equipment (especially submarines). A tactic that he found useful was to ask the locals if the Germans in front of them were still wearing their helmets. If they were, he could expect a fight, if not, then they were probably ready to throw in the sponge. When his unit got into Germany, he found the civilians there friendly and ready to talk, which prompted Patrick Job to reflect on their lack of moral fibre:

'I thought of my own mother and the machine gun from Norway which she kept under her bed in a suitcase.'

Patrick had given her the machine gun, along with a belt of ammunition, himself. He had salvaged it from a crashed German aeroplane in Norway in 1940.

Job's group was only one of several, with different aims.

The Americans took the lead on nuclear information (ALSOS mission), the British on coding secrets (TICOM). Sometimes there was a crossover. A joint group of British, American and Russian scientists were to have gone to Peenemünde – but the Russian army got there first and kept the Allied scientists out. This was par for the course for Stalin whose promises were, as Roosevelt (among many others) lamented, often simply lies. The Americans didn't play it exactly straight, either. They had a head start in that the German rocket scientists, fleeing the Russians, surrendered to them. The scientists told their captors where the V2 blueprints were stored – which was in the British zone. The Americans promptly went and collected them – without telling the British. All's fair in love and war?

After an interesting journey north, Job and his troop took the surrender of the city of Bremen. As he approached the end of the war, Patrick Job did so with 'a feeling of regret that he would not have to face enemy fire again.' He and his team ended up in the docks at Bremerhaven, on the north coast of Germany, still in front of the advancing Allied troops. Here he confiscated a modern German destroyer, the Z.29. It was fully manned and the crew were not happy. Job ordered that the British white ensign be hoisted in the ship and then, having many other targets in the port, left the ship (renamed the HMS *Z.29*) in the care of a navy officer and six marines. The job of these men was to make safe the guns, remove any scuttling charges and disarm the crew. Job realised afterwards that his action in leaving so small a force could have led to their death…:

'The crew was in a very dangerous mood, ranging from aggressive anger through sullen insolence to weeping hysteria… this was a fighting ship with an undefeated ship's company… everywhere they went on the ship, Bob Grenfell and his men were met with boos and hisses, threatening gestures, attempts to trip them in the gangways, and the ominous bunching of German seamen behind their backs.'

The German Captain, Commander von Mutius, did everything he could to help the marines; but the situation was for a time close to mutiny. Eventually things settled down.

In getting in front of the lines, Job was operating in what would, with the division of Germany, become American administered territory; so the day after the war in Europe ended, he handed the HMS *Z.29* over to the American Navy:

'A whistle sounded shrilly, and the guard presented arms with a smack and a stamp, as a US seaman hoisted the Stars and Stripes to the peak. The White Ensign was hauled down, I dropped my hand from the salute, the guard ordered arms and HMS *Z.29* became the USN *Z.29*. Looking back, I see our little ceremony, sadly, as symbolic of transfer of power and command which was soon to be taking place throughout the world on a far larger scale. It was the end of an era.'

Patrick Job was, of course, right. Britain had had its imperial century. It ended with the bloodbath of the First World war. The interwar years had seen an increasing dominance in America's industrial power. With the second bloodbath, which destroyed much of Europe, America had become the foremost world power militarily too.

The process was hastened by the transfer of Britain's military and technological secrets (atomics, radar, jets, antibiotics, communications and computing) to America, mainly by the Tizard Mission, as I've explained elsewhere.

The sharing of British intelligence was part of the handover, too. I have talked about how OSS (which would later become the CIA) grew from the SOE and SIS; and the part Ian Fleming played in this. Indeed Fleming claimed (exaggeratedly) to have written the rulebook for the CIA. The gifts of intelligence were worth having. They were, to a significant degree, how Britain had managed to progress from being a small island nation off the coast of Europe to the ruler of the largest empire in history.

Of lesser importance, but of significance nevertheless, the American special force, the Seals, grew from emulation of British forces; as later, would their Delta Force from their founder's secondment to the SAS. These were forces that America had not needed when it was an isolationist power. It would when it became the globe's policemen.

These gifts were not entirely beneficial. Along with the apples came some very nasty worms; in the form of the Cambridge Spy Ring. One of them, Donald Maclean, along with John Cairncross (who I wrote about earlier) and the German, Klaus Fuchs, passed so much nuclear information to Russia that the Russian Spy controller, Yuri Modin, said of them: 'Without fear of exaggeration, I can confirm that we in the USSR knew absolutely everything about the technical and political aspects of atomic bomb development.' This was, quite apart from its global implications, to poison relations between the American and British secret services for quite a while.

Pax Americana Day

The passage of people from Europe to the American continent has been going on since the 'discovery' of the continent by Columbus. The flow from Great Britain to America has been going on since around 1600. American Thanksgiving Day, which celebrates the birth of the United States as a nation, relates to the hundred or so English men, women and children who cast anchor at Plymouth Rock in 1620 and founded the first successful English colony in North America.

Another American holiday is, of course, Independence Day, which celebrates the day in 1776 when the thirteen colonies which had grown from that initial landing decided that they didn't want to be English (or British) anymore.

So the United States of America already has a holiday to celebrate the time when England founded them. And it has another for when the states took over their own management (England, in the meantime having become part of Britain). Maybe there should be another American public holiday relating to the misty islands on the other side of the pond; to celebrate the moment when the Pax Britannica (1815 until 1940) became the Pax Americana.

What date should Pax Americana day fall on? The day Tizard gave America Britain's secrets in 1940? Perhaps the day in 1941 that Churchill gave Roosevelt the United Nations to look after (along with the bill for running it)? Or should it be the day America began lend-lease? Personally I would plump for the 3rd of February. That was the day in 1945 when the cameras popped at the 'big three' in Yalta. There sits Roosevelt in the middle of his client kings, Churchill and Stalin, in the meeting where the three divvied up the world.

'Big three' in Yalta

They look cold (indeed Roosevelt was sick and dying); but it's pretty obvious who is the focus. America held the purse strings. Britain would not finish paying its war debt to the USA until 61 years later.

In terms of suffering, Russia dwarfed the other Allied countries; with over twenty five million deaths (Britain had 450,000, America 400,000).

What of the lands that the armies of these three victors occupied? Russia was given pretty much a free hand in the east; not a great day for democracy. The countries occupied by American and British troops would return to self-determination. And then there was Germany; it would lose a chunk of its land to Poland, which, in turn, would lose a chunk of its land to Russia. The three victorious powers would occupy what remained of Germany until they saw fit to leave; each being allocated their own Occupation Zone. Churchill asked that the French, too, be given their own zone. Roosevelt agreed, Stalin didn't argue.

At this conference, too, the three leaders firmed-up on who was to be at the top table in the United Nations. The three themselves, of course. America wanted China to be included as well; and so it was. Britain wanted France in; and so it was. Stalin had no wish to nominate anyone but Russia; and so he didn't. These five countries were given a veto in the United Nations, which meant that if they acted solely in their own interests, the others could not vote them into line. Not a good start for the world's police force, you might think; but that decision would, after much argument, be ratified by the majority of the United Nations' countries. The argument the big boys used was that they (and mainly America) would be paying; which was accepted. If arguments were to be decided by dollars and not arms, at least that was a move forward.

The end of the war in Europe came in May 1945, followed by Japan's surrender three months later.

Cheshire and Nagasaki

I spoke about Leonard Cheshire in a previous chapter. He was the man who was in charge of the Dam Buster (617) Squadron which finished off the V1, V2 and V3 sites in Northern France. For that work, and the many other bombing raids that he led (he flew 102 missions in all), he was given Britain's highest military award, the Victoria Cross. He was also selected by Winston Churchill to go on a last bombing raid; this time as one of two British observers aboard a United States Army Air Force (USAAF) plane. The raid was to be on Kokura, a seaside city in the southwest of Japan. Cloud cover was bad on the day, so the Americans went for an alternative city on the target list, Nagasaki.

The other Briton in the observer plane with Cheshire, William Penney, was the head of the British scientists working at Los Alamos on the bomb. As the chief adviser to the Pentagon on where the bomb should fall, it was he who had put together the target list. I have explained elsewhere that British research on the bomb – code named Tube Alloys – lay at the foundations of later American development; and that several British scientists continued to work with the Americans.

Cheshire wrote later:

'We were about forty miles from Nagasaki when we saw a flash, followed by the billowing mushroom cloud... the smoke pall seemed to be ever-increasing, and after watching for nearly an hour we left... all of us were in a state of severe emotional shock. We realised that a new age had begun and that possibly we had all made some contribution to raising a monster that would consume us all. None of us could sleep.'

Robert Oppenheimer 'the father of the atom bomb' said that when he saw the cloud he thought of Hindu scripture: 'Now I am become death, the destroyer of worlds.'

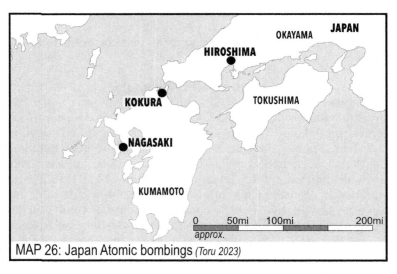

MAP 26: Japan Atomic bombings *(Toru 2023)*

Between forty to eighty thousand people died in Nagasaki; roughly half on the first day. For months afterward, large numbers of people continued to die from the effects of burns, radiation sickness and injuries.

I'm only seven though I died
In Hiroshima long ago
I'm seven now as I was then
When children die they do not grow

My hair was scorched by swirling flame
My eyes grew dim my eyes grew blind

Death came and turned my bones to dust
And that was scattered by the wind

I need no fruit I need no rice
I need no sweets nor even bread
I ask for nothing for myself
For I am dead for I am dead

(Nazim Hikmet; the girl child)

The bomb on Nagasaki was the second atom bomb dropped on Japan (Hiroshima had been the first). Emperor Hirohito ordered his generals to surrender six days later.

Leonard Cheshire saw the atom bomb as a necessary evil. According to his daughter, Elizabeth:

'He was very much of the view it was a dreadful weapon, but one that was necessary to end the war. He believed that had it not been used, a land invasion of Japan would have resulted in the immediate execution of all prisoners of war and probably three to four million lives would have been lost over the time it would have taken to win.'

A look at the figures backs Cheshire up. That wasn't much comfort to Nagasaki though.

Cheshire would go on to devote his life to providing shelter, care and comfort to the poor and sick, as did his wife, Sue Ryder. Their work continues to this day. There are hundreds of Cheshire and Ryder homes in dozens of countries.

What to do with Germany?

The news of President Franklin D. Roosevelt's death in April 1945 sent Adolf Hitler, in his bunker deep beneath Berlin, into ecstasies. The Fuhrer believed that the incoming president (Truman) would order America and Britain to sue for peace and join him in his holy war against communism.

As it had become more and more clear that their defeat was imminent, 'the holy war against communism' had become the Nazi's salvation myth. With their usual breath-taking cynicism, Hitler and Goebbels had reinvented their past. The Nazi state, it seemed, had not been about world domination at all; it had only been about destroying communism. Some in the west thoroughly agreed that would be a very good thing. America's greatest general, George Patton, made no bones of the fact that he was open to the idea of pushing his troops straight through Germany and on into Russia and thus get rid of two mass-murdering tyrants at once. Patton died in a car crash. The jury is still out on whether it was an accident or yet another murder ordered by Stalin. In terms of the war, it probably didn't much matter; whatever George Patton's feelings, he would never have been given his head. The President wouldn't have allowed it and even if he had Patton's own troops would probably have thrown down their arms. Just about all of the American and British fighting men (but not Patrick Job) wanted to stop fighting and go home.

The assault went on, Hitler shot himself and Germany surrendered.

What was the longer term plan for Germany? The Allies had been thinking about that for a while. Roosevelt is quoted by the American historian, John M. Blum, as having said to his Secretary of the Treasury, Henry Morgenthau that:

'We have got to be tough with Germany and I mean the German people not just the Nazis. We either have to castrate the German people or you have got to treat them in such a manner so they can't just go on reproducing people who want to continue the way they have in the past.'

He was preaching to the converted. Morgenthau wanted to turn Germany into a country of peasants with no industry and no potential to wage war ever again. In Britain, the sentiment was echoed by Churchill's aide, Frederick Lindemann (Lord Cherwell), who showed a deep hatred for his (fellow?) Germans. Russia was perfectly happy to see Germany stripped of its industrial capacity – a policy it would carry out in its own occupation zone.

Morgenthau drew up a 'Post Surrender Program for Germany', which was aimed at stripping Germany of industry and turning the country into a farming state. Roosevelt, who signed off the document (the Morgenthau Plan), afterwards denied that he had intended to do so. This is entirely possible, the President was a very sick man who, towards his end, scarcely knew what he was doing.

Winston Churchill did not agree with the Morgenthau Plan. He said that if it were implemented it would be the equivalent of Great Britain 'being chained to a dead body'. As the Allies' greatest statesman, Churchill had thought long and hard about the future of the unhappy continent of Europe. That is why he had insisted on France being given a seat on the UN security council and also that France be given its own occupation zone in Germany.

As for Germany, he did not seek to wreak revenge on the German people for their Nazi party. Partly this was because he saw beyond Hitler; 'A country is not a person' and towards decency: 'In victory, magnanimity'. The cynic will point out – rightly – that Winston didn't preach forgiveness simply because he was a nice chap. As usual, he engaged his head as well as his heart. Bringing Germany into partnership was necessary for the health of Europe. A weak Germany would allow Stalin free access to the heart of the continent; and that wasn't at all Churchill's cup of tea. Winston preferred Josef to be as far away as possible, in hell preferably, for he was only marginally fonder of the Russian dictator than he had been of Hitler. Back in 1941, when Germany had invaded Russia, Churchill had joked to an aide:

'If Hitler invaded hell, I would at least make a favourable reference to the devil in the House of Commons.'

The British did not want, and nor could they afford, Germany to be a failed and starving country. They echoed to the heavens, however, Roosevelt's sentiment that Deutschland 'couldn't go on the way it had in the past'. Britain had fought Germany twice in thirty years at a cost of over a million of her men dead and twice as many maimed, blinded or otherwise wounded. Thirty years of suffering, heartbreak and 'each slow dusk, a drawing down of blinds'; but the way forward was to harness German talents, rather than turn her citizens into serfs.

In the end, there was no disagreement on the subject between America and Britain. When Roosevelt's deputy, Harry

Truman, took over as president, one of his first actions was to sack Morgenthau.

A lot to unlearn: Wilton Park

That Germany needed to change was obvious. It's reputation lay 'deeply buried under millions of corpses and under the shattered structure of Europe'; the result of what Sefton Delmer (who had himself been schooled in Germany and had monitored Hitler's rise to power) called:

'The ruthlessness which Germans of my generation had been taught in their school readers and history books to admire as a virile virtue.'

The evidence was everywhere; the goods trains full of semi-skeletons on the railways, the slave labourers across the Reich, the Jews and gypsies and weak-minded who had 'disappeared'. It surprised the occupying Allied troops in Germany how ignorant the German population was of all this. Even Admiral Karl Dönitz – who took over as Fuhrer after Hitler's death – was, apparently, unaware of the death camps.

To the common man and woman in the Third Reich, looking the other way was taken for granted. To question was likely to lead you into a concentration camp. Having the moral courage to stand up against Hitler's regime was naïve. Those that did so were killed. So, they 'didn't know' or were 'just following orders.' The secretly taped conversations from Latimer House, Wilton Park and Trent Park of German prisoners of war show that they knew right enough. Helen Fry's book *The walls have ears* about the taping of German captives gives chapter and verse. I only have space for a couple of examples. The first is from General von Cholitz, who spoke of:

'The worst job I ever carried out – which, however, I carried out with great consistency – was the liquidation of the Jews. I carried out this order down to the last detail.'

A German, captured in 1943 told of when..:

'Driving back... from visiting some staff near Lvov... they heard shots. They approached and found about two hundred Jews, the men in their pants and the women in knickers and brassieres... some of the women had children in their arms. They were all shot in the back of the head, two rounds with a tommy gun... We shall have to pay for that.'

Another internee, Johannes Bruhn, said:

'Have we deserved victory or not? No, not after what we've done. After the amount of blood we've shed knowingly and as a result of our delusions... I now realise we have deserved defeat. We've deserved our fate.'

And so on, and on, and on.

It should be noted that these atrocities were not only carried out by SS units, but by soldiers of the line. To go forward briefly, it is a credit to Germany that they admit and publicise this evil in their history. An exhibition of photographs of army units' killings – over a thousand of them – ran for 10 years in Germany and visited 33 cities.

How had Germany sunk to such a corrupt moral level?

The education system was at the root of the brutalisation. When the Nazis were elected to power in 1933, schools were one of their first targets. After removing all Jews, many women and any who openly opposed them, they gave the rest of the teachers a choice; join the Nazi Teachers Association and teach the new curriculum or be sacked. Ninety seven percent joined. In the new curriculum, racial ideology and spurious pseudo-sciences replaced traditional subjects such as biology and history. 'Race knowledge' was taught from the age of 6. Hitler said that under him:

'A youth will grow up that will horrify the world. I want to have a violent, lordly, fearless, cruel youth ...nothing gentle and weak in them must be left.'

He got his wish.

In the armed forces as well as in schools, the message was clear. Hitler was the saviour, never mistaken, always right. Anything but obedience to him was met with the punishment that such betrayal of the divine-will deserved. All troops were forced to take an oath pledging their life to unconditional obedience to him. Not to Germany, not to the Nazi party, to Adolf Hitler. Never question. Hail to the messiah. Heil Hitler.

The Allies demanded that the German people awoke from this evil trance. Britain and America agreed that the way to achieve that aim was not to force but to guide. In the words of Sefton Delmer:

'Another Germany survived which it was well worth trying to excavate from under the debris. A Germany which recognised its collective responsibility for Hitler and the need to expiate the infamies under the Fuhrer.'

The Allies would punish (somewhat cursorily) the torturers and murderers. The remainder must be helped to cure their own ills; to devise as soon as possible a constitution and education system that would not allow another Hitler to rise. A key part in this process was Britain's decision to turn Wilton Park, one of the camps in Buckinghamshire which had been used to eavesdrop on German prisoners, into an educational establishment.

The first attendees for the courses at Wilton Park were volunteers selected from among the German prisoners of war (POWs) held in Britain; captured soldiers who were largely employed on the land and in reconstruction in the bombed out cities. There were plenty of them to choose from; four hundred thousand at the peak. All were male. The selection wasn't straight forward, though. The prisoners had been categorised into three categories; 'black' - dyed-in-the-wool Nazis impervious to change (the majority); 'grey' – those who were not completely indoctrinated; and 'white' – those who could think outside Nazi ideology. It was, perhaps, inevitable that few of the students that went to Wilton were from among the youngest POWs. Many of those were Nazi soldier ants. The old Jesuit maxim 'give me a child until he is seven and I will give you the man' worked for the Nazi religion as well as any other.

Three hundred volunteers were selected initially. They ranged from privates to generals, from convinced anti-Nazi's to those more sympathetic towards the Nazi party. What they were volunteering for was a bit difficult to describe; 're-education' sounded a bit too close to what Hitler and Stalin got up to. There was no snappy title for the course they were to attend; it was described as being designed to 'help in the re-institution of democratic processes within Germany'.

What was needed, in fact, was put pretty clearly by a man who did not mix his words. Field Marshall Bernard Montgomery said that; 'the Germans had a lot to unlearn'.

The remit of Wilton Park was:

'At a time of bitter hatred and recrimination, to go to the root of evil, confront deceitful ideologies and begin to reconcile former enemies at a level of common humanity rather than divisive stereotypes.'

The courses lasted for six weeks.

The idea was to get the students to think, to question; to realise both that the Fuhrer was not 'always right' but that there was no such thing as 'always right'; there were opinions, and the more you listened, the more malleable your own were likely to become. There is a line in *The Second Coming* by Samuel Butler Yeats: 'The best lack all conviction while the worst are full of a passionate intensity', which sums up neatly the danger of following a charismatic messiah.

Question, discuss; be ready to justify your opinions before your peers; think for your selves.

All 'students' would attend lectures on politics, economics, and current affairs – amongst other subjects. The talks were by members of parliament, economic leaders, trades unionists and educationalists. All of the sessions were discussion groups, led by the attendees. Many said that the major lesson they learned was that they could question and discuss things with people of opposing views without coming to blows. In the meantime, they might modify their own views. These may seem simple truths, but for those who have grown up in a totalitarian regime they are new and often disturbing ideas.

The lecturers came from all political parties. One Conservative MP pointed out to the German POWs that the RAF aeroplanes which had beaten the Luftwaffe had all been developed by private enterprise. If the state had been left to do the job: 'You would be lecturing me, rather than me lecturing you.' That raised a laugh. Quite a few of the lecturers had the knack of doing that. The courses didn't take long to gel.

The prisoners who went to Wilton Park were almost all very enthusiastic. One said:

'He (Heinz Koeppler, who was in charge) gave us Germans the possibility to become partners. He did not 're-educate' us... he did not tell us how things ought to be handled in Germany, but he made us think for ourselves; he believed it to be vital that Britons and Germans should get to know each other and to understand the other fellow's point of view. I cannot describe the encouragement he and his colleagues gave to us German prisoners of war, by having ministers of the British Crown, economic leaders, professors and so on come to talk and discuss with us.'

Civilian attendees – men and women - were also sent from the Allied occupation zones of Germany. The communists, in East Germany, declined to send anyone. Most of their prisoners were in Siberian work camps; those who were selected for 'political re-education' underwent a somewhat different regime than that at Wilton Park.

This may all sound rather dry, but four thousand POWs, as well as many civilians, came out of Wilton Park and took up places in German society; to their, Britain's and Europe's mutual benefit. This has led to strong and friendly ties between Britain and Germany which have lasted to this day. Wilton Park continues still (though, confusingly, at Wiston House, in Sussex) as a talking shop between different countries. In Churchill's words 'jaw jaw is better than war war.'

For their part of the bargain, the Germans re-instituted democracy in their country, adding checks and balances such as make it all but impossible for a charismatic hypnotist to ever again seize power there.

German prisoners of war were well treated in Britain. Twenty-five thousand of them would pay the country the ultimate compliment of settling in the British Isles rather than going back to Germany.

From a purely parochial point of view, of course, one could question Britain's wisdom in teaching Germans the value of cooperation. As with cricket, football, rugby, hockey, tennis, rounders (baseball if you're American) and so on, England has a knack of inventing great team games and then being totally outplayed by those it teaches them to.

Two ladies, one flame

The end of the war would see many changes. A broken Europe, threatened from the east, a new weapon which threatened the destruction of mankind, the birth of computing and the blossoming of communications. These latter would transform the world into a close community where anyone, anywhere, can speak to anyone else immediately (governments permitting). Much of this book has been about how and why many of these world-changing changes came to fruition in one small area of England – the Intelligence Zone. I hope that it has piqued your interest and broadened your knowledge of these subjects.

Statue of Liberty

Britannia

I would like to end it by talking briefly about the warriors for freedom, Britain and the United States. Their rewards had been vastly different. America was now the most powerful and richest nation on earth. The country had built a vast manufacturing industry and superb research laboratories; and it had boundless energy - that defining 'can do now' approach that had so often impressed visiting British generals in search of new ships, aircraft or proximity fuses. If Britain was licking her wounds and watching sadly as her empire's flags were struck around the globe, Uncle Sam was ready to show he meant business.

Energy. The United States of America owes its very existence to those who wanted a better life and were prepared to roll up their sleeves to get it. The country has grown from them. Firstly they came from the British Isles; originally from those hundred or so English who landed at Plymouth Rock in 1620. The flow continued and continues still – Biggins is a Yorkshire surname; but there are now more of my tribe in America than in Britain. The same goes for an endless list of British names: Bush, Clinton, Owen, Biden, Kennedy, Bell, and Spittles for example. Millions more fled from Europe. Never has there been such an industrious, inventive and hard-working tide of peoples. The slaves and native Americans, of course, had no choice in the matter.

America. Can do! Will do! Do! America, first among nations. Raring to go.

In Britain the outlook was rather less rosy. Many British cities were in ruins and needed rebuilding. The country was all but bankrupt. It had used up its vast reserves of gold and foreign currency on supplies from America and still owed a huge amount to the USA. Indeed, as I mentioned earlier, it would take 61 years to pay off the debt. A large part of the cost of feeding Germany had landed on its shoulders. Instead of coming to an end, food shortages in Britain would actually increase. Bread, which had never been rationed during the war was rationed after it ended, to allow grain to be sent to Germany, which was on the point of starvation.

The flow of people from Britain to America would continue. One hundred thousand British women were charmed across the Atlantic by virile American GIs and the better chances their country offered. They would be followed by thousands of British scientists and technicians.

When the United States of America became the undisputed leaders of the free world, they inherited quite a bit from Britain;

as this book has explained. Did they also inherit Britain's global foreign policy?

Inherit? Most parents know that it is pointless trying to advise their offspring. The older generation is quite deluded if they imagine that their lifetime's experiences can possibly be of use to their children; who are (as they will tell you) faster, smarter and more savvy than any other generation who have ever lived.

The analogy is far from perfect, I know. The incomparable motto of the USA is 'E Pluribus Unum' (many uniting into one); Britain is but one root of that mighty land. That said, it is the tap root. Britain and the United States share a language; and large parts of our laws, roots, sports, history and aspirations are the same.

It is not surprising, then, that America does, in fact, follow a very similar foreign policy to that with which Britannia once 'Ruled the waves'. It was well described by the Duke of Wellington, who was then the Prime Minister of Britain (which he, like many others, confused with England), in 1833. As such, he was in much the same position as the President of the United States is now:

'The foreign policy of England should be to maintain peace, not only for herself but between the powers of the world.'

Apart from substituting 'America' for 'England', that's pretty much how America conducts its foreign affairs now. And, like Britannia, the President keeps his eyes peeled.

But the President should never, I think, forget the lesson that the young German officer who Patrick Job saved from being lynched by the French resistance had yet to learn. Don't mistake subservience for love.

***

And what of Britain?

In all the long story of the world, no nation, perhaps, has ever fought a more just war than she did between 1939 and 1945. For much of that time, she fought alone. To her, first and foremost, the free world owes its survival.

It must be acknowledged, though, that in holding the guttering flame of freedom too long, Britannia had badly burned her fingers; a massive debt to America, rationing which would continue for thirteen years after the end of the war, rubble filled cities, the dismantling of the last of the British Empire and a decline in national power. The fact that this was the *best* the British could ever have hoped for was predictable enough from the start. That's what made their sacrifice so magnificent.

Mustn't grumble though.

The British people got far more than just a warm glow from the experience. The uniting of the nation in a fight to the finish (for the second time in twenty five years) had taught the majority the value of striving for a common purpose. Better still, it had taught them an ambition for the future. Things must improve. The rewards, just as the danger and struggle, must be shared fairly. When bulldozing the bombed sites, the slums must go too; to be replaced with decent housing and enough roofs for all. The sick should be cared for by a free National Health Service. All, including the young, the old and the weak, should have food, a roof, and enough for their needs. Children should be educated according to their ability, rather than their parents' money or their sex.

In short, the British wartime generation strove to leave their children a better future. In this, too, they succeeded pretty well.

And what of Winston? He would lose power in 1945, when the party he led, the Conservatives, was beaten at the ballot box by the Labour party. The chief disagreement between the two parties, which had ruled together during the war, was whether or not to implement the recommendations of the Beveridge Report. This report, which had been commissioned by the (joint) government, proposed radical improvements in health care, housing, education and pensions. The Labour Party wanted to enact it, the Conservative Party thought it would be too costly. Labour won. The idea of being cared for as a birthright proved even stronger to the British people than the love and admiration they felt for their greatest leader. In this, democracy triumphed; and it was for democracy, as Churchill himself ruefully remarked, that Britain had fought the war.

In the new Prime Minister, Churchill's ally and war-time deputy, Clement Atlee, Britain got another great man. Attlee was to say on Churchill's death (20 years later): "We have lost the greatest Englishman of our time - I think the greatest citizen of the world of our time." While I agree wholeheartedly with that, I prefer to remember Winston's own words "We are all worms, but I do believe that I am a glow-worm."

At end of fearful night
the glow-worm fades from sight
But not from memory

Appendix A: Oradour

The Oradour massacre took place on the 10th of June 1944 and was a direct result of attempts by the French resistance to slow down the movement of the 2nd SS Panzer (tank) Division, *Das Reich*, which was moving from Southern France to Normandy to counter the D-day landings of the 6th of June.

On their route north, *Das Reich* committed an atrocity of a type typical of the SS in Ukraine and Russia. It destroyed the village of Oradour-sur-Glane, which the Germans suspected of containing partisans (they got the wrong place, the partisans were actually in Oradour-sur Ayres, twenty miles distant.) They shot the men in the streets then herded the women and children into the church and set light to it, killing 642.

A farmer, Fernand Hyvernand, looking for his two sons, of thirteen and six, made his way into the church afterwards:

André Hyvernaud

'I found one of the boys. He was my youngest. He lay on his side and was half-charred… he still had one of his wooden shoes on. His other leg was completely out of joint and twisted behind his back. His throat was half cut through… but I did not find my older boy. Behind the altar, crammed closely together, lay at least twenty small children who had tried to find shelter there… they had all been suffocated by smoke or burned to death. I also saw prams with dead infants in them. Some were burned, others were riddled with bullets. Then I went home. That evening we dug a grave for André in our little yard.'

Max Hastings describes the division's movement across France in his book *Das Reich*. He interviewed survivors and perpetrators and reports the conversation between two SS veterans, one who had been there and one (Muller) who had not, about Oradour: "In our circle, Herr Muller, it was nothing."

The Nazi creed was perhaps the worst that has ever infected mankind. The depths of suffering it inflicted on the peoples of Europe are so upsetting that even the 'nothings' move one to tears. This is what the Allies were fighting against. This is what man is capable of.

Forgive and forget? Only those who have been sinned against have the right to forgive. Only the foolish forget.

Appendix B: de Gaulle's D-day speech

Made on the afternoon of D-day (6th June 1944) on the BBC from London

"After much fighting, here is the decisive battle. The battle so hoped for; the battle of France, for France. The immense attack – help for us – has come from the shores of old England; the last bastion of Western Europe, where the high tide of German aggression was stopped. It is today the base of the offensive of freedom.

France, submerged for 4 years but never broken or vanquished; France stands to take part. For the sons of France, wherever they are, the sacred duty is to fight however they can to crush the detested enemy who will try to hold our land as long as he can. But he has been pushed back from Stalingrad... Tunis and Rome and knows defeat. France will take part in the battle, furiously, in good order, as for 1500 years we have won each of our victories; we will win this one (with our) sea, land and air forces... never more disciplined and strong. Africa, Italy, the ocean and the sky have seen their reborn strength and glory and their native country will see them tomorrow; arm in arm, marching as one against the well-armed aggressor. Good battle-order demands certain conditions. First the orders of the *French* (de Gaulle stresses the word) government and *French* leaders must be closely followed.

Second, our actions behind the lines must be coordinated with the allied and the French armies. The resistance must fight long and it must fight hard.

Third, no matter what the trials, all must fight to their utmost to achieve the defeat of Germany... The battle of France has started. All have but one wish and hope; that by our blood and tears, from behind the clouds will reappear the sun of our greatness."

7: Rites of passage

Dear reader,

I hope that you have enjoyed this book. It has been the result of many years of research. If you bought it on online and like it, please leave a review. Better still, buy copies for your friends – they'll probably like it too!

I have researched it as closely as possible. If, however, you have seen anything which you have good reason to believe to be inaccurate, please tell me. If I agree, I will amend it.

My contact email is theintzoneuk@gmail.com

Thank you. And thank you for reading it.

Alan

March 2023

The map opposite gives an overview of the chapters in both books.

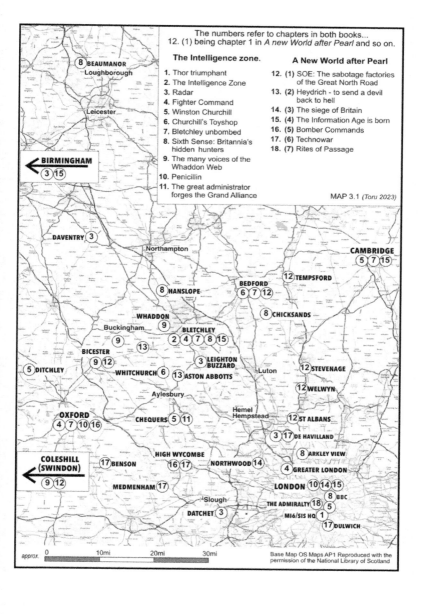

The numbers refer to chapters in both books...
12. (1) being chapter 1 in *A new World after Pearl* and so on.

The Intelligence zone.

1. Thor triumphant
2. The Intelligence Zone
3. Radar
4. Fighter Command
5. Winston Churchill
6. Churchill's Toyshop
7. Bletchley unbombed
8. Sixth Sense: Britannia's hidden hunters
9. The many voices of the Whaddon Web
10. Penicillin
11. The great administrator forges the Grand Alliance

A New World after Pearl

12. (1) SOE: The sabotage factories of the Great North Road
13. (2) Heydrich - to send a devil back to hell
14. (3) The siege of Britain
15. (4) The Information Age is born
16. (5) Bomber Commands
17. (6) Technowar
18. (7) Rites of Passage

MAP 3.1 *(Toru 2023)*

8 BEAUMANOR
Loughborough

Leicester

← BIRMINGHAM
3 15

DAVENTRY 3
Northampton

CAMBRIDGE
5 7 15

12 TEMPSFORD

8 HANSLOPE
BEDFORD
6 7 12

WHADDON 9
8 CHICKSANDS

Buckingham
BLETCHLEY
2 4 7 8 15

BICESTER
9 13
9 12

3 LEIGHTON BUZZARD
12 STEVENAGE

5 DITCHLEY
WHITCHURCH 6
13 ASTON ABBOTTS
Luton
12 WELWYN

Aylesbury

Hemel Hempstead
12 ST ALBANS

OXFORD
4 7 10 16
CHEQUERS 5 11
3 17 DE HAVILLAND

8 ARKLEY VIEW

COLESHILL (SWINDON)
9 12
17 BENSON
HIGH WYCOMBE
16 17
NORTHWOOD 14
4 GREATER LONDON

MEDMENHAM 17
LONDON 10 14 15

Slough
8 BBC

THE ADMIRALTY 18
5
DATCHET 3
MI6/SIS HQ 1

17 DULWICH

approx.
0   10mi   20mi   30mi

Base Map OS Maps AP1 Reproduced with the permission of the National Library of Scotland

Afterword: me and why I wrote this book

This book is the fruit of several of my interests and a lifetime of my experiences. My interest in military history is, in part, a result of having served in the Royal Air Force. My interest in Bletchley Park and its surrounding area also comes from experience. After leaving the air force, I worked my way through the early days of computing, from operator (when computers needed such help) through programming, software engineering and analysis. I got pretty close to the beast at times, programming at machine-code level, developing electronic mail and working on systems software.

My career, as were countless others, was based on the work of the geniuses – some of whom worked at Bletchley Park – who developed the mind-boggling device that I worked on. Bletchley Park was physically close to me. One rung of my own personal career ladder was when I became Information Technology Manager for the Milton Keynes Development Corporation; the organisation which was tasked with the development of the new city of Milton Keynes. As Bletchley is part of that city, I consider myself a very minor link in the chain that leads from 'B.P.' to the modern world.

Knowledge and interest aside, the book is also the fruit of many years walking. I have worked (and walked) for 50 years in the area that I call the Intelligence Zone. My walks are generally around 20 miles - so I have gone through a fair number of boots in my time. On many of my country walks I came across intriguing places: military sites relating to communications, radar, computers, intelligence, aerial photography, aircraft, weapon production, spies and saboteurs. There is little to commemorate most of these places. The huts where radio operators talked to the resistance movements of occupied Europe are broken down sheds in fields or mere marks in the grass. No plaques mark the houses where the great of Bletchley Park were lodged – or the mansions where SIS and SOE agents were trained. Few know where (or even why) the genius of Czech intelligence, František Moravec, planned the execution of the foul and efficient Nazi leader, Reinhard Heydrich.

259

Over the years, I came across more and more forgotten places with astonishing histories. For instance, I knew that there had been an escape organisation for Allied airmen – MI9 – somewhere, but never suspected that it was off a roundabout that I'd crossed a hundred times - or that an interesting house I had seen near the Thames had been the headquarters of the world's greatest aerial survey.

Walking in the cities was as revealing as walking in the country. In London is the hospital where Fleming discovered penicillin – 'the magic bullet' which has saved more lives than died in the Second World War. In Oxford, in a back street, is the place where it was isolated and extracted. In Cambridge is the laboratory where the genie was let out of the bottle in 1932 when Cockcroft and Walton split the atom. At home, with piles of obscure books and a keyboard, I followed these stories – which often led to the new world – the New World – America.

All of this was a small part of my life. My wife, Ann, and I were mostly busy bringing up our children and steering our little family boat over the sometimes rocky shoals of life. Over the years, though, I realised how the sites in the Intelligence Zone related, one to another. The conviction grew that their stories – if I could tease them out and piece them together (jigsaws are another interest of mine) - were far more significant than merely local history; a task for retirement.

World War Two was a war like no other. Hitler and Hess sought peace with Britain – but Winston Churchill rejected their repeated overtures. Churchill decided on war not in the expectation that it would bring gains to his country, but as a necessity, for the good of mankind. There has never been a more risky exercise of a moral principle. To lose the war would have meant the enslavement of the British people and the removal of the entire male population of breeding age. Victory brought crippling debt to Britain and the decisive shift in world power to America. What I had not realised until I worked on my jigsaw was the primary importance of the places I had walked through – the Intelligence Zone – in all of that.

If this epic was not a good enough reason to write my book, there are others. The British tend to be a reticent people. I have also written it to remind them that when Churchill described their sacrifices in World War Two as 'their finest hour', he was not exaggerating.

And this book is my homage to those of all nations who fought for freedom, on the battlefield or in the shadows.

Perhaps most importantly, I wrote the book to do my tiny part to remind my readers how near 'the new dark age' was to falling on the whole world. It could happen again. The price of liberty is, as the American moral giant Wendell Phillips pointed out, eternal vigilance. This, like all lessons, must be learned anew by each generation – for those who forget, or neglect, their history are in danger of repeating it.

In writing the book, I was faced with the challenge of how to weave a regional and national story into a global one: the passing of the Pax Britannica – the time when Britain was the world's policeman and the pound sterling was the world's currency – to the Pax Americana – the American age where the dollar reigns supreme. And then there is the little matter that the Information Age – the world of computers and communications – was born in the Intelligence Zone. I hope that you feel that I have acquitted myself satisfactorily in my evening task.

In writing the book, I feel like a curator of a vast library of knowledge who has picked out some choice and rarely seen exhibits to make a new and – hopefully - illuminating show. If this book has piqued your interest, I urge you to dip into the library.

Alan Biggins

Acknowledgements

My thanks to those who have read and commented on this book over the period of the five years that it took me to write it; John Ahern, David Biggins, Colin Bell, Mark Owen, Steve Parkinson and Roger Spittles.

I would also like to thank Amazon KDP; who allowed me to publish this work without involving me in an enormous expense. Without their innovative and excellent technology I would never have written it.

And I thank my artist, Kai Toru, for her excellent and sharply intuitive work on the covers, maps and layout of the books. Kai's website is at http://www.kaitoru.co.uk/

Bibliography

Chapter 1. SOE and the sabotage factories of the Great North Road
Books

Braddon, Russell. *Nancy Wake*. Pan, 1974.

Cowburn, Benjamin. *No Cloak, No Dagger*. Casemate Publishers, 2009.

Faramus, Anthony. *Journey into Darkness*. Grafton Books Harpercollins, 1991.

Farmelo, Graham. *Churchill's Bomb : A Hidden History of Science, War and Politics*. Faber And Faber, 2014.

Foot, M R D. *Memories of an S.O.E. Historian*. Casemate Publishers, 2009.

Foot, M R D. *SOE in France : An Account of the Work of the British Special Operations Executive in France, 1940-1944*. Frank Cass, 2006.

General Service Research. *Partisan Leader's Handbook*. Createspace Independent Publishing Platform, 1939. (also available online)

Manderstam, Len H, and Roy Heron. *From the Red Army to SOE*. 1985.

Manus, Max. *Underwater Saboteur*. 1953.

Marks, Leo. *Between Silk and Cyanide : A Code Makers's War, 1941-45*. The History Press, 2013.

Marshall, Bruce. *The White Rabbit*. Praeger, 1987.

Millar, George. *Horned Pigeon : The Great Escape Story of World War II*. Cassell, 2003.

O'Connor, Bernard. *Churchill's School for Saboteurs*. Amberley Publishing Limited, 2013.

Riols, Noreen. *The Secret Ministry of Ag. & Fish*. Pan Macmillan, 2013.

Shields, Pamela. *Hertfordshire Secrets and Spies*. 2009.

Turner, Des. *Station 12*. The History Press, 2011.

Verity, Hugh. *We Landed by Moonlight*. Allan, 1978.

Chapter 2. To send a devil back to hell
Books

Guderian, Heinz. *Panzer Leader*. Must Have Books, 2018.

Macdonald, C A. *The Assassination of Reinhard Heydrich*. Birlinn, 2007.

Moravec, František. *Master of Spies*. Time-Life Books, 1991.

Norden, Peter. *Madam Kitty*. Ballantine Books, 1974.

Rees, Neil. *The Secret History of the Czech Connection : The Czechoslovak Government in Exile in London and Buckinghamshire during the Second World War*. Neil Rees, 2005.

Schellenberg, Walter. *Hitler's Secret Service : The Memoirs of Walter Schellenberg*. Jove Publications, 1977.

Chapter 3. The Siege of Britain: Defeating the U-boats
Books

Baveystock, Leslie. *Wavetops at My Wingtips*. Crowood Press, 2001.

Beesly, Patrick. *Very Special Intelligence*. Ballantine Books, 1981.

Bowyer, Chaz. *Coastal Command at War*. Ian Allan, 1979.

Cremer, Peter. *U333: The Story of a U-Boat Ace*. Bodley Head, 1984.

Frank, Wolfgang. *The Sea Wolves*. Random House Publishing Group, 1981.

Gannon, Michael. *Black May*. Dell Publishing Company, 1999.

Goebeler, Hans, and John Vanzo. *Steel Boat, Iron Hearts*. Savas Beatie, 2005.

Hendrie, Andrew. *The Cinderella Service*. Casemate Publishers, 2006.

Macintyre, Donald. *U-Boat Killer*. Orion Publishing Co, 1976.

Nesbit, Roy. *Ultra versus U-Boats*. Casemate Publishers, 2009.

Nudd, Derek. *Castaways of the Kriegsmarine*. Createspace Independent Publishing Platform, 2017.

Sanders, James. *Of Wind and Water*. Airlife Publishing Ltd, 1989.

Schaeffer, Heinz. *U-Boat 977*. William Kimber, 1952.

Werner, Herbert A. *Iron Coffins*. Weidenfeld & Nicolson, 1999.

Whinney, Bob. *The U-Boat Peril*. Burns & Oates, 1986.

Media and Online sources

Helgason, Gudmundur. "*The U-Boat Wars 1939-1945 (Kriegsmarine) and 1914-1918 (Kaiserliche Marine) and Allied Warships of WWII - Uboat.net.*" *uboat.net*, 2019

Wikipedia Contributors. "*RAF Coastal Command.*" *Wikipedia*, 2023, en.wikipedia.org/wiki/RAF_Coastal_Command.

Chapter 4. The birth of the Information Age
Books

Cairncross, John. *The Enigma Spy*. Random House (UK), 1997.

Gannon, Paul. *Colossus : Bletchley Park's Greatest Secret*. Atlantic, 2007.

Haswell, Jock. *Spies and Spymasters*. Thames and Hudson, 1977. – A short, general, but excellent book on spying; especially useful as an introduction to the Lucy (Russian) spy ring, in Switzerland (but he doesn't mention that their English radio operator, Alexander Foote, probably worked for MI6 and was therefore feeding Russia with information from Bletchley Park).

Hayter, Sir William. *A Double Life*. Hamish Hamilton, 1974.

Heiber, Helmut, and David M Glantz. *Hitler and His Generals : Military Conferences 1942-1945 : The First Complete Stenographic Record of the Military Situation Conferences, from Stalingrad to Berlin*. Enigma Books, 2003.

Hinsley, F H, and Alan Stripp. *Codebreakers*. Oxford University Press, 2001.

Jennings, Christian. *The Third Reich Is Listening*. Bloomsbury Publishing, 2018. – Excellent book on the German WW2 intelligence organisations.

Modin, Yuri. *My Five Cambridge Friends : Philby, Burgess, Maclean, Blunt, and Cairncross*. Knopf Canada, 1995.

264

Smith, Chris. *The Last Cambridge Spy*. The History Press, 2019.

Media and Online sources

Brigadier John Tiltman a Giant among Cryptanalysts. National Security Agency, 2007. https://www.nsa.gov/portals/75/documents/about/cryptologic-heritage/historical-figures-publications/publications/misc/tiltman.pdf

"The National Museum of Computing." *The National Museum of Computing*, www.tnmoc.org/.

Chapter 5. Bomber Commands. The warlords of Wycombe

Books

Baveystock, Leslie. *Wavetops at My Wingtips*. Airlife, 2001.

Bennett, Donald. *Pathfinder*. Crecy Pub, 1998.

Charlwood, Don. *No Moon Tonight*. Goodall Publications Ltd, 2019.

Currie, Jack. *Lancaster Target*. Goodall, 2012.

Currie, Jack. *Wings over Georgia*. Crecy Pub, 1989.

Daniel, Glyn. *Some Small Harvest*. Thames and Hudson, 1986.

Doolittle, James Harold, and Carroll V Glines. *I Could Never Be so Lucky Again*. Bantam Books, 1992.

Dugan, James, and Carroll Stewart. *Ploesti : The Great Ground-Air Battle of 1 August 1943*. Brassey's, 2002.

Dumais, Lucien A, and Hugh Popham. *The Man Who Went Back*. Sphere, 1975.

Hastings, Max. *Bomber Command*. Pan, 2012.

Hastings, Max. *Das Reich*. Pan Macmillan, 1981.

Makos, Adam, and Larry Alexander. *A Higher Call*. Berkley Books, 2013.

Neave, Airey. *Saturday at MI9*. Coronet, 1973.

Nichol, John. *Lancaster*. Simon & Schuster UK, 2021. – I found this after having finished writing this book; but I include it here as it is excellent.

Probert, Henry. *Bomber Harris His Life and Times : The Biography of Marshal of the Royal Air Force Sir Arthur Harris, the Wartime Chief of Bomber Command*. Greenhill, 2006.

Richard, Michael, and James Maydon Langley. *MI9*. Bodley Head, 1979.

Speer, Albert. *Inside the Third Reich : Memoirs*. The Macmillan Company, 1970.

Stiles, Bert. *Serenade to the Big Bird*. Pickle Partners Publishing, 2014. – I have not used any of this in my book but it is one of the great books to come out of the war. Bert Stiles was an American pilot who flew – and was killed in – the war. He was 23 when he died, but already a man of great wisdom and compassion. I want to quote a little here:

> "In a steady endless procession, wars have swept the world, eaten away at its heart, growing from stupid little brawls with clubs and rocks to the mechanical perfection of a city flattened out in the night, so many bombs to the acre, so many planes for the job.

…maybe the Americans and the Russians and the English and all the others who have learned to fight together can crawl out of their Yaks and Liberators and Lancasters and General Sherman's and LST's and maybe they can sit down and have a cigarette or smoke a pipe of peace. Maybe they can go off and get good and drunk first, and make love for a while, and throw darts, and get good and hung over.

Then maybe they can sit down somewhere, where it's quiet, and take a good long look at the world."

This book is a masterpiece.

Stubbington, John. *Kept in the Dark*. Casemate Publishers, 2010.

Terraine, John. *The Right of the Line*. Pen and Sword, 2010.

Wilhelm Johnen. *Duel under the Stars*. New English Library, 1975.

Wilson, Kevin. *Bomber Boys*. Phoenix, 2006.

Yates, Harry. *Luck and a Lancaster*. Twayne Publishers, 1990.

Zukerman, Solly. *From Apes to Warlords*. Hamish Hamilton, 1978.

Media and Online sources

"*1-Lt. Col. "Rosie" Rosenthal WWII Hero -- from Brooklyn to Berlin*." *www.youtube.com*, youtu.be/9g-HazD1AwA.

"*RAF CASPS Historic Interview | Sir Arthur Harris*." *www.youtube.com*, youtu.be/UCWK-O7cKvc.

Wikipedia Contributors. "*Area Bombing Directive*." *Wikipedia*, 22 Oct. 2021, en.wikipedia.org/wiki/Area_bombing_directive.

Chapter 6. Technowar -the attack on London
Books

Barker, Ralph. *Aviator Extraordinary - the Sydney Cotton Story*. Chatto & Windus, 1969.

Braddon, Russell. *Cheshire, V. C.* Evans Brothers, 1954.

Currie, Jack. *Mosquito Victory*. Crecy Pub, 2004.

Dejonghe, Etienne, and Yves. *Le Maner. Le Nord-Pas-De-Calais Dans La Main Allemande*. Voix Du Nord, 1999. – in French

Dowling, Taylor. *Spies in the Sky: The Secret Battle for Aerial Intelligence during World War II*. Abacus, 2011.

Holmes, Jamie. *12 Seconds of Silence : How a Team of Inventors, Tinkerers, and Spies Took down a Nazi Superweapon*. Houghton Mifflin Harcourt, 2020.

Irons, Roy. *Hitler's Terror Weapons: The Price of Vengeance*. HarperCollins UK, 2013.

Irving, David. *The Mare's Nest*. Focal Publications, 2010.

Jones, R.V. *Most Secret War*. Penguin UK, 2009.

Jones, Vincent. *Operation Torch : Anglo-American Invasion of North Africa*. Ballantine Books, 1992.

Martelli, George. *The Man Who Saved London, the Story of Michel Hollard*. Doubleday, 1961.

Michel, Jean, and Louis Nucéra. *Dora*. Sphere, 1981. – In French – about the death camps where V weapons were made

Morpurgo, J E. *Barnes Wallis*. Longmans, 1973.

Phelps, Stephen. *The Tizard Mission : The Top-Secret Scientific Mission That Changed the Course of World War II*. Garsington, 2011.

Pile, Sir Frederick. *Ack-Ack*. George G. Harrap & Co. Ltd, 1949.

Speer, Albert. *Inside the Third Reich : Memoirs*. Ishi Press International, 2009.

Wilhelm Johnen. *Duel under the Stars : The Memoir of a Luftwaffe Night Pilot in World War II*. S. Greenhill Books, 2018.

Wyman, Bill, and Ray Coleman. *Bill Wyman, Stone Alone : The Story of a Rock "N" Roll Band*. Da Capo Press, 1997.

Younghusband, Eileen. *One Woman's War*. Candy Jar Books, 2011. – worked in radar & tracking V weapons

Media and Online sources

"*Early Life – Bill Wyman*." *Billwyman.com*, billwyman.com/early.

"*FlyingBombsandRockets,v1 & v2 Statistics*." *www.flyingbombsandrockets.com*, www.flyingbombsandrockets.com/stats_summary.html.

"*FlyingBombsandRockets,V1,V2,Rockets,Flying Bombs,*." *Flyingbombsandrockets.com*, flyingbombsandrockets.com/index.html.

"*The V-1s*." *Hawkertempest.se*, hawkertempest.se/index.php/action/thev1s. - (gives stats of what destroyed by guns and what by fighters)

"*V1 Arme Du Desespoir Yannick Delefosse Offensive Ete 44*." *V1armedudesespoir.free.fr*, v1armedudesespoir.free.fr/ete_44.htm. – in French but has a superb map of V1 launch sites and where they were aimed at.

Chapter 7. Rites of passage
Books

Annan, Noel. *Changing Enemies: Defeat and Regeneration of Germany*. Cornell University Press, 1997.

Boyle, Andrew. *No Passing Glory: Biography of Leonard Cheshire*. HarperCollins Distribution Services, 1972.

Burman, Ben Lucien. *The Generals Wear Cork Hats*. Taplinger Pub. Co., 1965.

Cowburn, Benjamin. *No Cloak, No Dagger*. Casemate Publishers, 2009.

Dalzel-Job, Patrick. *Arctic Snow to Dust of Normandy*. Pen and Sword, 2003.

Foot, M R D. *SOE in France : An Account of the Work of the British Special Operations Executive in France, 1940-1944*. Frank Cass, 2006.

Fry, Helen. *The Walls Have Ears : The Greatest Intelligence Operation of World War II*. Yale University Press, 2019.

Hue, Andre, and Ewen Southby-Tailyour. *The next Moon*. Penguin UK, 2009.

Kenyon, David. *Bletchley Park and D-Day : The Untold Story of How the Battle for Normandy Was Won*. Yale University Press, 2019. – I don't address this subject at all in this book (due to lack of space)– but this is an essential read for anyone interested in BP and the war.

Lycett, Andrew. *Ian Fleming*. St. Martin's Press, 2013.

Macintyre, Ben. *Operation Mincemeat : The True Spy Story That Changed the Course of World War II*. London Bloomsbury, 2016. – It is unusual to list a book that I didn't use. If I had come across it earlier in the writing process I would have done so. Britain's intelligence services pulled off two astoundingly successful deceptions during the war. Firstly Operation Mincemeat persuaded the Axis leaders that a landing was not be expected in Sicily; while the later Operation Bodyguard made the Germans defend the French coast immediately opposite England more heavily than the coast of Normandy. Ben Macintyre's excellent book tells of the Sicily deception.

Mayne, Richard J. *In Victory, Magnanimity, in Peace, Goodwill : A History of Wilton Park*. Whitehall History Pub. In Association With Frank Cass, 2003.

Millar, George Reid. *Road to Resistance*. Arrow, 1981.

Purnell, Sonia. *A Woman of No Importance : The Untold Story of the American Spy Who Helped Win World War II*. Viking, An Imprint Of Penguin Random House Llc, 2019.

Rankin, Nicholas. *Ian Fleming's Commandos : The Story of 30 Assault Unit in WWII*. Faber, 2012.

Roland, Paul. *Life in the Third Reich*. Sirius Entertainment, 2021.

Stourton, Edward. *Auntie's War : The BBC during the Second World War*. Black Swan, 2018.

Troy, Thomas F. *Wild Bill Donovan and Intrepid : The Origins of CIA*. Yale University Press, 1996.

Media and Online sources

Borden, Mary. *Journey down a Blind Alley. Internet Archive*, University of Michigan, 1 Jan. 1946, archive.org/details/JourneyDownABlindAlley-nsia/page/n15/mode/2up.

"Morgenthau Plan." *Military Wiki*, military-history.fandom.com/wiki/Morgenthau_Plan#CITEREFBlum1967.

List of terms and acronyms

ATS – Female member of the British army in WW2

AXIS – the alliance of fascist powers (principally Germany and Italy and later Japan)

BBC British Broadcasting Corporation. The state-owned radio and television service

GC & CS The government Code and Cypher School. The department of the SIS/MI6 which dealt with cryptography and was at Bletchley Park (later renamed GCHQ)

GPO – General Post Office. At the time, the state-owned monopoly for postal and telephone services

HF/DF (huff-duff). High Frequency detection. The equipment which was used to determine the physical source from which enemy transmissions were coming

Luftwaffe – the German air force

MI5 – The British domestic (as against overseas) intelligence service

MI6 – see SIS

NID – Naval Intelligence Division (of the Royal Navy)

RAF – Royal Air Force

RFC – Royal Flying Corps. Merged with Royal Navy Air Service (RNAS) to become the Royal Air Force in 1918

RN – Royal Navy

RNAS – Royal Navy Air Service. The navy's flying arm. Merged with the RFC in 1918 to become the Royal Air Force

RSS – Radio security service. The civilian counterpart (GPO and secret services) of the military listening ('Y') services

SIS. The Secret Intelligence Service, also known as MI6. Britain's external intelligence service (i.e. dealing with overseas intelligence)

SOE – Special Operations Executive – organisation set up for overseas sabotage

Ultra – The highest classification of British security. Often used to refer to Bletchley Park's output

USAAF – United States Army Air Force (preceded the USAF)

WAAF – Women's Auxiliary Air Force (female member of the RAF in WW2)

WRNS (WREN) – female member of the Royal Navy in WW2

Y services. The listening services the British armed forces and secret services used to puck up Axis messages. The letter 'y' came from the original 'WI', which was short for Wireless Interception.

Index

i

Index

Index

Index